W9-CHU-830

* HOTTER THAN A *
MATCH HEAD

JUL 3 1 2014

782.42166092 Boone

Boone, S.
Hotter than a match head.

PRICE: $18.95 (3559/he   )

STEVE BOONE

Life on the Run with
THE LOVIN' SPOONFUL

With TONY MOSS

* HOTTER THAN A *
MATCH HEAD

ECW PRESS

Copyright © Steve Boone and Tony Moss, 2014
Published by ECW Press
2120 Queen Street East, Suite 200, Toronto, Ontario, Canada M4E 1E2
416-694-3348 / info@ecwpress.com

All rights reserved. No part of this publication may be reproduced, stored in a retrieval system,
or transmitted in any form by any process — electronic, mechanical, photocopying, recording,
or otherwise — without the prior written permission of the copyright owners and ECW Press.
The scanning, uploading, and distribution of this book via the Internet or via any other means
without the permission of the publisher is illegal and punishable by law. Please purchase only
authorized electronic editions, and do not participate in or encourage electronic piracy of
copyrighted materials. Your support of the authors' rights is appreciated.

To the best of his abilities, the author has related experiences, places, people,
and organizations from his memories of them. In order to protect the privacy of others, he has,
in some instances, changed the names of certain people and details of events and places.

Library and Archives Canada Cataloguing In Publication

ISBN 978-1-77041-193-7
also issued as 978-1-77090-602-0 (EPUB) and 978-1-77090-603-7 (PDF)

Boone, Steve, 1943–, author
Hotter than a match head: life on the run with the Lovin'
Spoonful / Steve Boone with Tony Moss.

1. Boone, Steve, 1943–. 2. Rock musicians—United States—Biography.
3. Lovin' Spoonful (Musical group). 4. Rock groups—United States—Biography.
1. Moss, Tony (Anthony Lyle), author 11. Title.

ML419.B724A3 2014   782.42166092   C2014-902518-1
C2014-902519-X

Editor: Jennifer Hale
Cover design: David Gee
Cover and title-page images: © Henry Diltz
Interior image (pg 310): Courtesy Steve Boone
Type: Rachel Ironstone
Printed and bound in Canada by Norecob   1   2   3   4   5

TABLE OF CONTENTS

PROLOGUE

I stood on the deck of what qualified as a rescue boat, a bottle of Mount Gay rum in my hand, watching the *Do Deska Din* disappear beneath the waves and into the predawn black of the Atlantic Ocean.

She had been a 68-foot Rhodes Motorsailer, a behemoth of metal with two giant 100-horsepower diesel engines and enough room to house a crew of 12. I had been her captain on a voyage from Antigua to Santa Marta, Colombia, and back northward through the treacherous open ocean to what would be her final resting place, off the coast of Ocean City, Maryland.

And though I was standing on the deck of a rescue boat, this had not been an accident.

In addition to me, my younger brother Mike and his high school buddies, who had made up our crew, there had also been enough room on the *Do Deska Din* for 19,000 pounds of the finest Colombian reefer money could buy in June 1979. The pot was long gone, having been unloaded near Ocean City onto two vessels during the final phase of what would be considered — boat sinking and all — a successful operation.

I was a pot smuggler, and an unapologetic one.

In these pre-Reagan years, that didn't make me so special. Before the 1980s, when the heat was turned up on drug offenders in the U.S., there were a lot of guys just like me running these missions, which weren't anyone's definition of easy money but could make you some decent income if you knew what you were doing.

I'd come of age in the 1960s and was indifferent about the use and proliferation of recreational drugs like pot. I'd smoked marijuana for 15 years or more and had never thought ill of the fellow travelers who sold it or smoked it. I was part of that world and I understood that world, so I didn't think much of profiting off that world. Most of my cohorts in the smuggling trade fit that same profile.

But in the back of my mind, I must have known I was an outlier.

As far as I know, I was the only international smuggler whose face had been beamed out multiple times to millions of viewers via *The Ed Sullivan Show*. I can't say that I'd encountered anyone else in the drug transport trade who had written or played on a No. 1 hit, or who'd hung out with The Beatles backstage at Shea Stadium.

Although in a lot of ways what I was doing in June 1979 made more sense to me than what I'd been doing in June 1966 as the bass player and a songwriter in The Lovin' Spoonful, there was no doubt it had been a strange journey from there to here. But in the moments and hours immediately preceding that bottle of Mount Gay winding up in my hand, there hadn't been time for such navel-gazing reflection.

The call to action had been prompted by something I'd seen as the *Do Deska Din* made its way north toward the mainland. That something was the Coast Guard cutter *Dallas*. As the ship passed by slowly, I stared in the direction of eight uniformed officers on various bridges, photographing and filming us.

We'd been spotted. The *Dallas* didn't stop — it wouldn't have mattered if it did, as there was neither stem nor seed left on our boat — but there was a good chance the Coast Guard knew we weren't out there doing some early morning fishing. From that moment, the *Do Deska Din* was damaged goods. Trying another expedition like the one we'd just pulled would have been a suicide mission, knowing the Coast Guard had intelligence on our vessel. Even having the craft visible and easily traceable back to us could cause unwanted attention.

With the *Dallas* safely out of range, I radioed to the boat's owners, my partners. "We've been auditioned for the movie," I told them.

"Unplug the electronics," was the response. We all understood the code.

And though I never would have made this analogy at the time, sinking a steel-hulled boat in the middle of the open ocean without using explosives was just like laying down tracks in a studio to arrive at a completed master. Get any of the steps wrong, and you are going to have a hard time living with the result.

We cut the rubber hoses that brought seawater into the boat for cooling and other uses like toilets, thus initiating the flow.

Next, we broke off the bronze fittings that normally returned used seawater to the sea.

Then we disconnected the stuffing boxes for the propeller shafts and pushed the shafts out, allowing a good flow of seawater to enter the *Do Deska Din.*

And finally, we opened all the hatches and portholes so that when the water got high enough, it would rush in, and the end would be near.

Then it was all aboard the friendly trawler yacht that awaited us — not an insignificant transfer of crew from one boat to another. As the captain, I went last, carefully stepping from the sinking boat onto the rescue ship rocking beside it so as not to get smashed between the two and seriously injured or worse. We all made it.

As the last tip of the mast fell beneath the surface of the 200-foot-deep ocean, I took a long slug off that bottle of rum.

Three months later I'd be onstage at the Concord Hotel in the Catskills, bass guitar in hand, once again standing before a rabid audience and a film crew. The Lovin' Spoonful was back together for the first time in more than a decade, and I was playing a show with my former bandmates.

My old life had returned. But I'd be setting sail again before long.

Chapter 1

YOU'RE A BIG BOY NOW

I was supposed to be a military man, just like my dad.

I was born John Stephen Boone — named after early naval heroes John Paul Jones and Stephen Decatur — at Camp Lejeune, North Carolina, during the height of World War II, on September 23, 1943. My first memory is looking up from the crib at a couple of my dad's Marine buddies in their dress blues. At my christening, the commander of the Marine Corps base proclaimed that I'd be "the future commandant of the U.S. Marine Corps." No pressure, kid.

My dad, Emmett Eugene Boone Jr. (everybody called him "Junie" for short), was doing air and sea rescue for Marine aviators who were training there on the Carolina coast before being deployed. My pop, who had previously worked directly for FDR in the "summer White House" in Warm Springs, Georgia, had training in seamanship and small-boat handling, which helped him into this job working with young men waiting to ship off to the Pacific and World War II.

Still too young to understand why certain people were our enemies or grasp the carnage that accompanied war, I developed a deep respect for the United States military and in particular the Marine Corps. This

1

respect and exposure drove my early desire to become a naval aviator and, for at least the first 16 years of my life, becoming a member of the armed services was all that I ever considered for a career.

I built all the models of World War II and Korean War aircraft, both the newer plastic and the balsa wood, which required a lot more concentration and patience. I also learned how to fly control-line powered model airplanes and was fascinated by both oral and written histories of World War II and the Korean conflict.

We moved a few times when I was a kid, with every move having a deep impact on the various interests I'd develop.

After my dad was discharged from the service, we moved to Buck Hill Falls, a resort village in the Pocono Mountains of eastern Pennsylvania. His background before he'd joined the military was in the hotel business, and it was at another Pennsylvania resort that he'd met my mother, Mary, some years before. My father and grandfather ran the inn at Buck Hill Falls, which was connected to a 36-hole championship golf course and country club. Since my dad and granddad both worked there in management positions, I pretty much had the run of the place.

It was while living in Buck Hill Falls that I learned to hunt, fish and swim, as well as play tennis and golf. I developed into a good enough athlete to take first place in the Junior Olympics at summer camp. I learned how to shoot a rifle and march in time as a member of the Marine Corps League Junior Rifle Association, though one notable incident from my youth would instill in me a healthy respect for the dangers of firearms.

My parents were out for the evening when Skip, my older brother by six years, found the key to my dad's rifle cabinet. Out came the .30-06 deer rifle, and with childish humor, knowing the rifle would never have been put away loaded, Skip pointed it at me. He raised the barrel just enough to clear my head, pulled the trigger and . . . *BAM*. The sound was so loud that the house shook. In stunned silence, Skip and I stared at each other, then at the golf-ball-sized hole in the wall of the family living room.

I wasn't dead, but knew that might change when Mom and Dad came home.

We carefully placed the rifle back in the cabinet, put the key back where it belonged and came up with the brilliant, sitcom-ready plan to move a framed picture from another part of the house to cover the huge hole in our wall.

It took my parents about 15 seconds to size that one up. I remember a lot of yelling, and Skip stepped up and took the brunt of their anger. I guess since I'd almost taken a bullet for him, he was willing to take one for me . . . in a manner of speaking.

Life was idyllic in Buck Hill Falls, but it was just before my 11th birthday that a different family trauma would necessitate another move for the Boones.

One day while Skip and I were at school, my six-year-old brother Charlie reached up to the stove in the kitchen and pulled a pan of boiling hot water onto himself. He was wearing cowboy boots and heavy clothing at the time, which helped trap the scalding water against his skin, making the burns more serious. He was rushed to the hospital and given what was then considered experimental skin graft surgery. Charlie very nearly died.

To facilitate his healing, doctors recommended we move to a humid climate. As it happened, my grandfather was in the process of retiring to St. Augustine, Florida (along with his much younger secretary) to a small truck farm off the Tolomato River, just north of downtown. He had been going down there for the past few winters, and my family had been joining him for a month each winter in a cottage next to the one he rented at Aldea Del Mar on St. Augustine Beach. So we were familiar with the terrain, and since my dad wanted to leave hotels anyway to start a business building custom wood furniture, the decision was made to move in the fall of 1954.

While I'd liked living in the Poconos, I immediately fell in love with St. Augustine, its warm weather and its ocean. We wound up in a nice little house on Anastasia Island, in the Davis Shores development, and sailing, surfing and waterskiing became a regular part of my routine. My schoolmate John Heagy and I built our own little motor-powered go-carts to drive around the then-unpaved streets of Davis Shores. I joined the Boy Scouts and had two paper routes, one in the morning and one in the evening. I had yet another brush with death while working that job. I was pedaling my bike furiously across the Bridge of Lions on the way to my route, when my foot slipped off the pedal and the locked coaster brake flipped me completely over the handlebars, headfirst. I spilled out onto the roadway where, as it happened, one of my brother Skip's best friends barely brought his car to a stop with the right front tire just a foot from squashing my head. The newspaper business can be tough.

But the water was everything to me from the time we set foot in Florida. I devoured C.S. Forester's books about Captain Horatio Hornblower, the fictional hero of the Royal Navy. I was captivated by the *National Geographic* spreads written by the champion yachtsman Carlton Mitchell, who wrote about the joys of cruising the Caribbean, of living on a small sailboat and of racing his 38-foot yawl *Finisterre* to victory in the Newport Bermuda Race three times in the second half of the 1950s.

Noting the aquatic passions of his second son, my dad started the St. Augustine Optimist Pram fleet in a joint effort with the local Rotary Club. Optimist Prams are simple little eight-foot dinghies that are the entry-level boat for sanctioned sailing in the U.S. I took to the little boats naturally and was soon the club champion. It was a huge confidence builder, though I'd get an early dose of humility that would mean more than all the victories put together.

The best six or so sailors in the club were entered to compete in a big out-of-town regatta in St. Petersburg, a regional event that was going to be my first experience sailing outside the club. While I'd been competing against 10 or 15 sailors in my local races, I looked around at the start of this regatta and saw 200 boats, sailed mostly by people with much more experience than me. I was completely overwhelmed, got caught in the wind shadow and soon fell to dead last. I finished slightly better — third from last. Complete humiliation. I stalked off to the station wagon and sulked.

Soon came the announcement to prepare for the next race, and my dad walked up to the car and said, "You better be getting ready, you've only got 15 minutes 'til the start."

"I'm not racing this race, or any race," I said in tears.

"And why not?" he demanded. I said nothing.

With less patience in his voice, the order came: "Get yourself down to the boats!"

"No," came my reply. "I can't do this anymore."

Now his tone went from impatience to Marine Corps gunnery sergeant and he got in my face and said, "I am going to give you two choices: number one is to go sail this race as best you can, and number two is . . . you know what number two is."

I was there in plenty of time for the second race, and finished a reasonable seventh or eighth in that race and the third and final one. After we'd loaded up the boats and were headed home, my dad broke the terrible silence by saying, "There is absolutely no way you can be a winner if you quit. No son of mine is going to be a quitter, is that clearly understood?"

It was. My dad taught me that there was more shame and failure in quitting than anything else, and it was advice that would stay with me throughout my life.

Rock 'n' roll would arrive later for me, but it would indeed arrive.

I'd loved music from an early age, when my family would gather around the piano at holiday time and sing Christmas carols. I enjoyed the classical music I heard at home, particularly Liszt and Chopin, and also knew the soundtracks to Broadway musicals like *South Pacific* and *Annie Get Your Gun* by heart. I'd wedge myself between the speakers of my dad's hi-fi, which was set up in the library of my grandfather's house in Buck Hill Falls, and listen for hours. I took piano lessons for about a year in Pennsylvania but didn't continue amid my new, outdoors-based life in Florida. I also tried tap dancing for one semester, which, while it may have helped with my sense of rhythm, did not evoke a young Gene Kelly.

All of that said, rock 'n' roll was something completely different — and magical.

I'll never forget one day, on my way home from crewing for a neighbor who raced a D utility class boat on the St. Johns River, when "Peggy Sue" came on the radio. Now, I had heard of Buddy Holly before and thought his hits were great, but when I heard this record I almost flipped. The rhythm was unique and the singing style was beyond cool. If there was any one moment in my life that made me want to be a musician, this was it.

During this time Skip had started playing guitar well enough to begin a band with some friends of his. They named the band The Blue Suedes, after the Carl Perkins song that had also been a hit for Elvis. The Blue Suedes even got to meet the boy King on his way through Jacksonville, as they were dispatched to find Elvis an acoustic guitar when his got lost in airplane baggage. Skip and the Blue Suedes' lead singer, Arthur Osborne, got far enough to record two songs in Nashville for new producer Chet Atkins at RCA Records. All of this was really getting my attention. Skip was six years older than me, so there wasn't much hope of tagging along or hanging out with the band, but the exciting stuff they were doing wasn't escaping me either.

Before long I decided to try my hand at performing, like my older brother. I'd been singing in the grade school choir, mostly because everyone sang in the choir, when my seventh-grade home-room teacher, Sister Mary Gemma (whom I had a huge crush on), suggested I understudy for the lead role of Ralph Rackstraw in the school's performance of the Gilbert and Sullivan operetta *H.M.S. Pinafore*. What the heck, I said. It was something to do, I'd meet some girls, and the lead, Paul Emory, would surely show up, so I could enjoy watching the play like everyone else.

Wrong.

Paul got laryngitis and I had to go out there and basically talk my way through all of the songs that poor Ralph had to sing to win the fair maiden's heart. Stage fright and I were already second cousins, but at least I did it. Once it was over, there was no denying that performing had offered quite a rush.

Still, my long-term objective remained the military. I had the required crew cut and my parents had enrolled me in a small Catholic school, St. Joseph's Academy, with the hopes that the nuns there could get my grades up enough that I could try for an appointment to the Naval Academy. St. Joe was a great fit for me. It was small and a good environment for learning. Most of the students were female boarders, many of them from Cuba and South America, and there was a very small percentage of boys. I was even able to go out for the football team — the coach needed every possible body just to fill out the roster. Another check off my list for service academy appointment.

Then, in the summer of 1958, as I enjoyed myriad outdoor activities in the terrific weather, preparing to start another year at this great school where I really felt I belonged, my father dropped an atom bomb on me: we were moving again.

With the woodworking business struggling, Dad announced he was taking a hotel job in East Hampton, New York, right next to his old hometown of Westhampton Beach.

I was beside myself. I had been in Westhampton Beach once or twice when we lived in Pennsylvania, but I could not imagine spending another winter anywhere colder than Jacksonville. What about sailing? Waterskiing? What about the Navy? This was going to mess up all of my plans.

In a fit of personal crisis, about a week before we were set to move, I hitched a ride up to the Navy base at Mayport to plead my case to the recruiters. I carefully and passionately explained the situation, and asked what I'd have to do to join the Navy right now.

"The first thing you have to do is get about four years older," the recruiter told a frenzied boy of 14.

I'd be joining my family in the Hamptons, where old money goes to die and new money tries to get old. This would not be my idea of a good time. East Hampton was and still is the summer home of many wealthy people — in the 1950s it was truly the summer playground for the old-money set from the city. Because my family was not part of high Hamptons society, access to sailing was not going to be as easy as it had been in St. Augustine.

East Hampton High School was huge, and I was growing taller and skinnier, which also meant my high school football career was over — I took one look at those potato farmer linemen and ran the other way. I hated leaving Florida and never fit in very well with most of the students in my new class.

At 15 — the worst possible time to lose your self-confidence — I was bottoming out.

There had always been tension in my house. I loved and admired my dad, but he was a rum drinker and a bit of a tyrant. I'll never forget him slamming his fists down on the dinner table when anyone dared to defy him, particularly when it came to his largely right-wing politics. My mom was a beautiful Irish-Catholic lady who had to put up with a lot, including my dad's philandering. Now I was adding to the bubbling toxicity in the house with my rebellion.

I introduced a motorcycle jacket and longer, "ducktail" haircut to my look, and in what had been a mostly formal, buttoned-down military household, the changes were noticed. I also started drag racing on weekends with the few friends I had.

My parents were hopeful that what I was going through was just a phase, and that I'd get my act together and get back on track toward a military career. Honestly, they were probably right. By the end of my junior year at East Hampton I was starting to snap out of my funk and get back to normal. That's when it happened — June 26, 1960 — the day everything changed.

It was the last day of junior year, and I went bowling with my friend, Bob Schwenk, to celebrate. At about midnight, after bowling a few games, Bob and I decided to hitchhike home, a mode of travel that was not such a big deal in East Hampton in 1960.

Just then, one of our schoolmates, an older guy named Jim Harkness, drove up in a tri-powered Chevy Impala, a big, fast car that his parents had bought for him.

"Come on, guys," Jim said. "I'll give you a lift."

Jim had a reputation as a drinker and reckless driver, but getting in a car with someone who had been drinking just wasn't a concern back then like it is today — it especially wasn't a concern for a couple of invincible 16-year-olds like Bob and me. We dropped Bob at his house and headed into town toward mine. It was getting foggy, and Jim was driving way too fast down a long road, appropriately known as Long Lane, that had a reputation as the town's most dangerous.

At a speed of what seemed like 100 miles per hour, in the thickening fog, Jim missed a turn at the corner. That's the last thing I remember about that night. I do remember the aftermath. I've had to piece together the interim second-hand, and it went like this: We hit an oak tree head-on. Jim was walking around with no more than a scratch on his head when the ambulance arrived. Meanwhile, the paramedics took one look at me lying motionless inside the badly mangled car, assumed I was dead and set about treating Jim.

One of them must have seen me stir, because he said, "Hey, this kid's still alive!" Which I was, but barely.

I woke up in the Southampton hospital the next day, though at the time I kind of wished I hadn't. My right leg was completely shattered, as were my pelvis, my hip and my shoulder, which was also dislocated. My right foot was paralyzed. The lower half of my body was in traction. Throw in a concussion for good measure. That hospital room would be my home for the better part of two months, and I'll never forget the sound of kids laughing and carrying on through my window, which opened right onto the road to the beach.

When I was finally discharged, I had to come to terms with the fact that a career in the military was probably a non-starter at this point. The biggest problem was my foot — they don't accept kids with paralyzed feet into flight school. Dr. Farrell, my family doctor and a retired Air Force pilot, confirmed the bad news: given my injuries, the military was out of the question. One mistake by an acquaintance in the nighttime fog on a winding road, and the predicted future of the commandant of the U.S. Marine Corps became a "what might have been" story. More than 50 years later, I now know that "what might have been" was perhaps my being shot down in a rice paddy in Southeast Asia, as far too many young men of my generation were. In that regard, Jim Harkness very well might have saved my life. There was no way to know that at the time, of course.

My injuries aside, for a kid who had been extremely active for his entire existence up to that point, my convalescence was hell. Pain, boredom and a state of mourning over watching a dream disappear do not mix particularly well.

Luckily, my family was not about to allow me to mope. My sainted mom came through and bought me a Gibson LGO acoustic guitar with money I'd later learn had been loaned to her by my maternal grandfather, who was living with us. My brother Skip showed me a few chords, and I had nothing to do but to learn them. Soon, I started trying to play along to the faint, late-night signal of WKBW in Buffalo, and religiously watching Dick Clark's *American Bandstand*.

In the movie version of this story, you'd now probably jump-cut to me standing on the stage at the Hollywood Bowl, playing before throngs of screaming fans. The ultimate symbol of perseverance and redemption despite stifling, life-threatening odds. But because real life is never that easy, I'll tell you what really happened: my family fucking moved again and I was as miserable as ever.

We relocated that summer from East Hampton to Westhampton Beach — which, while not a long physical distance, was a pretty big deal for a 16-year-old who had spent the better part of the last two years trying to fit in at a school he'd never set foot in again.

I showed up at Westhampton Beach High School for my senior year at about six-foot-three and 150 pounds, on crutches, not knowing a soul. The acting out would become worse. The crowd I hung with would get rougher, and with a military career no longer an option, there was no incentive to shape up. I became fascinated with hot rods and drinking and behaving badly with other kids of low ambition.

Luckily, two things would be there to save my life — music and Peter Davey.

Chapter 2
GOOD TIME MUSIC

The Palm Terrace wasn't a club as much as it was a rock 'n' roll roadhouse.

It was a secluded, non-residential spot in the middle of the pine barrens, with no neighbors to call the cops. At the same time, it was in a most convenient location, a short drive from the substantially populated town of Riverhead, the county seat of Suffolk County, Long Island, and also not far from the Air Force base in Westhampton, a critical, fully staffed location for the military at the height of the Cold War. The Air Force guys showed up at the Palm Terrace looking to blow off steam after protecting and maintaining the military's missile silos all day long, converging with the Riverhead locals to guarantee good crowds.

And in 1961, when I started going there to see my brother Skip play in his latest band, the Palm Terrace had great crowds. The owner, Tony Moreno, looked the other way regarding underage drinkers. I was among them, even in this era when the drinking age was 18.

I'd stand in the back in the shadows with my beer and watch Skip and his band, The Kingsmen, a five-piece R&B-type combo made up of some of his buddies from the Air Force (Skip was not in the Air Force himself, having done his military service in the National Guard), as they grooved their way through the hits of the day and a few standards from yesteryear. The Kingsmen were fronted by Joe Butler (drums/vocals), Sonny Bottari (rhythm guitar/vocals) and most notably King Charles, an older, black saxophone player and New York City expat who must have been about the hippest guy on Long Island in the early '60s, without even trying.

From the first time I had seen Skip play in a band, way back in St. Augustine, I always thought he looked so cool onstage. I fantasized about being up there as well, but flying jets had always been my top priority. Even with that prospect out of the picture, and with a brother up on the bandstand, I'd never really thought about becoming a performer. My early attempts at playing the drum set that belonged to Jan Buchner, another sometime bandmate of Skip's who stayed with my family for a while, did nothing to make me think I'd missed my calling.

But one day when we were both bumming around the house, almost in passing, Skip threw it out there: "Why don't you come out to the Palm Terrace with your Gibson and sit in on a few songs?"

"My Gibson?" I said, squinting my eyes at him. "You know that's an acoustic guitar, right?"

"Yeah . . . so?"

"So it doesn't have a pickup. Who the hell is going to hear it?"

"I'll hear it," he said. "The other guys in the band will hear it. Let's try it out on a couple of numbers and see how it goes."

I still have no idea what motivated Skip to ask me to come onstage. It wasn't my musical virtuosity. It wasn't like Skip to feel sorry for me, so the fact that I was still hobbling around and mopey after the accident couldn't have been it either. As best as anyone can remember all these years later, the invitation may have been made at the behest of Sonny Bottari, who much preferred being a frontman to a guitar player.

By this time, I had gotten pretty good on that Gibson acoustic.

Skip had taught me the basics, and I was able to figure out most of the simple songs of that time by listening to them on the radio and playing them over and over. In my bedroom I might as well have been Duane Eddy or Buddy Holly. After a while I got good enough to accompany myself at beach parties or at friends' houses. But was I good enough to play a real gig with a working band like The Kingsmen? I sure couldn't play any leads. Even if I could, I didn't have an electric guitar to play them on. Did they even have rhythm guitars in rock bands? How was I, a tall, skinny teenager with a dark brown acoustic Gibson, going to look standing with these seasoned older guys?

On the opposite end of the scale from these worries were the girls.

I'd seen from my vantage point in the wings how women looked at my brother and his bandmates onstage, and man did I want a taste of that. I'd spent the last three years in high school as a prisoner of my insecurities, and I was ready to get my mojo back. Not that I knew what my mojo was.

I shrugged my shoulders. I took the gig.

On a cool fall night in October 1962 I put on a white shirt and dress slacks and went out to the Palm Terrace to give being a rocker a chance. The Palm Terrace was the archetypal no-frills rock roadhouse. The place would be jammed on Friday and Saturday nights, evenly split between Air Force grunts and townies. Despite the good time vibe of the music, there was plenty of tension in the room. The girls were mostly local, so the competition for their attention and affection among the Air Force guys and the townies, combined with the steady stream of alcohol, was like a petri dish for violence.

Having witnessed and sidestepped these conflagrations as a spectator, I already knew what to do should a skirmish break out during my inaugural performance. The Kingsmen would just link arms in front of the amps and drum kit to keep the fighters from falling into the bandstand.

The other guys in The Kingsmen were all good players and singers. In addition to Sonny, Joe, King Charles and my brother on lead guitar was Clay Sonier on bass, a great guy and native Louisianan whom I'd get to know well. When Joe came up front to sing a lead, our old houseguest Jan, now a full member of The Kingsmen, would fill in on the drums.

Fortunately, not a lot was expected of me that first night. I wasn't getting paid, so no one was giving up any money. As it turned out, I wasn't going to steal anyone's girls — The Kingsmen were all chick magnets — and I was welcomed enthusiastically that first night by the guys onstage. I strummed along and tried to stay out of the way.

The material was mostly Top 40, the same fare I'd been playing in my room for weeks and months. The Isley Brothers' "Shout" was a popular request, and the slow songs were usually older standards brought to the band courtesy of King Charles. It all went down pretty well. The guys in the band were aces, as players and as people. I don't even remember any fights on the dance floor.

I loved the feeling of being up onstage and couldn't wait to get back up there, but I was still feeling more than a little out of place. Playing in an electric band with an acoustic guitar was not really doing it for me — I still wasn't sure anyone could hear me — so I sat down with Skip the next day and asked if I could get a paying gig in The Kingsmen if I bought an electric guitar and worked hard at learning the band's full repertoire. He said he'd talk it over with the other members. If anyone balked at having to give up a cut of their pay to include his kid brother as rhythm guitarist, Skip never told me so. He said he'd discussed it with the rest of the guys and back came an enthusiastic yes. I was in.

Excited, I rushed right down to the small music shop on Mill Road in Westhampton Beach, run by a cool older guy named Bud Leimsidor who'd also given me a music lesson or two in the past. Right in the window of his store, sitting in an open case with shiny brown padding, was a beautiful, gently used 1957 Gibson Goldtop Les Paul. In 1962 Fender was the guitar to have for rock 'n' rollers. Gibsons, especially the Les Paul model, were highly regarded guitars, but all the buzz was being created by the Fender Telecasters and Stratocasters, and soon the Jazzmaster would wow everybody who wanted rock star credibility. I knew playing a Gibson would set me apart from the prevailing fashion. The price was $125, which was a lot of money in 1962, but I had to have this guitar. I appealed to my mom and dad, reminding them that I had insurance settlement money coming because of the accident. They scraped the money together, God bless them, and I was a fully plugged in, guitar-playing member of an established local band, The Kingsmen. I happily plugged my guitar into another band member's amp — the art of mic'ing and mixing live sound had not been fully developed, at least at our level — and suddenly could hear myself playing. Quite a thrill.

All this happened just in time for a bass to be put in my hands. Not more than a couple of weeks after I strode onstage with that gorgeous Les Paul, Clay Sonier announced he was leaving the Air Force, and the band, to return home to Louisiana. He'd be gone within a month. Clay pulled the newest member of the group aside.

"Steve, why don't you become the bass player?" he said. "I think you could pick it up real fast."

"Holy cow, Clay," I said, "how can I learn to play the bass in a month?"

"I'll teach you," he replied. "You've got good rhythm and you already know most of the songs on guitar. You'll be fine."

The bass was a necessary instrument in every rock band, but then as now, no one lay awake at night dreaming of riding it to fame and fortune. To wit: a satirical article from *The Scoop News* made the rounds a couple of years back, with a headline that screamed "Groupie Accidentally Sleeps With Bass Player." "If I'm going to sleep with someone, they'd better be important," said fictional article subject Victoria Jorgensen. "I mean, I could find someone here in town as important as a bass player."

Mike Watt, who played bass for the influential '80s punk band Minutemen, summed up the job by saying, "In the hierarchy of rock 'n' roll, bass is where you put the lame dude, the retarded friend. Kind of like right field in little league — no one's gonna hit it out there."

But the best way to capture the mystique of the bass probably came from a line in the 1997 autobiography by Dave Davies of The Kinks. Talking about the formation of the band and the fate of member Pete Quaife, Davies wrote, "We drew lots to see who would play bass guitar and Pete lost."

The road of rock history has been littered with many a frustrated guitarist who agreed to play bass for the good of the team. Paul McCartney is probably the most famous example. I'm another.

"Well, what the fuck," I said.

Even before the strings were broken in on that gleaming Les Paul, I was feeling the heavier weight and foreign touch of Clay's loaned bass against my body.

On the inside I was thinking, "I can't do this," but Clay and King Charles both helped me a lot. Clay had a strange style that I had to modify — a holdover from his days as an upright-bass player — where he held the neck almost against his face. Since bass guitars were smaller, easy to hold and had frets, the idea was that you could hold it just like any guitar. Clay taught me using the old school vertical positioning, but as I got more comfortable I held the bass in the more familiar manner.

Clay also showed me how to use restraint with the notes I played. It wasn't until I picked it up that I realized how much I listened to the bass guitar, and how the instrument can hold the entire sound of a band together, even if the casual listener doesn't realize it.

King Charles, meanwhile, taught me my most valuable piece of musical learning. I was picking up the basics from Clay, but was still extremely unsure about playing the complicated charts to the standards that were part of our repertoire.

"You can play major and minor scales, can't you?"

"Well, K.C., I'm learning, but yes, I can," I replied.

"Well . . . I'll signal to you what key the song is in using my hand, and will let you know whether it's in a minor or major key. Just play the major or minor scale for that key and keep in time with the drummer, and you will be just fine. You'll get a couple of off notes, but over time you'll figure it out."

Man was he right. There were definitely some clams in the beginning, but they got fewer and fewer the more we played together and the more comfortable we got. Having my arm twisted into playing bass ended up being a tremendous blessing. I'd never been comfortable playing lead lines on a guitar — it just didn't come naturally to me. Bass lines, on the other hand, came easy.

I learned about how the bass and the bass drum are practically married to each other, so I got a sense of Joe's rhythm and style and played as a unit with him. I developed my confidence and before long even enjoyed playing the instrument.

Marijuana helped too. It was after I started smoking pot — the summer after my postgraduate year at Westhampton Beach High School, along with some guys I'd been lifeguarding with — that I started hearing the bass in a different way. I couldn't quite put my finger on it, but whether I was listening to music or playing it, there was a clarity there when I was high that helped me hear the relationship between the bass and drums better than ever before.

Other important awakenings for me around this time came in the form of Bob Dylan and Lenny Bruce. I was introduced to Dylan's music by Skip, and like many of my generation found myself completely enthralled by his words. Up to this point I'd thought pop music had one of two purposes: to make you dance fast, or to make you dance slow. Listening to songs like "Masters of War" showed that music could have meaning. Dylan inspired me to start writing songs — albeit silly, bad folk songs. But at least I was writing . . . and thinking.

Lenny Bruce opened my mind in much the same way, taking on the establishment with an irreverence that was both hilarious and shocking. I studied his records, and even got a chance to go see his show at the Village Vanguard in December 1962. I went with Joe Butler and Skip down to this club in Greenwich Village and listened as Lenny brought the house down. I was sitting in the rear of the club next to Joe, who has always had an extremely loud, unique, bordering-on-obnoxious laugh, and was laughing a lot on this particular night, for obvious reasons. In the middle of the show, Lenny stopped cold:

"Who is laughing like that?" he demanded.

Silence.

"I know it's somebody in the back . . . well, that's the kind of laugh that mugs old ladies in Central Park." Joe may have been embarrassed, but I think he enjoyed the attention even more.

Dylan and Bruce would have a huge impact on the way I looked at the world. Meanwhile, thanks to Clay, King Charles and pot, I was on my way to bass stardom, which is an oxymoron if there ever was one.

But a notorious New Year's Eve gig at the Palm Terrace — and a little misunderstanding with the club's owner, Tony Moreno — almost cut my fledgling career short.

When I was playing rhythm guitar, my small share of the night's pay came from the other five guys in the band, who would all chip in to make sure I walked home with something in my pocket. It wasn't close to a full share — it was more like a group of waiters tipping out a busboy — so having me onstage did not cost the Palm Terrace a dime beyond the extra electricity it took to power my guitar.

But when I took over bass duties for Clay, I asked the band for a full share and they obliged. Since they were swapping Clay's salary for mine and wouldn't have to tip me out at the end of the night, it was a net gain for them anyway.

Somehow this message did not get relayed to Tony Moreno, however, and the situation would come to a head on New Year's Eve, 1962. Traditionally the band gets double pay on New Year's, to account for the bigger crowd and an extra set that came about due to the club being open later on the holiday. Tony was prepared to pay the band double, but since I'd been a part-timer, he'd only counted on paying five guys, not six. At the end of the night, when he handed Skip our cut, it was one double-share short. Skip explained the situation to Moreno, and as I watched from the wings while cleaning my bass, I could see Tony starting to wildly gesticulate.

Tony loved The Kingsmen but he was also a minor mobster — God only knows how many wiseguys had their hooks in him for a cut of the night's take. Now we were asking him for more, which probably felt like another shakedown. His face was beet red.

"I'm not fucking paying you guys that," he screamed. "I never agreed to pay that, and if you don't like it you can pack up your gear and get the fuck out."

Skip was a tough, no-nonsense guy who had been around the block with club owners during his career as a musician — so, mobster or not, he wasn't going to take any shit from Tony Moreno, especially when it came to doing right by his younger brother.

"There are six people in this band, Tony," Skip yelled back. "You agreed to pay us, you never said anything about not wanting to pay the new guy. You're going to pay, and that's final!"

"Oh shit," I thought. I put my head down and wiped my bass strings even harder, pretending not to notice the commotion. When I looked back up, Tony was coming out of the kitchen with a double-barreled shotgun in his hand. He pointed it to the ceiling and pulled both barrels at the same time. KABOOM. I dove under a table.

After a couple of minutes of stunned silence I looked back up and saw everyone still in the restaurant — bouncers, bartenders, the band — frozen, staring at Tony, the still-smoking shotgun in his hands.

"Now do you believe I ain't gonna pay ya?" he said.

Ultimately we came to an agreement. He wouldn't pay me my double-share, and we were free to come back and keep our house band gig at the Palm Terrace. He'd also agree not to kill us. That all sounded like a reasonable compromise to me. A deal we could live with. Literally.

Apart from that incident and a couple of other scrapes here and there, being a member of The Kingsmen was a rush, and I rode the wave.

College was in the back of my mind, but for now it could wait. I was making good money — enough to buy a smart little bright red MGA Roadster — and zipping all over Long Island to play shows before groups of appreciative patrons, including throngs of cute girls.

In addition to the Palm Terrace we had a steady gig at a place called the Cottage Inn in East Hampton, which was a different experience altogether.

East Hampton in the late '50s and early '60s was a community located on the South Fork of Long Island, which was by all appearances a comfortably integrated, working-class set of small towns situated within an improbably wealthy township. The "summer set" of mostly rich folks was and is the background of the town of East Hampton, and by 1962 a lot of the land that had previously been used for farming was being sold to land developers who were creating even bigger and more expensive homes for the Hamptons summer set.

A service community had sprung up to serve these part-time Hamptonites in the area's hotels, restaurants and storefronts, and it was these folks who helped form the South Fork's black middle class. Many were people who had made enough money working in service jobs in New York City to buy homes in the then-affordable communities of East Hampton — Springs, Bridgehampton and Sag Harbor. While there was no open policy of segregating neighborhoods, as a practical matter many of these smaller subset communities had their own little village centers, apart from the white villages. The Cottage Inn was in one of those small villages. Located on Springs Road about two miles east of downtown East Hampton and owned by an NYC transplant named Noah Simmons, the Cottage Inn served as a restaurant, bar, liquor and convenience store as well as a gathering spot for locals. When the dinner hour was over, Noah would convert the restaurant part of the store to a dance hall with a stage. At first he brought in small blues and jazz combos to play there on weekends. The quality of the food and the music led to the venue becoming very popular with the locals, and the Cottage Inn began to grow via word of mouth.

King Charles was The Kingsmen's entree into this world. Never one to miss an opportunity, K.C. sensed that the Cottage Inn could use a house band in the summer and told Noah he knew just the band the place needed. Whatever his reservations may have been in hiring a band that was five-sixths young white guys, Noah knew and trusted K.C. and agreed to give us a shot.

I'll admit that it was awkward at first, playing to a mostly black audience that was older than the one we played for at the Palm Terrace. But the audience did grow to like us, and we in turn helped cultivate a new demographic for the Cottage Inn. The rich Hamptonites and their kids began trickling into the club on weekends during the early summer of '62, and by summer's end the Cottage Inn was the place to be and be seen by the swingin' set of New Yorkers partying out in the Hamptons.

With the convergence of the black middle class and the rich white folks, The Kingsmen were able to pack the place night after night. With that success Noah was able to lure bigger and bigger names to the Cottage Inn. Amazing acts like Dinah Washington, James Brown, Ray Charles, Ike & Tina Turner and Etta James would come out to East Hampton to play Sunday night shows, after having played in New York City on Saturdays. The Kingsmen would be the house band on that same stage through all of this, and the best thing was we never had to change our repertoire from what we'd been playing at the Palm Terrace. The same music that got the Air Force dudes and Riverhead toughs up dancing had the black construction work-ers and beauty shop owners out on the dance floor twisting and doing the Shag along with the Hampton socialites.

For a couple of years it was quite the scene, and our following began to extend beyond the Palm Terrace and the Cottage Inn.

We'd play the Out of This World Inn off the highway in Wainscott, where we'd spy rich part-time Hamptonites like Henry Ford Jr. We'd also play the Surf and Sand on the Low Road in Montauk and the rockin' clubs like Billy DePetris' place in Bridgehampton. On weekends we'd throw a hootenanny at a little hole in the wall called the Jack of Eagles, on the Montauk Highway just as you came into East Hampton on Route 27. Some Friday nights the crowd would get so big it would spill out into the street, and the police had to come out to keep the traffic flowing. Through 1963 and 1964 we had the band circuit pretty well wrapped up, and my bass playing had gotten much stronger. We probably had a 50-song repertoire, and we'd morph into a seven- and eight-piece show band for the bigger summertime gigs. This included a great singer, Seth Weinberger, who was also the only guy I ever saw challenge Joe Butler for chick magnet status. It was fun to watch Seth and Joe go into competition mode whenever a hottie or two would come on the scene.

By this time I was playing with a group of guys I felt as close to as my own family (well, one of them really was my family). Joe and I would race back from Montauk after gigs at the Surf and Sand, with him taking the high road in his big Chevy Impala and me in my MGA, in an effort to get to Sam's Bar on Newtown Lane in East Hampton before closing time. Loser bought the round then we'd head out to the beach, where there would always be a party happening.

The only thing threatening to put an end to that life was the draft notice that appeared in my mailbox in the fall of 1963.

Once the accident took aviation off the table, I hadn't given a second thought to serving in the military. Vietnam was not yet building toward a climax, but I knew enough to know I didn't want to end up slogging it out with a rifle in the jungles of Southeast Asia. Guys I knew were cooking up all sorts of ways to avoid service, but there was no way, with the military background in my family, that I was going to be a draft dodger.

When I got my notice, I responded to an office in Riverhead, where a group of guys and I took a bus down to Whitehall Street in lower Manhattan for physicals. I'll never forget standing, buck naked except for my underpants and the brace that kept my injured leg straight, along with 30 other guys waiting to take pre-induction physicals.

A burly ol' sergeant came right up to me. "What are you doing in this line, boy?" he said.

"Waiting to take my physical, sir."

"Get in that office," he demanded and pointed toward a door. I went in and he asked for my draft notice, wrote something on it and handed it back before saying, "Get out of here, son, you can't fight no war."

I was not going to try to talk him out of it. Because of my injuries, I was 4F, physically unfit for military service.

I'd continue on with The Kingsmen into 1964, though after a couple of years of playing the same joints, with the same cover songs and the same stale beer, I have to admit I was beginning to get bored. The group had gotten far enough to record a few demos at Dick Charles Studios in Manhattan (I think it was "You Belong to Me," "Unchained Melody" and a couple of originals written by Skip, including one called "Second Time I Fell in Love"), and although I got to see what it was like working in a big New York recording studio, and Dick Charles himself praised our efforts, nothing ever came of them. It felt like the band was starting to run its course. The emergence of The Beatles and the other British groups in early '64 had put the music The Kingsmen were playing out of vogue pretty quickly. The gigs hadn't dried up yet, but they would. Our audience was changing, growing up, and we'd need to too.

I was going to be 21 in September, and the thought of college and a proper career had begun to appeal to me. I had some money sitting in the bank from my insurance settlement, so I'd be able to support myself as a student for a while until I chose a profession. I made the tough decision to leave the band in the summer of '64. The guys understood. Joe and Skip were talking about starting up a new band with a couple of other musicians from the Island and moving down to Greenwich Village, where there was a thriving music scene. King Charles would always be OK — his skills as a bandleader and sax player could be valuable in lots of different setups, so there'd be plenty of work for him.

I was the one who would be leaving the musical life for a new racket. But before I set to acting like an adult, I decided to take a trip that would extend my boyhood a little further.

Sometime in the summer of '64, my friend Peter Davey and I had dreamed up the romantic notion of traveling through Europe via motorcycle. Peter was an old-money kid from Connecticut whose family summered in nearby Remsenburg. I met him there, at a beach party. Peter and I had all the same interests, the same sense of rebellion, and were inseparable almost immediately. My first time living on my own had been in an apartment with Peter and another friend of ours named Doug Dickson in the summer of 1962, which is when we'd first started fantasizing about a bike trip. By the summer of '64, that discussion got serious.

The Beatles were really hot by this time, of course, sparking interest in tourism across the pond. Though some guys my age had resisted it, I thoroughly enjoyed the Merseybeat music and thought it would be cool to hear it in an authentic setting. In addition to the music, as a certified car nut I wanted to go to Italy to check out the Ferrari factory. And more than all that, I was a 20-year-old kid who had a little money in his pocket and wanted to go on an exciting adventure with a buddy. Peter and I were hell-bent on experiencing the real Europe instead of the tourist traps.

We flew from New York to Newfoundland to Scotland to London via Icelandair (a mere 26 hours) and set about buying the bikes that would carry us on our journey. We were sitting sipping rum-and-Cokes at our hotel in Soho when we saw an ad in one of the local papers for a huge bike-dealer in Surbiton, in the southwest suburbs of London. The dealer had hundreds of motorcycles for sale and was asking a price that sounded reasonable enough to us.

We took the train out to the 'burbs and made the deal, with Peter snagging a Triumph Tiger Cub twin cylinder 500cc bike, and me taking the 500cc Matchless G80 single cylinder. We'd made a slight miscalculation, though. By the time we picked through the hundreds of motorcycles and closed the deal, we not only had to learn how to work the bikes (shift, brake etc.), we also had to get them back to our hotel — 20 unfamiliar miles of left-side driving, complete with roundabouts, in rush hour traffic. A baptism by fire if there ever was one, but it started the trip on a much-needed cautionary note.

We'd get the hang of the bikes before long, moving on from a couple of atypically sunny days in the U.K., where the highlight was the Grand Prix we took in at Brands Hatch, through the countrysides of France, Germany, Denmark and Scandinavia. Once in Copenhagen, I agreed to go with Peter to the tattoo parlor, where he picked out a black skull tattoo that would have been positively terrifying . . . had he not fainted the second he saw the needle come out.

We came to France after a rainy week in Northern Germany (where we couldn't go to Berlin — the communists had closed off the Autobahn because it went through East Germany), and the bad weather gave us a chance to stay off the road, get dried out and have some repairs done on our bikes. It was a Sunday when we arrived in Paris, driving around looking for a sign in French indicating motorcycle repair. When we found one, I knocked on the door, and though the man who answered was a bit perturbed, he offered to fix my throttle right then. After he'd opened his shop and turned on the lights he saw my guitar case and asked in broken English what kind of music I played. I seemed to surprise him with my ability to speak high-school-level French, and he asked me to play some *"américaine"* music on the guitar. Not quite sure what would be a suitable song to play, I picked "Louie, Louie," a big hit for another band called The Kingsmen (the hitmaking group was a surf act from Portland, and had no relationship to our Kingsmen), and one in which Peter and I were well rehearsed. The motorcycle mechanic called his whole family down to hear us sing and play this American pop song. From then on, we played it everywhere we went in Europe, sometimes with better results than others. In this case, "Louie, Louie" earned us not only free bike repair but a delightful home-cooked Sunday meal and accommodations for the night. I think about that day every time I hear the song.

It was while venturing from Lyon, France, to the Swiss Alps — where the temperature went from 70 degrees Fahrenheit to zero Celsius and back to 70 — where things really took a turn for the interesting.

Peter and I had been traveling single file, with the lead driver alerting the following one to hazards ahead. I was in the lead as we came out of a tunnel, and when I came around a corner I saw the unmistakable glare of black ice on the road. This particular road was all switchbacks, with no guardrail, and beyond the outside shoulder was a steep drop-off of hundreds of feet of mountain rock. I immediately slowed down gently, put both feet down for stability and as I came to a stop I turned on my seat to signal Peter to slow down and stop. Unfortunately he was about 100 yards behind me and around a curve by the time he saw me. By then he was already in the black ice. As he attempted to slow down, he fell instantly. I watched as he hit the ground and, in what seemed like slow motion, slid from the inside of the road to the outside shoulder, heading off the cliff toward probable death. By some miracle he came to a stop just inches from going over. Peter was battered, dazed, but not dead. He managed to get back up on his bike and we ventured down the road to a rest stop.

We pulled ourselves together at a roadside stop area, just before a long tunnel, when we were told by highway workers we'd be the last motorcycles to be allowed through for the winter, as the roads would become too dangerous due to the weather. As Peter set about confirming that he hadn't broken any bones or suffered any serious injuries during the spill, I looked around to see the odd sight of two 18-wheel semis, painted white and bearing the big, unmistakable blue-and-white oval Ford logo.

I was a car guy, so this immediately raised my interest. On a complete whim, I went over and started talking to one of the truck drivers, an American who had stopped to have a cup of coffee after coming out of the black ice. I told him I was a car lover from America and asked what was in the trucks.

His voice lowered to a whisper. "Don't tell anyone I told you, but it's the first GT40 prototypes." I'd been reading in the American car magazines I devoured about the GT40 race cars Ford was developing to try to compete in the Ferrari- and Jaguar-dominated 24 Hours of Le Mans race. The GT40 would win four straight races starting in 1966, but this was 1964 and hardly anyone had seen the car. "We're taking them to Monza for testing," he added.

Monza, Italy, was the site of the famous Monza racetrack with the "Monza Wall" and its 40 degrees of banking on the corners. It was one of the fastest racetracks in the world, and it was where Ferrari took its race cars for testing. I'd been thinking of visiting Monza before I knew the GT40s were going to be there. The truck driver told me the cars would be there within two days, and that if I could make it up to the track he'd try to get us into the course to see them run. There was nothing anyone could do to keep me away now. I told him not to forget us, as I definitely planned to take him up on the offer.

The trip into Switzerland then became little more than a necessary stop before we could reach Italy, and we stopped for the night in Lugano, where Peter nursed his wounds from the fall and I got out the map and plotted the next two days down to Milano. Switzerland was nice and all, but it was a way station.

We approached Monza around lunchtime. The weather had become dreary and cold, but I could hear high-performance engines running at high rpm in the distance, and that got the adrenaline flowing. Astonishingly, the gates were wide open to the track and we pulled in and drove as close to the trackside pits as possible. Just as an official-looking person began heading our way, probably to question why we were there, I spotted our friend the truck driver and shouted out to get his attention. I think he was amazed to see that we'd really made it. He came right over, convincing the track official that we were there with Ford's permission. This driver was also part of the trackside crew and told us where to observe so as not to be in the way or draw the team manager's attention.

And there right in front of me, idling with the hardiest growl I had ever heard from a race car, was the GT40, gleaming white with Ford-blue racing stripes. The next thing I knew, the driver put the car into gear and headed out onto the track with the most beautiful sound, like a bass guitar on hyperdrive. After a lap or two it was up to full speed and, to put it mildly, I had just become witness to a unique event in sports car racing history, seeing in person what up to that moment had been viewed by only a few in the car racing world. When the car came to a stop, who got out but Dan Gurney, one of only two Americans to win a Formula 1 race, and one of my godlike heroes. Peter and I were stunned — Pete was not quite the racing fan I was, but he knew we were witnessing history.

As if that wasn't enough, the driver of the truck who had made all of this possible came over and asked how I'd like to go around the track for a couple of laps in the GT40. I'd like it, I said. But just as I was getting into the car, the team manager rushed over and said a ride wouldn't be possible, citing insurance concerns. Ironic, since car-insurance-related matters were the reason I was able to travel to Europe in the first place! But as a compromise, the Ford guys let us drive our motorcycles up on the steep-banked track at Monza for a few laps, which was both a thrill and a challenge.

We did fine on the flat part of the track, but navigating that curve requires a rider to speed up to 60 to 70 miles per hour, otherwise you'd just fall over in the corner. It gave me a whole new understanding of how something made to look so easy on TV or in the movies can be very difficult to do in real life. I approached the turn with extreme caution and as the wall came up, I would slow down and turn around and reverse course for a few yards before mustering up the courage to drive again. Maybe my accident, or the episode with the black ice, had given me caution. But I knew I'd never get this chance again, and finally got up the nerve to go up onto the wall. Getting up to about 60 mph, I steered up onto it and to my amazement, did not fall down or go flying off the outer edge of the track. After a few laps at high speed on the bikes we bid farewell to our new friends at Ford Motorsports and Monza.

I walked out of Monza flying sky-high, a feeling that endured for the remainder of my time in Europe. The rest of the trip was pretty much a blur, though eventful in its own right.

On my way to the Ferrari factory in Maranello, I stopped at a small hotel, where I encountered Mike Parkes, the retired Formula 1 driver who had become the director of competition for the Ferrari racing team. Parkes graciously arranged an exclusive, private tour of the factory, another tremendous privilege and thrill. I wondered, as I watched the work that went into making those high-performance vehicles, whether I'd ever be able to dream of owning one. In October 1964, owning a Ferrari was not on my radar screen, but anything was possible, I thought. Maybe some day.

After visiting some of Peter's extended family in Florence, we headed down to Rome and somehow ended up at the American embassy on the night of the 1964 presidential election. As luck would have it, as Lyndon B. Johnson danced with Lady Bird at the inaugural ball a continent away, I ran into an old girlfriend of mine from East Hampton High School, Judy Pontick, who was living with someone working in Rome. Another strange coincidence on a trip full of them.

Then it was on to Spain, where we stayed for two weeks in Sitges and met two wonderful Canadian girls about our age, Carolyn Liddle and Judy Gunn, who accompanied us to a bullfight in Barcelona, and were our constant companions during this part of the journey. We were all treated like family at Ricky's Tavern and Hotel, our accommodations while in Sitges. (Nearly 40 years later I would reunite with Carolyn and Judy at a gig in Canada, and we have stayed in touch ever since.) We again impersonated the other Kingsmen and "Louie, Louie" for our Spanish hosts, eventually having to own up to not being *those* Kingsmen.

After eight weeks of travel and innumerable repairs to our bikes, we were exhilarated but ready to shut it down. Exhausted, we put our bikes on a cargo ship in the port at Barcelona, eventually made our way up to Madrid, and flew back to the States.

It had been the trip of a lifetime, but my journey was over, and it was time to get serious about life. Little did I know that a different kind of adventure, one I never could have foreseen, would be starting when I returned stateside. As it turned out, that trip would include some similar hairpin turns.

Chapter 3

DO YOU BELIEVE IN MAGIC

It was the second week of December 1964, and I was just back from Europe. It was good to be home and seeing family and friends, telling them stories and lies about our adventures overseas.

I returned from Europe thinking I'd better get a college degree. Having given my notice to The Kingsmen, I no longer had a regular gig playing music. While completing my postgraduate year at Westhampton Beach High School, I had passed a test qualifying me for an entry-level job with New York State as a civil engineer, but having met the Ford GT40 team and toured the Ferrari factory in Europe, I was motivated to get a full engineering degree and start a career in automobile design. When I saw that Southampton College was offering enrollment for spring semester classes on the new campus in the Shinnecock Hills, I registered for classes that were to begin in January 1965.

Meanwhile, I was eager to get my motorcycle back stateside. I'd had it sent home by steamship from Barcelona, and it was to be delivered by customs to a pier on the West Side of Manhattan in mid-December, so I called my brother Skip and arranged to stay with him in Greenwich Village for a couple of days until the bike was released. Since I'd left for Europe, Skip and Joe Butler had changed the name of The Kingsmen to The Sellouts and moved to the Village, where they'd become the neighborhood's first rock band, playing a residency at one of Village icon Trude Heller's clubs on West Eighth Street. Rock 'n' roll had been the domain of midtown places like the Peppermint Lounge on 45th Street and Metropole Cafe on Seventh Avenue near 48th Street, where I'd taken plenty of cues from the hipper bands on how to dress and act like a rocker. The Village, meanwhile, had mainly been about folk music. It was odd to see a rock band there, but The Sellouts were gaining a nice foothold.

Most Manhattan-going guys my age, those not in a band, would head to Bleecker and MacDougal at the epicenter of the Village in search of entertainment. The whole atmosphere of Greenwich Village was less touristy than uptown, and, not insignificantly, it was where the girls were. Skip was living in a typical low-rent apartment with a couple of other guys on Carmine Street in the West Village. Before I hopped on the train to Penn Station, Skip suggested I bring along my bass guitar. I thought twice about lugging it, since music was not on the front burner for me at the moment and dragging it on the train was a hassle, but I ultimately complied with the request. I would soon learn why that idea was floated.

I got on the train in Westhampton Beach and switched at Penn Station for the subway to take me down to the Village. After trudging up the steps of the Sixth Avenue subway, I was greeted by a cold and windy December day, along with sights and sounds that were brand new to a relative country bumpkin like me. I'd been to the entertainment district at the central part of the Village plenty of times, but had never really experienced the West Village, and as I headed down Carmine Street, I felt like I was walking into *West Side Story*. An endless array of little street-front shops selling produce and groceries. Pizza parlors and cleaners, and tough-looking kids hanging out on front stoops. Also, it was occurring to me that cities have a smell you don't experience in the country, that potpourri of diesel exhaust and garbage, stirred to life by the constant commotion of any big city. It was an aroma I'd first noticed in London and would later come to recognize in most every big city I would visit. But for now, it was all a little intimidating for suburban Steve Boone.

I tried not to look like a hick from the country, but my reticence and fear of this ultra-urban neighborhood must have been evident. I was here to get my motorcycle and go back to Westhampton, and if I got to meet some new musicians and jam a little while I was here, I was up for that too, but I sure didn't want to get my ass kicked while doing it.

I finally found the number on Skip's building — 64, I think it was — and scanned the broken metal nameplates for something familiar amid the Italian and Jewish surnames. I pushed what I hoped was the right button and waited for a voice to come out sounding like my brother's.

Instead, I heard a female voice.

"Who's there?"

Taken by surprise, I muttered, "Skip's brother." A buzzer sounded, the door rattled and I pushed it open. As I started to walk up the well-worn wooden steps to what I thought was my brother's apartment, this attractive girl says, "Hello, Skip's brother." It sure sounded like a come-on, but maybe she was just being nice.

With my bass in one hand and a small bag over my shoulder, trying my best to stay cool, I agreed that yes, I was Skip's brother. "I'm Ruth," the woman replied. She opened the door to an apartment, and with very little light to see by, in I went. The smell of pot was in the air, as was the smell of youthful spirit. With sheets hung on the windows to block the light, not much in the way of real furniture, some strange paintings on the walls and some Bob Dylan on the phonograph, I was smack-dab in the middle of a beatnik lair. There were Joe and Skip and some more girls, and a couple of guys I did not know. In its own way it was a very cool, relaxed scene. You definitely didn't think anyone's parents were going to come walking into the room.

"I can see you guys have moved uptown," I said to no one in particular.

A couple of people turned to look at who had come in, and I couldn't help but notice that Ruth was checking me out. Ruth was tall and not skinny but also not overweight, and carried herself confidently.

Joe spoke up as usual: "It sure beats the street. Who are you, Boone, *Better Homes and* fucking *Gardens*? Where are you living nowadays — under a rock, or staying at Mommy's house?"

Joe and I always talked to each other this way, but to the unacquainted it sounded like a fistfight was about to break out. Everyone was looking at us, so I lightened the mood.

"Well, at least it's a step up from that shithole you were crashing in out in Bridgehampton."

I got introduced around and made some small talk before Joe spoke up again. "Hey, you want to put that bass to use?"

"I don't know, Butler, is it going to get swallowed up by this rancid trash heap you call an apartment?"

"Not here, dummy. There are a couple of guys rehearsing down the street. They're putting together a group, and . . ."

"I'm done with groups," I insisted, looking around. "The rock 'n' roll lifestyle has become a little too *extravagant* for me."

"Suit yourself, but these guys are legit. They've done some recording. They're real musicians, so I doubt you would fit in."

"Fuck it," I said. "Spending another second in this rat's nest is bound to be hazardous to my health anyway. Where can I find these virtuosos?"

Joe and Skip directed me to take my bass down to a little music club on West Third Street called the Village Music Hall. As I took the damp, chilly 15-minute walk to West Third and MacDougal, where the Music Hall was, I must have looked a sight. Though I didn't know the term "mod," that was my look — kind of a mix of what I had seen in Europe and what the guys in the bands uptown were wearing — with tight jeans, boots and a denim or leather jacket.

My hair was long, but having the roadster made keeping my hair in the fashionable "DA" style impossible, so it just kind of flopped on my head. People always accused me of fashioning my hair after The Beatles, but that wasn't the case — it was tailored to meet the needs of my car. I wasn't sure whether these Village folkie types I presumed I was about to meet would share my look, sense of fashion or general sensibilities about music or anything else.

As Carmine Street changed to Sixth Avenue and West Third Street began, I headed east, passing a fabled outdoor basketball court called "the Cage," where all manner of past and future basketball greats played pick-up games; a fortune teller, where I was tempted briefly to get a quick reading; parking garages; and of course a pizza shop. I also noticed a small storefront called the Night Owl Cafe that would be featuring some folk artist that night. I glanced in the window and thought, "That room doesn't look big enough for live music." But I hurried on, as it was a chilly day and I didn't want to miss these guys who were expecting me. Suddenly there it was, one of those sandwich-board folding signs on the sidewalk announcing what was going on inside, and in crudely painted letters both on the sign and the overhead awning: the Village Music Hall.

I walked in, and here were these two really different-looking young guys. They both had long hair like mine, but one was very folkie-looking, à la Kingston Trio, with little round granny-type eyeglasses and jeans and a T-shirt. The other one had darker, Jewish features, with long hair all messed up. He'd soon reveal himself to be a funny, outgoing sort but looked like the type of guy you might meet at a Civil Rights march. Clothing-wise, they didn't look terribly different than me, which was a relief. The wild-looking one shouted out, "You must be Boonie." I nodded and then the other guy walked over, reached out his hand and said, "Hello, and come on in," in a real friendly way. I'd just been introduced to John Sebastian and Zal Yanovsky.

I put my bass down and we did the name thing and were all talking fast and excitedly. I was already feeling good about meeting these guys. Zalman Yanovsky — now there was a name, with a personality to match. His dark eyes, giant smile, nervous chatter and high energy were magnetic. His mannerisms and sense of humor reminded me of a cartoon character, not unlike a Jewish comedian in the Don Rickles vein. Luckily I'd had an introduction into this personality type and offbeat sense of humor via Diana Hirsch, a Jewish girl who was my East Hampton girlfriend in the summer of '63. I didn't really speak Zally's language, but thanks to Diana and her family I understood it.

John, the guy with the glasses, was more reserved and looked eccentric in his own way. In addition to his guitar he had this belt-like strap with about a dozen harmonicas attached to it. Now that was something I hadn't seen before. He projected a very confident aura.

We seemed to hit it off right away in conversation, not least due to the fact that they had the same musical influences I did: Elvis, Chuck Berry, The Everly Brothers, Buddy Holly, Motown, and more recently The Beatles and the rest of the British invasion. John and Zally both had more of a background in Delta blues and traditional folk than I did, but their passion for this kind of music made an uninitiated guy like me interested real quick.

"I've been working with this Delta blues singer named Mississippi John Hurt," John said. This was a name I had heard in conversations with King Charles and some of the musicians who would come through the Cottage Inn.

Zally did his share of name-dropping too, citing some of the performers he knew and had played with while working the folk club circuit. Zally had met John earlier that year at their friend Cass Elliot's apartment, and they'd both played briefly with Cass in a band called The Mugwumps — though John's building relationship with Zally had become too distracting for the manager of the band, Roy Silver, and John was fired. The Mugwumps broke up soon after. (Some of this history is recounted on The Mamas and the Papas' 1967 hit "Creeque Alley.")

But these guys weren't just trying to impress me with their résumés. They saw a business opportunity here, and made their pitch.

"I've got some songs I've written by blending the traditional sounds of the R&B records with folk-style guitar," John said, launching into a tune called "Good Time Music." The tune sounded familiar to me — it was a ringer for the recent Tommy Tucker R&B hit "Hi-Heel Sneakers" — but the lyrics were a statement of intent, diminishing the music that was being passed off as rock 'n' roll in the early '60s, while simultaneously praising The Beatles, their English brethren and the type of vibe they'd brought to the radio.

Though the song was derivative, I was impressed. These guys had their shit together. When he finished, John said, "All we need now is a bass player and a drummer to pull it off."

"And some decent amps," Zally interjected.

"When we saw The Beatles on *The Ed Sullivan Show* we knew this is what's coming next," John added.

You could tell these two fellas thought they were on the cusp of a new movement, and it was easy to get sucked in by their enthusiasm. There was talk of producers and managers. John and Zally were just a couple of 20-year-old guys, but they were not going to be content playing covers for a bunch of partygoers. I was impressed. These were serious musicians.

John concluded by asking if I'd like to jam a little bit. "Well, I didn't come to paint," I said. That cracked them up, and I opened up my case and out came my ice-box-white Fender P Bass.

I wasn't too used to jamming without a drummer, but for some reason we seemed to be really clicking on the tunes we picked to play, including some Chuck Berry covers and R&B-type jams. John, who was the Village-bred son of a classical harmonica virtuoso and recording professional (also named John Sebastian, though he'd grown up as Giovanni Puglese), could really lay down a good solid rhythm on the guitar, and would also pick up one of the mouth harps and tear into some great riffs. All the while seeming really concentrated on his playing, without saying much.

Zally, who was from Canada and had played coffeehouses in Toronto before striking out in The Halifax Three and later The Mugwumps with Cass and another future Papa named Denny Doherty, was all over the neck of his guitar. He had this outrageous Guild electric, and was working the whammy bar like it was a gear shift, all the while letting out whoops and grunts as he played. A very excitable guy, but man was he good. I hadn't seen too many folkies play like that.

What struck me more than anything was that these guys played loud. This of course was before the age of Marshall stacks, when Fender and Ampeg were the standard for guitar amps. Out on the Island we had been using Silvertone amps bought straight out of the Sears catalog, which were much less expensive than Fender or Ampeg and would distort without much encouragement. In my experience you did whatever necessary to minimize the distortion, so it was striking to me that John and Zally were intentionally making their amps sound like fingernails on a blackboard. I would become a convert to this new sound in time.

In spite of all this, I could not have been more fascinated. The more we played, the better it seemed to get, and before I knew it we had spent a couple of hours at the Village Music Hall — which, like Zally, I would soon begin referring to as the "Music Tit" — just thrashing away. I seem to remember a joint being passed around, which made the session even more enjoyable. A couple of passersby stuck their head in while we were playing, and by the time we put the guitars down a small stir was already erupting on and around West Third Street. People were talking about us.

After packing up I was invited by the guys to a party at an apartment on MacDougal Street just across from the Kettle of Fish, a place I knew as one of the tourist spots to feature real folk talent. I was pretty impressed that these guys knew someone who lived on the street where all the action was in Greenwich Village. Looking back, the rest of that day seems like a dream, or like something a bad screenwriter would dream up out of a need to crowbar a bunch of new characters into a story. Though it seems unbelievable, I really did meet some of the most important people in the Greenwich Village music scene, and in a matter of hours, The Lovin' Spoonful's story had begun.

When we knocked on the door of the apartment, a tall, skinny blond-haired guy answered the door and introduced himself to me as Erik Jacobsen. He was a banjo player in a folk group called The Knob Lick Upper 10,000 (it was time I got used to strange band names), which had recorded a couple of albums for Mercury Records and even played Carnegie Hall. Erik explained that he was looking to move from playing to production. The first thing I noticed about Erik wasn't Erik at all but his beautiful girlfriend, Tinker, who had long, straight black hair and the cutest smile. I could not take my eyes off her.

I was trying to act cool, but inside I was not really sure how to act around all these new friends, so at first I just listened and tried to piece together who they were from the stories they told. The guys played some more of the tunes they had been working on, and though I felt a little out of my element, I liked what I was hearing. Some pot had started going around the room when the doorbell rang, and everyone got nervous that it might be the cops. But when the door opened another tall, skinny guy, this one with red hair, came in and played a disc he had just been working on. He was introduced to me as Jerry Yester, from a Village group called The Modern Folk Quartet. The demo he played was called "Lady Godiva" and was a unique combination of California surf music and electric folk, with John Sebastian contributing vocals. Man! These guys were up to something. Then Erik put on a demo of this singer/songwriter he was producing by the name of Tim Hardin, singing a tune called "Don't Make Promises." Wow, what a song. So far I was pretty impressed. I was beginning to feel like I had stumbled into the inner circle of cool musicians in Greenwich Village, which I'd later realize I had. At some point, the party moved to a bar on Sullivan Street called Googie's, where we fortified ourselves against the December chill with some tequila and beer. Little did I know I had just met a group of people who would be an almost daily presence in my life for the next three years.

Whatever it was that these guys were up to sure was starting to sound good to me, and I decided to stay on for a few more days in New York. My extended stay would give me a chance to see John play live at that tiny folk club I had passed on West Third Street, the Night Owl. John said the players he would be jamming with were really good, and convinced me to stick around.

I showed up at the Night Owl Cafe the next night and wasn't sure what to make of the scene. The club was small for live music, not to mention strangely configured. It was a long, narrow room — basically a railroad flat, with the stage positioned in the middle of one of the long walls, facing the other long wall. The audience mostly sat on either side of the stage, with fewer patrons in the middle since there were banquettes that broke up the continuity of the room and little space for in-front seating. It was definitely more like a coffeehouse than a nightclub.

When I got there before the show, the place was almost full, and John introduced me to some of the players. First was the singer whose name and wonderful demos, produced by Erik Jacobsen, I had heard at Erik's house a few days earlier: Tim Hardin. Tim was an ex–U.S. Marine, like my dad, and that alone caught my attention. Who would have thought a Marine could write such wonderful, sensitive songs? Next John introduced me to his crazy-haired roommate, Buzzy Linhart, who was playing the vibraphone and acted about as high-strung and eccentric as he looked. Felix Pappalardi, who was going to play bass, was very friendly, and got my attention with his guitar-bodied electric Guild bass, unlike anything I'd ever seen. Onstage, I saw John and a very beatnik-looking guy whose 12-string guitar John was helping to tune. This was Fred Neil, who I was introduced to as he was tuning up.

As the room filled up with cigarette smoke and people, despite the fact that there was no alcohol served, the atmosphere was electric.

The crowd in this club looked very hip. You could tell it was not the usual day-trippers from the Island and Jersey, but more like the types that would come out to the Jack of Eagles in East Hampton on summer nights. Very artistic and serious-looking, but still with an almost childlike enthusiasm once the show began.

After about a half-hour of tuning, the lights dimmed and a comedian/MC named Al Mamlet got up and told a couple of jokes. Then, with an almost eerie silence in the room, the entertainers were introduced. It was billed as a Fred Neil appearance, but it was obvious that the sidemen were all just as well known to the audience. Then Fred introduced the first song, and as he began singing "The water is wide/ I can't cross over," I was completely blown away. Fred's voice was so warm and sonorous and the backing instruments so perfectly suited for the accompaniment — with Fred on that difficult-to-tune but beautiful-sounding 12-string, John on a second guitar and harmonica and Buzzy, Tim and Felix filling in perfectly — that I think my jaw actually dropped open. I remember thinking after that first song that this was the best live entertainment I had ever seen or heard, even better than Lenny Bruce!

Tim sang a few of his songs, with John accompanying on harp and guitar, Buzzy playing vibes in a way I had never heard before and Felix on bass, equally locked in. It was as though these guys were a band that played together every day. By the end of this set, though I hadn't quite forgotten about cars or college, I was totally convinced that I wanted to be part of this scene.

All the players on the Night Owl stage would become more famous than they were that night. Tim Hardin, who wrote staples like "If I Were a Carpenter" and "Reason to Believe," made several highly acclaimed albums in the late '60s before succumbing to heroin addiction and dying of an overdose in 1980. Felix Pappalardi was a founding member of the band Mountain and went on to produce albums for Cream and others before being shot to death by his wife under mysterious circumstances in 1983. Buzzy Linhart made albums and was in great demand as a vibraphonist throughout the

'70s, in addition to co-writing Bette Midler's theme song "(You Got to Have) Friends." And Fred Neil, who wrote the likes of "Everybody's Talkin'" (Harry Nilsson) and "Candy Man" (Roy Orbison), made several influential albums in the mid-to-late '60s before later retiring from music. He died in 2001.

I left that night and practically floated back to Skip's apartment. All the reasons I had for going back to school and getting myself started in a proper career were disappearing into the dark sky above New York City. I knew there were no guarantees, but a voice was telling me, "Follow your dream where it leads you. You'll never know 'til you get there." This would be a mantra I'd turn to for the rest of my life.

I got to Skip's apartment and found myself in the middle of a full-blown party, with seemingly everyone, including my brother, stoned and laughing. Me, I was just tired. Before I could even get my jacket off, Ruth — the girl who'd let me in the day before — walked up and said, "You look tired, do you want to go over to my apartment and get some rest? It's not going to quiet down here for a long time."

It was getting late and I asked, "How come everyone is talking at once and being real loud?"

"Oh, there are some 'trols going around and I think everyone took one or two," Ruth said.

"'Trols?" I asked.

"Escatrol, it's a diet pill or speed, you know — amphetamine? You want one?"

I had heard of diet pills, but at six-foot-four and 160 pounds I sure didn't need to go on a diet, so I had never taken one. Where pot will keep you in a talkative but mellow and subdued state, these 'trols seemed to have everyone testing the limits of the city noise ordinance.

"How long does the 'trol keep one in that state?" I asked.

"Oh you mean loud and speed-rapping? Well the main effect wears off in a couple of hours and then you can just drink a beer or a shot of whiskey and you're back to normal."

I took a long look at Ruth, obviously older and more experienced than me, and figured what the fuck.

"Gimme one," I said. "How long does it take to feel the effect?"

"When did you last eat?" she said with a glint in her eyes.

"Oh this afternoon sometime." I had been too busy to eat dinner before the show at the Night Owl.

"Well then, you'll feel it pretty quick."

Soon a joint came floating by and I took a hit. The next thing I knew, not only was I feeling stoned but this incredible warmth and confidence came over me. Ruth was staying by my side. I didn't feel out of control, but definitely high like I'd never been.

The party went on with a lot of talking, especially me raving about how great the show was at the Night Owl that evening. Everyone there knew or was aware of the players I mentioned, and I was answered with nodding heads and general agreement that these were some of the best musicians in the Village.

By now it was getting real late and Ruth came over to me and reiterated her previous invitation. "You're starting to look asleep on your feet, why don't we go to my house and get some sleep . . . you won't be getting any here for a while."

Now that was the second time tonight Ruth had invited me to spend the night at her apartment, but I thought she was with Tom Danaher, one of the guys I'd met at Joe and Skip's the day before, who would later become Skip's bandmate. I looked at her quizzically and she said, "We're just going to my place to get out of the noise and partying."

As we left, Tom said "See ya later" to both of us and off we went. It was just a few blocks to Ruth's place, which was a small apartment just south of Houston on Spring Street. The speed was having an effect on me, and despite needing sleep, I did not feel at all like going to bed. Once in the apartment, we both had a beer and then another beer, after which I started to feel a little sleepy.

She said, "Why don't you lie down on the bed and I'll make some tea that will really relax you."

Ruth had long hair that had been in a ponytail, and as she made the tea she let her hair down, brought the tea over and said, "Let's get comfortable." She slipped into the bed beside me.

At this point it's probably appropriate to mention that I was a 21-year-old virgin. One of my goals in going to Europe had been to get laid. Ever since my accident, which happened right at the peak of my teenage horniness, I had developed an incredible case of insecurity about my appearance. I had lost a lot of weight and also grown a couple of inches since the accident and looked like the proverbial beanpole. Being in a rock band like The Kingsmen made it much easier to meet girls, but being in a rock band also brands you as someone who must be incredibly sexually experienced. I was the exception to that rule. The combination of insecurity and inexperience caused me not to be very pushy with the girls I dated, including my high school sweetheart, Lynne Bishop. My friend Peter, on the other hand, was the quintessential ladies' man and had no problem with promiscuity at all. Our trip to Europe was to be a bacchanal for us both. Our first stop was in London, and on the second night in our hotel room Peter said to me, "I'm gonna get laid, do you wanna come with me?" Well here it was, and I said, "Let's go." We headed down to Carnaby Street and turned off into a smaller side street where the girls were hanging out in the windows of obvious brothels. Peter immediately found a lady to his liking, but after two or three looks I chickened out and went back to the hotel. This scene would repeat itself several times on the trip. I surely wasn't a prude; I just had a mental block and did not know how to overcome it.

But here I was, in Ruth's bed, and another moment of truth had arrived.

The virgin in me was screaming, "You've never been laid and this girl is giving herself to you — do it, dummy," but my brain was saying, "What if her boyfriend walks in unannounced?" So I said, "What about Tom?"

"Oh, we have an open relationship," Ruth replied. I had no idea what she was talking about.

"What if the door opens and he comes in?" I asked.

She laughed and told me to be quiet. This was it, I finally was going to get laid and at last become a man. Unfortunately, even after an hour of trying, my little man would not cooperate. This would be the first but not the last time I would find out that certain combinations of drugs and alcohol can make having sex for a male all but impossible. I was crushed. Ruth must have had this happen before and gave it the good ol' college try but finally said, "Let's both get some sleep and see what happens in the morning."

By this time I was totally exhausted and fell right off to sleep, boyfriend or not, and woke up the next morning to a still-ready Ruth. Within minutes of opening my eyes, I could finally say I wasn't a virgin anymore. It wasn't the best sex I would ever have, and surely not for Ruth, but I had crossed the Rubicon.

A new phase in my personal life had begun, and now it was on to the professional.

By this point John, Zal and I had already decided to move forward together as a band, but we'd need a concrete plan before we proceeded. The competition in the Village was getting fierce, and since all three of us had been working musicians, we were all weary of venturing down the slow road to glory. Either the concept was going to work fast or it was going to fail fast, and we could all move on to our next hustle. For me, that meant a temporary delay in my studies. I agreed not to attend the spring semester at college, instead dedicating six months to seeing if we could get a band off the ground.

We wanted to record some demos, and having a professional producer like Erik Jacobsen in the fold would help with that important part of the project. But we'd also need to play some gigs and try to find ourselves a record deal, and for that we'd need a savvy manager. Zally and Erik knew a guy named Bob Cavallo who had managed The Halifax Three and The Mugwumps, and had told Zally to look him up when he was ready to start his next project. So the day after the Fred Neil gig we had our first band meeting with Cavallo. I joined up with John and Zal and headed over to the site of said meeting — Erik's apartment. We were sitting around smoking a joint when we saw a short, round, 20-something guy with an open-collar suit walk through the door. It was then that we got a quick primer on Zally's special relationship with Bob Cavallo.

"Hey, everybody! Big fat Blob is here! Hi, big fat Blob! Come meet Steve."

You could tell by the look of resignation on Cavallo's face that he'd heard this particular schtick from Zally before. We did our introductions and made some small talk, and as if on cue Zally spoke up.

"OK, Bob, tell us now, like you told me the last two times, how you're going to make us all rich."

"Well, I always told Zal I'd be interested in anything he did, and I am interested in managing you, though just to warn you, Zally told me about the band, and you guys have to be realistic that you're different from most of the acts making records. I think you know what you're up against."

We knew what that meant.

"Because we're not British," John said.

"Exactly," Cavallo said. "Look, right now everyone is trying to copy The Beatles' sound, and from what I heard of Zally and John's playing and how good some of John's new songs are, I think we can pitch you guys as something that can work alongside the Merseybeat sound. Between Erik and me, we've met some of the top people in the record business, and if you guys make me some good demos, I will get you a record deal. The fact that you're bringing a fresh twist to the kind of thing The Beatles are doing can work in your favor if we find a label that wants to stay ahead of the curve."

That was music to our ears, but given that we hadn't played any actual music in a public setting, the conversation shifted to how we'd survive while this band went from concept to reality. I had already paid my registration fees at Southampton College, and though I still had a bit of money left from my insurance settlement, it was bound to evaporate fast if I was living on my own with no income to offset expenses. At least on the Island I could play pickup gigs for pocket money. This six-month plan gave little consideration to making gig money, and we still had to pay the rent and eat. We had to talk about how we were going to keep ourselves alive and well.

"I can probably make some money doing sideman gigs in the studio," John said.

Zally noted that he was used to living on the street, but offered what would become one of the most important suggestions in the folklore of our band. "I think Cass is staying at the Albert and we might be able to crash with her for a while."

The Albert Hotel, on West Tenth Street and University Place, not far from Bleecker and MacDougal, was a crash pad for folkies who were in New York for an extended gig or trying to find a more permanent residence. It was in disrepair but was conveniently located and had developed a reputation as a friendly place for would-be musicians. Cass and Denny Doherty were still in New York looking for the next stop on their path out of folkie purgatory. Hearing Zally talk about Cass' talent and gregarious personality made meeting her a must, and the Albert — more or less a flophouse — is where that would happen.

Meanwhile, Cavallo explained that he had an interest in a night-club in Washington, D.C., called the Shadows — where he'd met Zal — and with some additional financial help from Bob's dad, we would collectively have a means of keeping starvation at bay. Cavallo also had connections among other club owners that could get us some decent-profile gigs. He was closer to our age than most management types, seemed to understand and sympathize with what we wanted to accomplish musically and was a known quantity who had been introduced into our circle by one of our own. We also had no other options, as managers were not beating down the door of an unknown group without a name, a drummer, a realized concept or any established track record.

"OK, you're hired," John said, as Zal and I nodded in agreement. "Congratulations on making your life truly miserable."

Cavallo looked a little surprised at the haste of the decision, but shrugged his shoulders, shook our hands and was officially the manager of our unnamed band.

The drummer issue would be settled next. Tapping into the same vein that had made me a member of the band, my brother Skip and Joe Butler, The Sellouts' drummer, recommended Jan Buchner, our part-timer from The Kingsmen and a solid player. Though he wasn't really a drummer, Buzzy Linhart's name was mentioned as a fallback option, but Jan would be the first target. Fortuitously, or so we thought, Jan not only agreed to try out for the band, he also offered us a rehearsal space. He was the manager of a small inn out on eastern Long Island called the Bull's Head Inn, which was owned by a member of the DuPont family and was right on the Montauk Highway in the heart of Bridgehampton. It was not a large place, but it would be big enough for us to rehearse and crash at for a couple of weeks. Since it was December, the inn was closed, which meant that in addition to a rehearsal space in the main sitting room, we could have the place to ourselves when not rehearsing.

So we gave Jan the gig and took a couple of weeks to get our affairs together over the holidays before starting the band in earnest. What I remember most about this period was the bone-chilling drive on my motorcycle from Manhattan back to the Island. Right after Christmas 1964, when I had broken the news of my plan to my highly disappointed parents, I reconvened with the guys in the Village. We managed to get the gear and instruments into Jan's customized '53 Ford and the Austin-Healey 3000 MK II I'd been keeping at my parents' house (another handy by-product of the insurance settlement) and took the Long Island Expressway to our new rehearsal space. It was there that our story nearly came to an end before it had even begun. As we drove out the LIE that cold winter afternoon — in typically heavy traffic, with me driving, Zally in the passenger seat and John in the jump seat in back — an accident started happening right in front of us. Cars were swerving and skidding out, and as I tried to steer away from a collision, it was almost as if I was guided by a magical hand, and a lane opened up and we blew right through untouched by anything save the sweat on all our brows.

John, who was a city kid and didn't drive, let out a "holy shit." Zally tried to scream but nothing came out except a cigarette from his pack, which he promptly lit with shaking hands. And I gave a silent thanks to whatever saint watched over me that day. While this to me was good luck combined with the great reflexes I had been blessed with, I think it elevated me in John and Zally's eyes to an exalted status as a driver. As we recomposed ourselves, I remember thinking, "This band has the angels on its side." This wouldn't be the last time I'd feel that no matter what, this band would survive, though that feeling was put to the test early and often as we tried to find our footing.

The arrival of a small British sports car, loaded up with three long-haired guys and as much equipment as could be crammed into every available crevice of the vehicle, at the Bull's Head Inn in Bridgehampton, New York, must have been a strange sight to behold. It was certainly strange to us to be pulling up to a closed-for-the-winter hotel in this little farming town to begin what we were planning as a journey into rock 'n' roll fame and fortune. Today Bridgehampton is much more sophisticated and urbane than it was in 1964, but up to that point its major claim to fame was as the home of the famous baseball player Carl Yastrzemski, who would become a Hall of Famer for the Boston Red Sox. The Bull's Head was a historic building that had become slightly run down. In the summer it was still a destination, but in the winter it could have been the set for an Alfred Hitchcock movie — nothing in this potato-farming community was going on around the Bull's Head, much less inside of it. Jan was the hotel manager in the summer and the live-in caretaker in the winter.

After setting up the basic equipment to rehearse, with a lineup of Jan on drums, me on bass, John on guitar and mouth harp and Zally with his Guild electric guitar, we set about learning a few songs. At first we just played some standard rock stuff we all knew, like Chuck

Berry and some blues songs, and we also began to learn a couple of John's originals. We again tried our hand at "Good Time Music," which went down pretty well. We played some traditional folk-type tunes that I had never heard and never would have expected to make suitable material for a rock band, but songs like "Wild About My Lovin'" were easy to learn and turned me on to a new way of looking at the type of material a rock band could play.

"Wild About My Lovin'" in particular gave me a taste of John's unique singing style. With the exception of ballads, most of the rock songs that I played in The Kingsmen were sung with a lot of gusto — if not just slightly ahead of the beat, then right on the beat and forcefully. John, on the other hand, had this way of delivering a vocal on medium-tempo folk and blues songs like "Wild About My Lovin'" that trailed the beat ever so slightly. It was almost like a talking style of singing, and I had never heard beat songs done that way before.

Another facet of John's talent was the Marine Band harmonica, an ideal instrument for blues- and folk-style playing. It had a soulful resonance like a saxophone, whether John played it in the folkie-style neck brace or held firmly in hand. It brought another dimension to our sound, as we were able to add some pure bluesy instrumentals to our repertoire, including what would become our signature song at the Night Owl — "Night Owl Blues." It was when John played the mouth harp that Zally would call him "Creefy John." I never did know what the hell that meant, but it was typical Zalman-speak.

Putting a rock beat to traditional songs was the brainchild of John and Zally, both of whom had a background in folk music. There was also constant mention of a group called The Jim Kweskin Jug Band. In addition to never having heard of this group, I had no idea what a "jug band" was. I'd soon learn that John was a big fan of the genre and had recorded an album with an urban jug band called The Even Dozen Jug Band, of which he was briefly a member. The sound came from a combination of homemade instruments — like a gallon jug you would blow into to make a sound, or a washtub bass — and folk-style instruments like autoharps and even kazoos and stringed instruments. The idea of combining jug band music and rock 'n' roll — which was purely John's — was a way-out idea in 1965 but sounded worth trying. Within a few days we had about a 10-song repertoire and were practicing daily. Bob Cavallo and Erik Jacobsen came out to Bridgehampton to hear how we were developing, and while they might have been forcing it, they gave us words of encouragement that helped a lot. I'm sure a casual listener might have said this band was going nowhere — we were still mighty raw — but as we improved as a unit during our residency at the Bull's Head, we felt we were on to something. Real friendships were also developing in front of the burning fireplaces of the otherwise unheated inn. We'd play music all day and hit the blue-collar joints and the bars like Billy DePetris' club in Bridgehampton at night. In fact, for all the perception of Bridgehampton as having a small-town attitude, everyone we came into contact with was very supportive and encouraging.

It was during this period of dues-paying that I suddenly and unexpectedly found myself playing with the most influential musician on the planet at that moment. About a week into rehearsals, the phone rang at the Bull's Head and the voice on the line asked to speak to John. After a short conversation, John hung up and casually said, "That was Bob Dylan. He wanted to know if I could come into the city and play some bass on his new album." I was a major fan of Dylan's, so to say I was shocked would be putting it mildly. John had mentioned that he knew Dylan from their mutual time in the Village, and I didn't doubt it, but to be invited to play on a session showed that John wasn't just blowing smoke. Since John needed a ride into the city, I was deputized to shuttle him to Columbia Records' studios in my Austin-Healey. This was getting interesting. We loaded up the Healey with me and John, and brought along my Fender P Bass since John didn't actually own one.

All the way into New York I was thinking, "This can't be happening." Bob Dylan was up there with The Beatles on the short list of music stars I'd like to meet and whose music I was really attracted to, though I kept telling myself not to act too "groupie" about this. Living adjacent to the upper crust in the Hamptons and playing in some of the area's hot nightclubs, I had met my fair share of celebrities and famous people. I was determined to stay cool. Then again, this was Bob Dylan.

We got to the studio and sure enough, there was His Bobness, wearing an Oxford shirt, blazer and jeans. The producer was the famous Tom Wilson, whose name I had seen on many LP jackets. Tom was a smartly dressed black man and Harvard graduate who had cut his teeth recording cutting-edge jazz players like Sun Ra and had graduated to Columbia staff producer. I had a few casual words with Dylan and Wilson, and did my best to maintain a friendly but businesslike demeanor while John described what he was up to with this new band he was in. There was some talk about the songs Dylan was recording before Bob directed John on what he wanted him to play on these songs. After about an hour of overdubs and not getting what either Bob or Tom wanted, John said, "Why don't you let Steve take a try at this? He is an actual bass player."

Whoa, Nelly. Dylan looked at me and asked if I wanted to try. At that point, had he asked me to jump off the building, I would have made tracks for the roof. I couldn't say anything but OK. Dylan gave me a general idea of what he wanted the bass part to sound like, but also directed me to "play what you hear for the part." We went over three or four songs, including "Maggie's Farm" and "Love Minus Zero/No Limit," and I did a couple of takes on each of the songs. Though I was nervous, I also felt confident — I was a bass player, after all, and didn't feel hesitant. I play my style and play it well. I have never been a quick learner, but the songs did not have complicated charts so I played as many takes as were asked of me and that was that. A photographer snapped some pictures of me (which were later published in a book about Dylan by Daniel Kramer), capturing the place and time. I eventually received a pay-check from Columbia for this session, which at the time helped pay the bills and later would offer proof of the session to anyone who doubted that I had been there. Though there is some debate among the cottage industry of Dylan biographers on the issue of whether my parts ended up on any of the finished tracks, I'm almost positive it's my bass you can hear on "Maggie's Farm," from the *Bringing It All Back Home* album. If it's not me, then it's someone who listened to my parts and was asked to copy my style exactly (it's a style that I adopted from Clay Sonier, and it differs greatly from that of Harvey Brooks, Dylan's usual bass player of this era).

When the session was over for the night, Bob invited John and me, along with his friend Bobby Neuwirth — who was essentially Bob's road manager, and was very easy to get along with — to hang out and drive around Manhattan in his Plymouth station wagon. (Yes, Bob Dylan, iconic voice of a generation, got around in a Plymouth wagon.) We drove around for about an hour, shared a joint and bullshitted back and forth like we'd all been friends our whole lives.

As we drove around Manhattan with Dylan driving and a joint seeming to stay lit the whole time, we talked mostly about motorcycles and rock music. I slipped in a little groupie stuff by telling Dylan how cool I thought his music was, but we never talked about anything heavy or controversial, as I was still kinda new to the left-leaning politics of the folk crowd. Before we parted company, I remember Bob asking John to keep him up to date on the progress of the band, and thanking me for sitting in on the bass. Considering how casual the whole evening went, I had to keep reminding myself how far up the music world food chain I had just traveled. The episode gave me a good dose of confidence that would serve me well in the coming months.

Later that year, we'd run into Dylan again after he came to our gig in the Village, and he invited us up to his apartment to play an acetate of a song he'd just finished and seemed pretty excited about. It was in Bob Dylan's flat in Gramercy Park that I first heard a drumbeat and organ intro preceding the lyrics "Once upon a time you dressed so fine . . ." The song Bob was so excited about was called

"Like a Rolling Stone." The whole world was set ablaze by that song despite the fact that it stretched on for six-plus minutes, longer than anything previously heard on Top 40 radio. I told Bob that although the track was a jaw-dropper, like a lot of people I didn't think radio programmers would go for it due to the length. I'm happy I turned out to be dead wrong. I'm also proud to say I was one of the first in line to be knocked out by one of the great tunes of any generation.

After the heady experience with Dylan in the studio, it was back to the Bull's Head to rehearse for what was to be our first gig, taking the same Night Owl Cafe stage where I'd seen John and Fred Neil thrill that audience a few weeks earlier. Joe Marra was the owner of the Night Owl, a tough-talking Italian guy from the neighborhood who John knew from his time backing up other artists in the Village. Joe knew John was trying to put a band together and, intrigued by the possibilities of the folk-rock combination, told John that whenever he was ready, he'd have a place to try it out for the public. John and I talked about the gig on our way back out to the Island, and while I wasn't sure we were ready, the experience with Dylan wasn't hurting anyone's confidence.

Buzz about the gig started growing in the tight-knit community of the West Village. I'll never forget an unseasonably warm day in February 1965, when I was driving through the Village and celebrating the nice weather with the top down on my Austin-Healey. I had just turned onto Eighth Street from Sixth Avenue when who did I see but Tinker, Erik Jacobsen's cool and pretty girlfriend. She wished me luck on the gig and we spoke for a few minutes. When we parted ways I remember thinking life could not get any better. It was a beautiful day in New York, I was flirting with a gorgeous "Village girl" and was part of a band that now seemed destined to me to make great music and be famous . . . Tinker wouldn't have talked to me otherwise!

At that moment I felt ready for anything.

Of course, before we could take the stage at the Night Owl and deliver on all this presumed greatness, we'd need to decide on a name.

I came from a place where the band was usually named something very mainstream, like The Kingsmen. Problem was, that name was so original that it was shared by at least five other bands. So trying to come up with a unique name was a mystery to me. I was pretty much open for whatever was put on the table. We were all sitting around talking about it one day and John came out with, "What would you guys think about 'The Lovin' Spoonful'?"

"The Lovin' what?" I said.

John repeated the name, arguing that it defined what our music would be all about. Well, I didn't know about this. It made no sense to me. I thought the name sounded too fey, and I didn't think it said anything relating to music. As I thought about it, "Lovin' Spoonful" also conjured up images of drug use — heroin addicts using a spoon to cook up their potion. Would other people see it that way too? Maybe "A Spoonful of Rock" or "The Lovin' Bluesmen" would be better. John was insistent, though, and explained that it was a phrase from a blues song by Mississippi John Hurt, or "Sippy John." Later I would find out that Fritz Richmond, the washtub bass player from the Kweskin Jug Band, had recommended the name to John. I still wasn't happy with the name, but Zally liked it and John was really pushing it, so I decided to go with it at least until I could come up with something better. I also did not think the name would matter if the music we made was good. Would we have ever gotten out of the Village with the name "A Spoonful of Rock"? Who knows. But I'm glad I relented on "The Lovin' Spoonful." Turns out it would not hold us back, although it would cause some bumps in the road ahead. One thing was for sure: you would not forget it once you heard it.

Now we had to get a couple of sets together for our Night Owl gig, and that seemed much more important to me. Our sound was going to be different than the rock 'n' roll fare I had played in my career up to that point, and was also going to be substantially different from the folk being played in the Village coffeehouse scene of the time. John had introduced the autoharp into the band — a very interesting stringed instrument, to say the least. It was a small, trapezoidal wooden box with about 30 strings, related to a zither. It looked very much like a small piano, except instead of striking the strings with hammers, you would either pluck them with a pick or strum them like a guitar. A set of crossbars, accompanied by spring-loaded push pads, muted all the strings except the ones that would make a chord. I loved this instrument. It made the coolest sounds, and John played it beautifully. We had worked up some of the songs using the autoharp, and it made us sound different than anything I'd ever heard. (There were also some issues that made it difficult to use in live performance. For one, it had to be tuned constantly. John would have to find a quiet spot and slowly tune every string. Tuning devices were very expensive at that time, so at first John would tune it with either a simple tone generator or a harmonica.)

Walking into the Night Owl in February 1965 for our first gig, I was convinced this band was something special. It would take an audience just a little bit longer to reach that same conclusion.

We set up at the Night Owl and were all amped up and excited for our debut. John, Zally and I helped tone down our nerves by smoking a joint in the small dressing room in the basement of the club. Smoking pot before playing a gig was new to me. I had been high at beach parties where I played my guitar and sang along, but getting up for a paying gig at a club full of strangers in Greenwich Village could be a problem.

I'll never forget the feeling of walking up the stairs from the Night Owl basement for The Lovin' Spoonful's first gig — the nervousness; the difficulty of maneuvering those steep, narrow steps; and the good buzz off some Mexican weed. The stairs were directly behind the stage, and I knew that when I came up from the dressing room I'd be stepping right off the staircase into a room full of folks looking to hear the next cool thing in the Village.

I don't think that pressure was lost on any of us.

"Pow," Zally said as we began our ascent. "There's no turning back now."

After we hit the stage, the nerves began to show, as did the limitations of this particular facility, coupled with the kind of sounds we were making.

The Night Owl, as mentioned, was not configured like a normal rock 'n' roll club and was thus less than ideal for an amplified music show. Meanwhile, John and Zally — both experienced folk players — were kinda new to guitar amplifiers, and certainly did not have an extensive background in working with them in small clubs. Zally was always on overdrive in the volume department, and it was hard for John to play guitar and use a mouth harp brace at the same time, through the same amp. (Controlling the sound of the autoharp with a surface contact mic was another job unto itself, though John would not introduce the autoharp on this night.) Sound systems in those days were primitive at best, and the Night Owl's was no different. Added to this was a full drum kit. I doubt there had ever been a full drum kit onstage at the Night Owl before, and it took up a lot of room. John and Zally were up front, on either side of the drums, and I was in the back alongside Jan. We had just enough room to stand up there and play. With the drums in my right ear and the guitar amps in front of me, the little Ampeg was pumping out all it had as I strained to hear the vocal cues and leads. John has always been able to lay down a terrific rhythm guitar part, but it was hard for me to hear him over Zally.

Plus, our lack of good amplifiers and stage gear put us behind the eight ball. The Fender Bassman amp I'd used out in Westhampton was on permanent loan and was hard to fit in my car, so I'd rented an Ampeg Porta B from the legendary Manhattan institution Manny's Music, figuring it would be fine for a small venue like the Night Owl. Trouble was, Zally and to a lesser degree John liked to play loud, and it was tough for the rhythm section to be heard.

In spite of all this, it was hard for me to tell how it really sounded to the audience. There were no stage monitors; we just turned up the amps and played. It was during our first gig at the Night Owl that I came upon the discovery that when I was high, everything sounded great even when it didn't, and I also found out that if I looked out into the audience I would have a mini-panic attack, which caused me to stare straight down at my shoes for most of the show.

Still, from what I could discern, the audience was into it. We played most of what would become our early repertoire, including a couple of John's originals ("Good Time Music," "Didn't Want to Have to Do It"), a couple to appease the folkies ("Wild About My Lovin'," "My Gal"), and a few of the early rock staples that we all loved ("Route 66," "Alley Oop," Chuck Berry's "Almost Grown"). It seemed to be going OK, but as the set wore on, you could see people holding their hands over their ears and making faces of discomfort. We played about a dozen songs and left the stage to modest applause. And the crowd goes mild.

After a quick huddle with Erik Jacobsen and Bob Cavallo and some nervous talk about the amps being crappy, we headed quickly over to Googie's and downed a couple of tequilas and beers, a little unsure of what we had just done. But we had done it, launched this baby, no matter how inauspicious it may have been. The Lovin' Spoonful was born, and though changes were coming, I felt pretty good about what had just happened. It may have been the tequila or the pot wearing off, but I was actually looking forward to getting back to the Night Owl.

We did another set, playing the same tunes with similar sonic results, only the crowd was much smaller for this one. After the show was over, we were greeted by a pretty displeased-looking Joe Marra.

"Hey, I don't know how to break this to you, but you guys suck."

We looked at Marra in stunned silence.

"The problem was . . ." John started.

"The problem was, people were walking out of your fucking show, and my fucking club, with their ears bleeding. Listen, go back and practice, turn down the amps and come back and see me when you figure out what the hell you're doing."

Joe was a straight-talking guy and he kind of scared me, but even after his harsh words I came away thinking that he really did like us, we just had to learn how to use our amplifiers better. For now, however, we were fired. And for the first time in weeks, visions of Southampton College began dancing in my head.

As it turned out, Erik Jacobsen had brought along a small tape recorder that preserved the Night Owl show for posterity. Keeping in mind that it's difficult to translate the sound of the audio mix of the recording to what patrons actually heard that night at the Night Owl — as most listeners know, live recordings rarely sound anything like the gig — listening today, one can hear we had some strong moments during what was, after all, our first gig. Zally was far too loud, but he was great, the star of the show. Even then, Zally was the kind of performer who could smile and entertain no matter what else was going on. John also had plenty of nice moments. Trying to be objective, I wasn't terrible. But in addition to the adventure of amplification, we had a problem behind the drum kit.

Jan (going by the stage name Jan Carl that night) was technically a decent drummer but was six years older than us, with a style better suited to an older form of rock 'n' roll, which did not mesh with our arrangements. Visually, he didn't fit in with the rest of us, and the fact that he wasn't into smoking pot — a substance the rest of us enjoyed, albeit casually — concerned us. Jan was a nice guy, and his landing us the Bull's Head as a rehearsal space was critical to our development, but the chemistry, both on and offstage, had to be right if this was going to work. The next day, after Jan had gone back to Long Island, we sat down with Erik and Bob Cavallo to discuss what had happened and where to go from here. The consensus was that while we all had a lot of growing to do musically, it was obvious we needed another drummer to attempt the next step. I can't remember who fired Jan — it was probably Erik. The Beatles didn't fire Pete Best face to face, and The Lovin' Spoonful followed the same (you might say cowardly) playbook. Jan, if you're reading, we're sorry, and it was strictly business.

With Jan and the Bull's Head both in the rearview mirror, we had two very real, very immediate issues: Who was going to be the drummer, and where were we going to rehearse?

The latter would be decided first. One of the selling points for musicians who were staying at the Albert Hotel was a big, divided, decaying space, where the proprietors of the Albert allowed its residents to rehearse. That filled a particular need, although the confines of that room made the unheated Bull's Head Inn look like the Four Seasons: pools of standing water that gave you pause every time you plugged in a mic or an amp, paint peeling off the walls and ceiling and falling on your head while you played, bugs of mysterious origin patrolling the floor at all hours. If ever there was a place that inspired a musician to make it big, it was at the Albert Hotel — not a person went in there who wasn't inspired to get the hell out.

As for the drummer issue, even before the deed had been done with Jan, we knew who headed our list of prospects. Joe Butler, my old bandmate from The Kingsmen, had already grown disenchanted with Skip and The Sellouts. The Sellouts were a great band — there had even been demos and some interest from record labels — but they lacked any real songwriters. In the wake of The Beatles, that was a death sentence for an aspiring band, and Joe knew The Sellouts wouldn't last. In addition to being a more-than-capable drummer, Joe also had the ability to help with vocals, and his versatility, experience and leading-man looks, which turned the head of many a Greenwich Village female, were not selling points to be discounted. Joe wasn't exactly champing at the bit to be in The Lovin' Spoonful — The Sellouts' manager, Herbie Cohen, who would later manage the likes of Frank Zappa, Tom Waits and Linda Ronstadt, had signed Joe to a solo management deal, so he had some prospects and a little cash — but Joe had seen The Spoonful, he liked us and he knew we had original songs that could set us apart.

Joe agreed to play some rehearsals with us at the Albert, and since we weren't really talking to any other drummers, the pressure was low. Until he walked into the Albert, that is.

I'll never forget the sound I heard that day as I walked into the Albert with Joe, John and Zally — the distant sound of drumming that got louder with every step. By the time we reached the lobby-level room where Joe would give his audition, the drums were almost deafening, and we hardly even noticed the rest of this band, which was laying down some really crisp, tight Chicago blues. We looked around the corner and there was this black dude, with the biggest arms I'd ever seen, beating the life out of these drums. The drummer was Sam Lay, and the rest of the band was Elvin Bishop, Mike Bloomfield, Jerome Arnold and Paul Butterfield. When the song broke down, they introduced themselves to us as The Paul Butterfield Blues Band, rehearsing in preparation for their first recording sessions for Elektra Records. A friendly bunch of guys, and man could they play the blues. And here was Joe Butler, getting ready to play his first rehearsal with a new band, and he had to follow Sam Lay? If I was him, I might have left my drums behind and run right out the door.

But to his credit, Joe stuck around, and though he might not have had Sam's power, it was immediately apparent that he brought a dimension to our sound that Jan hadn't. He understood the material, he looked the part, and he was a "gamer" — which we saw in the middle of that first rehearsal when he broke a drumstick but kept on hitting the crash cymbal with his hand, until he was bleeding all over the drum set. It was almost like an initiation rite — Joe Butler was in.

Soon after, the newly rendered version of the group took some speed and began a four-hour middle-of-the-night journey to Cambridge in pursuit of a much-needed amplifier. John had loaned an amp to Timmy Hardin some weeks before, and given the decaying state of our equipment, we needed it back. The trip had been dreamed up when we were sitting around John and Michelle Phillips' apartment in the sketchy East Village and a girlfriend of Joe's named Leslie Vega agreed to loan us her English Ford. I drove, and John, Zally, Joe and I speed-rapped and talked about the future all the way from the Village to Cambridge. When we got to Cambridge, we were greeted at the door by a strung-out looking Tim Hardin.

"Sorry, man, the amp's gone," he said. He had sold it to buy heroin the week before. The trip back to New York was not quite as jubilant.

Through the next few weeks at the Albert, we tightened our sound and bonded, both as a group and with our fellow residents. In addition to Cass, Denny and the Butterfield guys, there was Butchie, a full-time resident who was about five years older than us but acted as sort of a den mother for the artists who came through the hotel. She always made sure we were fed and sheltered. Her dad had named her Butchie because he wanted a boy, but she was a tall, blonde, attractive and most of all supportive lady who said whatever was on her mind. She'd eventually marry and divorce actor Bob Denver (a.k.a. Gilligan), but in 1965 she may have been The Lovin' Spoonful's biggest fan. She was never my girlfriend (I suspected maybe she wanted to be, though I never quite had the confidence to see it through), but in time she'd inspire one of our best-loved tunes, which I'd be moved to write after reflecting on what she'd meant to us. At the time, we had no idea that the relationship between her and John was more complicated than it seemed, but I'll get to that story a little later.

We didn't stay at the Albert long, but in addition to its role in our musical development, it was unforgettable as a scene. I'll never forget Cass and Denny lighting firecrackers and throwing them out the window, or sending Denny down multiple times to bat his eyelashes at the lady manager and see if she would forgive our overdue rent. Denny, with his charm and good looks, always got it taken care of.

Working Joe into the band really solidified our chemistry and brought out the best in our music and creativity.

One day when we were dodging cockroaches in the Albert rehearsal room, John brought in this song none of us had heard. He was working it out on the rhythm guitar — John was, and is, a tremendous rhythm guitar player — and it sounded promising. It wasn't a fully formed song, but John had a good first line that he said had been traveling around with him for a while: "Do you believe in magic/ in a young girl's heart." The melody was less derivative than "Good Time Music" and a little harder-edged than some of the other original stuff we'd played at the Night Owl, like "Younger Girl."

Meanwhile, John had been incorporating his funny-looking autoharp into more of our rehearsals. He played it beautifully, but I wasn't the only one who didn't quite see how this instrument would fit into the context of a rock ensemble. But somewhere John found a ukulele contact mic that he affixed to the back of it, plugged the mic into his amplifier and found the one spot in the Albert rehearsal room where he could play it without feeding back.

When he took those chords he'd been strumming and translated them to that autoharp, the new song went from great to amazing, and everyone knew it. The guys in the band looked around at each other, determined to capture whatever it was we had just done before it slipped into the creative ether. John finished the lyrics, which fittingly were about the transformative power of music, and we quickly put together an arrangement right there in the Albert. Everyone we brought around to hear the song — from Erik Jacobsen and Bob Cavallo to the guys in the Butterfield Blues Band and our other fellow boarders at the Albert — thought we had a hit. We'd talked for weeks about putting together a demo to shop to prospective record labels, and that discussion kicked into high gear once "Do You Believe in Magic" entered the picture.

Erik put up his own money to assemble a demo session at Bell Sound Studios, a somewhat cramped but popular New York studio where Buddy Holly, Burt Bacharach, Del Shannon and others had recorded. I frankly don't remember what else was on the demo. I seem to recall getting decent and representative versions of "Wild About My Lovin'" and "Younger Girl" committed to tape, but Erik told an interviewer a few years back that another of John's songs — a jug-band-style tune called "On the Road Again," sung by Zally, was the only other thing on the demo (and would end up being the b-side). Either way, there was no doubt that "Magic" would be the centerpiece of our audio sales pitch.

I don't know if "Do You Believe in Magic" is our best song, but I do know that it includes all of the elements that made The Lovin' Spoonful great. And if you want to know why we'd eventually turn away Phil Spector, whom we all idolized, as our producer, just listen to what Erik did with that track.

There's the distinctive sound of the autoharp that gets your attention right away, followed by John's fine voice singing lyrics that actually mean something — hardly a given in pop music in 1965. Erik also invited our friend Jerry Yester to play piano and add backing vocals along with Zally. Joe was still pretty new to the band and was having some trouble mastering the tempo, but he finally nailed the little fill that kicks off the song and turned in a fine performance.

Then there's Zally's playing. The depth of the wild man I had just met, with his crazy-shaped guitar and whammy bar, wasn't fully revealed to me until that session. Most people don't notice those brilliant little Floyd Cramer–like guitar figures Zally is playing under the autoharp in the verse, and Zally also contributes that creative, underrated little solo he overdubbed for the middle eight.

The whole thing came out sounding like a two-minute symphony. Even the structure of the song was unique. Although it's grounded in rock 'n' roll, "Magic" doesn't really have a chorus, so it's also subtly indebted to the folk tradition that John and Zally came out of. It was like nothing else on the radio in 1965. I was positive we had a hit.

Not that record companies had any idea what to make of it.

Erik and Bob took the song to probably 30 labels, and while some were more enthusiastic than others, the devil was in the (marketing) details. The sentiment was best encapsulated by Joe Smith, who was the A&R Manager at Warner Brothers and would eventually run the label. "I like it," Smith said. "But unless these guys start speaking in English accents, I can't sell it."

Though I know we were discouraged by the lack of immediate interest, I'm also sure Erik and Bob shielded us from how dire things had become. On a positive note, we'd gotten good enough in the

Albert to start playing gigs again, and things had started to click in a live setting. We were hired by the proprietors of the Café Bizarre, a little dump located a block south of Washington Square Park in the Village, which would later become famous for being the place where Andy Warhol discovered The Velvet Underground. We played every night at the Café Bizarre, for at least three shows a night, and were paid in either tuna fish or peanut butter and jelly sandwiches and ice cream. Given that we were literally on the verge of starvation in the Albert, we'd take it.

It was a short apprenticeship at the Café Bizarre, for while Andy Warhol didn't rescue The Lovin' Spoonful, Joe Marra did. In the weeks since we'd been fired, Joe had reconfigured the venue to better account for amplification, and had even tried out a couple of other bands who'd had better results. Joe ran into Bob Cavallo on the street in the Village, and asked what we were up to. Bob told him we were slogging it out at the Café Bizarre, and Joe offered to better our non-deal down the street. Marra liked us, thought we had potential, but knew we needed more seasoning. It was like he sent us down to the minor leagues for a couple of starts before bringing us back up to the bigs (and yes, compared to Café Bizarre, the modest trappings of the Night Owl were the major leagues).

Our second go-round at the Night Owl was much better than the first. The setup was indeed improved, and Zally and John met Marra halfway and turned down the amps enough for us to be comfortably heard. As he discovered that we now sounded like a real, live professional group, Marra performed what turned out to be a slick marketing trick — he took a six-by-eight-inch color photo of the band, blew it up to about eight by ten feet, and stuck it right in the front window of the Night Owl. You couldn't walk down West Third Street without noticing this photo, which gave the impression that we were already huge stars. It must have worked — we watched over the next few weeks as the Night Owl began to fill with more and more people. For a young band that was still somewhat unsure of itself, there was nothing more intoxicating than playing before a decent-sized audience that cared. Our stagecraft got better and better. We learned how to work the crowd, to play to the girls who were showing up with increased frequency. During the day, we started getting recognized more throughout the Village, which didn't exactly equate to decent food or shelter, but at least gave us a sense that this dream was headed somewhere.

The night Phil Spector walked into the Night Owl, that feeling was cemented.

I'll never forget watching from the stage as he sat at a table near the front — dark suit, dark sunglasses, completely expressionless, with his ear to the Night Owl wall. For two sets he sat there in that same spot, just watching, ear pressed to the wall, alone, listening. To us.

Apparently, someone had tipped Spector off to the buzz surrounding this different-sounding band down in the Village. He was doing most of his recording at Gold Star Studios in L.A., but by this time he ran his label, Philles Records, out of Midtown in New York. He was also a Bronx boy with lots of business and personal interests in the city.

Anyway, we all idolized the guy. I'll never forget the surreal feeling of playing "You Baby," a song Phil Spector had produced to perfection for The Ronettes, back to Phil Spector. When the second set was over, Phil came backstage. Despite his well known eccentricities, some of which we'd just witnessed with the ear-to-the-wall thing, he could not have been more pleasant or normal. I suppose he wasn't in the full throes of craziness at this point. Phil made it known to us and to Bob Cavallo that he loved our sound and expressed a wish to sign and produce the band. It was a great thing to hear, and proof positive that we were on the right track musically. There was no insider in the music business at this time whose hitmaking ability or knowledge was held in higher esteem than Phil Spector's. We agreed to talk over the informal offer with our management, and told Phil we'd get back to him soon.

But once we got over the high of meeting one of our idols,

reservations started to creep in about a working relationship between The Lovin' Spoonful and Phil Spector. As great an artist as he was, and despite his incredible track record, in many ways Phil was part of the old school of music-making, where the producer and label head (Phil Spector happened to be both) called all the shots, including choosing the musicians who would play in the studio. Once The Beatles came on the scene, writing most of their own material and playing on all of it, that old style of music-making had immediately become antiquated. We already had a producer whom we trusted implicitly in Erik Jacobsen. We were real musicians who wanted and expected to play on our own recordings. As hard as it was for four guys who were still basically living out of one room in a run-down hotel and now were being courted by one of the most powerful and revered people in the industry, we decided not to jump in bed with Phil Spector, at least not immediately. I don't think we turned him down flat — it would have been silly to burn what was at that time the only bridge out of town — but we decided to play hard-to-get for a little while longer.

It turned out to be the right move. Once Phil Spector made his presence known at the Night Owl, other label heads and music biz folks started talking amongst themselves, and the door began to swing open even wider.

In walked Elektra Records.

We certainly knew Elektra, which was a great label that had long been a fixture on the Village folk scene. John had already appeared on Elektra albums by the Even Dozen Jug Band, Fred Neil and others, and was friendly with the head of the label, Jac Holzman, and his house producer, Paul Rothchild. Our brothers in arms from the Albert, The Paul Butterfield Blues Band, had started recording their debut album for Elektra, with Rothchild at the controls. You could tell these guys really liked the "Magic" demo and our live act and believed in our talent. Jac made it very clear that they wanted us, and we listened. But again, as desperate as we were, none of us were sure Elektra was a fit. They were a folk label — we were not a folk act. They were big into albums. Our mission statement had been singles — including what we thought was a surefire hit in "Do You Believe in Magic" — that could be played on the radio. We couldn't come up with any Elektra singles that had really broken through to the pop market. We also wanted Erik Jacobsen to produce us, and though we liked Paul Rothchild, we didn't really want a producer forced on us (especially since we'd heard how hands-on he'd been with The Butterfield Band, who were forced to scrap their completed first album and start over at Rothchild's behest).

Like we'd done with Phil Spector, we put Elektra off and told Bob and Erik to keep turning over rocks in search of the right deal.

It was under one of those rocks that they found Charley Koppelman and Don Rubin.

Koppelman and Rubin were a couple of late-20-something Brooklyn boys who had started out as part of a college doo-wop group called The Ivy Three, somehow hitting the Top 10 in 1960 with a truly terrible novelty single called "Yogi," about the cartoon character Yogi Bear. The group eventually disintegrated, but Koppelman and Rubin were hired as staff writers by soon-to-be music impresario Don Kirshner, who ran a business that included a publishing house (Aldon Music) and a record label (Dimension Records). A number of Brill Building writing superstars were employed at Aldon, and the Dimension part of the business struck gold with Little Eva's 1962 No. 1 hit "The Loco-Motion." On the heels of that success, Kirshner's entire operation was sold to Columbia Pictures, and Koppelman and Rubin were appointed to executive roles within the music arm of the company. After a brief stint working for notoriously shady music business character Morris Levy at Roulette Records, it was in early 1965 that Koppelman borrowed $80,000 in seed money from his uncle Leo, and along with Rubin founded a new company that included a music publishing house (Char-Don Music) and a record production company (Koppelman-Rubin Associates).

Koppelman and Rubin already knew some in our camp, as Erik Jacobsen had produced a record for an artist they represented named Dwain Story, who had been in The Knob Lick Upper 10,000 along with Erik. The record was released on their own Stallion Records label, and John Sebastian and Jerry Yester had both played on the recording. All had come away with a positive feeling about Koppelman and Rubin. It was soon after they founded their new company that they walked into the Night Owl Cafe in search of some talent. To hear them tell it, they were blown away by The Lovin' Spoonful. And while that may have been true, I think they also saw an easy and convenient mark.

They charmed us right away with their enthusiasm. Whereas Jac Holzman had projected a paternal attitude to our music and our careers, Koppelman and Rubin were a couple of guys closer to our age who gave the impression that they really understood our concept and our music, and made it clear we could be huge. They had worked in every aspect of the business — as artists, songwriters, producers and publishers — and emphasized that they had all the right contacts. They'd heard the "Magic" demo and told us they had the network to get it into rotation on the radio, which was what we wanted to hear. Also, significantly, they wanted to sign our entire team lock, stock and barrel. They wanted Erik to produce us, would allow Bob Cavallo to handle day-to-day management duties and offered us our own publishing deal.

If anyone in our camp had negative feelings about Charley Koppelman and Don Rubin, they weren't made known at that time. Though this was a production/publishing team making a deal, and not a label per se (although their own label, Stallion Records, was an option), we believed Koppelman and Rubin when they said they had contacts at all the established labels in the industry. As it happened, they would only take our demo to one label before they made a deal, but in the meantime, we still had the Elektra offer on the table.

We let Jac Holzman know that we'd be turning down the deal, at least for now, though because we didn't want to create any ill will and since we had no cash in pocket yet from the Koppelman-Rubin agreement, we came to a side-deal compromise with Elektra.

Elektra had achieved some success with an artist sampler called *Folksong '65*, which included The Paul Butterfield Blues Band playing "Born in Chicago," and they were looking to repeat that success. We told Elektra we'd cut a few sides for their new sampler, which was to be called *What's Shakin'*, if they would give us a little bit of cash and buy us some much-needed new amps. The agreement was made, with the provision that the songs from the demo, and a couple of others, were restricted. We decided on a couple of John's originals, "Good Time Music" and the nondescript "Don't Bank on It Baby," along with covers of Chuck Berry's "Almost Grown" and The Coasters' "Searchin'," both of which were staples of our live act. None of the songs would ever appear on a Spoonful album, and frankly the results were a little bit sloppy. I personally thought we gave away a song in "Good Time Music" that had real hit potential as a single down the road. But the bottom line was we got what we needed out of Elektra, and although they didn't sign us to a long-term deal, they got what they wanted out of us. They'd end up releasing *What's Shakin'* in July 1966, after we'd emerged from the ranks of the unknown. Other artists on the sampler were The Paul Butterfield Blues Band, Al Kooper, Tom Rush, and Eric Clapton and The Powerhouse. (Clapton at the time was a member of John Mayall & The Bluesbreakers; The Powerhouse consisted of Stevie Winwood, Jack Bruce, Paul Jones of Manfred Mann, Ben Palmer and Pete York.) As Clapton and Winwood were not yet as famous, it was our photo that graced the cover. It's not a bad little album, though we would end up doing better on our own.

Soon after the Elektra sessions, we heard back from Koppelman and Rubin. Out of the blue, they'd signed a deal with a label called Kama Sutra to release our records. We'd never heard of this fledgling label, which was born of a production company formed by three old-school music business guys named Artie Ripp, Phil Steinberg and Hy Mizrahi. The newness of their label was less of an issue than the fact that they were close to a distribution deal with MGM Records, a major label backed by a major Hollywood movie studio that had a history of getting songs on the radio and more importantly on the charts. It all sounded pretty good to us, not that it would have mattered much if it didn't. We were never signed to Kama Sutra or MGM; we were signed to Koppelman-Rubin — a fact that would cause some major backroom dealings and complications down the road, not that we realized it at the time.

With the benefit of 50 years of hindsight and what we know now about the dirty dealing of record companies during what were still the early stages of rock 'n' roll, you could see some potential hazards when there were this many links in the chain: MGM distributed the records as part of a deal with Kama Sutra; Kama Sutra released the records as part of a deal with Koppelman-Rubin Associates; and since we worked for Koppelman-Rubin, our royalties and publishing income were to come on the back of that deal. That's a lot of transactions taking place between people we either didn't know or barely knew, but whom we would have to trust to loop us in on our share. Once we got past Bob and Erik, whom we could always trust, the system that put money in our pockets would have to hinge on honest accounting practices and honest people. We'd find out in time that both were in short supply in the music business in general, and particularly when it came to The Spoonful.

Of course, the focus when these agreements were signed in the spring of 1965 — when there wasn't a member of our band over the age of 23 — was on potential stardom and great music. A very familiar tale of rock 'n' roll naïveté. Kama Sutra took that demo of "Do You Believe in Magic," and seeing no need to improve on Erik's wonderful production, started pressing it in advance of its release and promotion. Management began making arrangements for our first serious live dates in the summer of '65. We were on the cusp of making it out of the Village, at the very least.

The wheels were in motion. Almost before we blinked, they were spinning out of control.

Chapter 4

DAYDREAM

It is the summer of 1965, and I'm standing on the roof of the fabled Brill Building at 1650 Broadway in midtown Manhattan. The man standing next to me is firing a machine gun into the air. That man, Phil Steinberg, also happens to own my band's record label. His associates at Kama Sutra Records — Hy Mizrahi and Artie Ripp — are taking turns firing their own rifles and shotguns they've retrieved from a closet in their office downstairs, and having a grand old time. They are celebrating the imminent departure of The Lovin' Spoonful on our first tour of the West Coast, and are doing so in what you might call an unusual way. They are jubilant. The members of the band signed to their label are a mixture of frightened and bemused.

"Here, you want to shoot it?" Steinberg asks me.

"Nah," I say, my mind swirling with visions of the cops busting onto the roof and finding me with a smoking machine gun in my hands. "The recoil might wrench my hand and I wouldn't be able to play my bass."

"Well, we sure don't want that to happen now, do we?" Steinberg says with a wink, as he fires off another round.

The other band members also decline to unload. "Yeah, I had to learn how to use one in the Air Force, they hurt my ears," Joe Butler offers while looking around, puzzled.

There is a certain exhilaration that comes from climbing the fame ladder, but there are also plenty of moments in those early stages that are strange and disorienting, where you find yourself constantly wondering, "Is this really happening?" After a while you stop asking the question, because all the events that once felt so strange and surreal begin happening frequently enough to become mundane. In the past six months I'd played a session with Bob Dylan and ridden around with him in a Plymouth station wagon smoking dope. I'd played in a band that was courted by Phil Spector and thought enough of itself to reject one of the all-time icons of rock 'n' roll. And now I'd signed a record deal with guys who were firing machine guns from the roof of the Brill Building in the middle of Manhattan. Things were getting weird, and somehow normal.

In the weeks between signing our record deal and that scene on the roof of the Brill Building, we'd been busy preparing ourselves. "Do You Believe in Magic" was to be released as a single during the second half of July, and we knew we'd be going out on the road to promote it.

Our standing gig at the Night Owl began taking on the air of a tour rehearsal. Our act was getting more precise the more we repeated the setlist — we were learning how to play together, how to amplify our sound properly and perfect our stagecraft. The crowds at the Night Owl were growing larger and larger, much to the delight of both the band and club owner Joe Marra. The NYPD was a regular presence, clearing the street of the overflow foot traffic that accompanied our live dates. Established stars began coming to see the act as well. One night Mary Travers of Peter, Paul and Mary came by. On another occasion members of the The Byrds, in New York for a promotional tour, stopped in to see us.

The Byrds had released their version of Dylan's "Mr. Tambourine Man" in April and it had shot to No. 1 in both the U.S. and England, a fact we found a little upsetting (we would have liked to be the first folk-rock act to break through on the charts) but mostly very encouraging. Roger McGuinn, David Crosby and Gene Clark had emerged out of the same folk background that had produced John and Zally — McGuinn had lived in the Village and worked in the Brill Building, and was a known face to both John and Zally. And although McGuinn's guitar was augmented by studio musicians on that first single, the fact that a band of American guys was finding a way to create something that would be heard in a British-dominated musical environment was highly encouraging. Since the foreign sound of McGuinn's 12-string Rickenbacker was being embraced, we thought the autoharp of "Do You Believe in Magic" might just stand a chance.

After the group came to see us play at the Night Owl, we were invited back to their rooms at the Hotel Earle — a place just a stone's throw away where Dylan and McGuinn had once kept apartments — to smoke some dope and bullshit about the biz. Crosby and Clarke raved about our show and our sound, which was a wonderful thing to hear from a band that had already made it.

Michael Clarke was actually new to the drums but had played in rock bands before The Byrds, and he and I gravitated toward each other for that reason. "I like the way you play bass, locked in with the bass drum," he mentioned.

"Yeah I always listen first to the bass drum and use the kick for my primary hit, a little different than the folkie bass players."

He laughed and said, "Yeah, I know what you mean, I'm still trying to find my strength at the drums. Hearing you guys gives me some good ideas."

"Well you sounded great on 'Mr. Tambourine Man,'" I said.

"Nah, that wasn't me, they used a studio drummer on the record. But I'm getting the hang of it."

The night was a great rush, and we promised to meet up with The Byrds again when we swung through their turf in L.A.

But for all our triumphs, like an audience of folk-rock royalty, there was evidence that The Lovin' Spoonful still had a distance left to run before we were ready for the big time.

Since we'd played only in the Village up to this point, and had been mostly nestled in what had become our insular cocoon at the Night Owl, our management decided we needed to play some different venues in front of some unfamiliar patrons. Charley Koppelman's Uncle Leo ran a joint called My Father's Place out in Manhasset, on the western end of Long Island. It was a huge rock club, which meant we'd be able to turn the amps up and play as loud as we wanted. If we were ever to play large venues around the country, and that was certainly the goal, we'd have to determine how to pull off our show in such a setting. That was the upside of playing My Father's Place. The downside, meanwhile, may have been apparent only to Joe Butler and me. We were from the Island and had played similar venues, though we hadn't played this specific one. We knew this to be the domain of the gum-chewing, lip-smacking, heavily made-up girls, and guys with T-shirts rolled up at the sleeve and slick ducktail haircuts. These folks didn't take kindly to long hair, and they were mainly there to dance to music they recognized. The Kingsmen had delivered what this type of crowd wanted. I had a sinking feeling my new band would not be received so warmly.

I also suspected we didn't really have the equipment to get over in a venue this huge, with its giant stage. Though this was before Marshall stacks became commonplace, the big-time Long Island rock clubs all had decent PAs, and the guitar players had more than one little puny amp, which is what each of us would take to the stage. Zally had been bugging Bob Cavallo for weeks about getting him a new amp, but Bob said we couldn't afford it yet.

I'm sure John and Zally, and for that matter Bob and Erik Jacobsen, didn't really know what they were about to face in Manhasset. Charley Koppelman and Don Rubin might have, but maybe they thought throwing us in the deep end and getting us out of our comfort zone would do some good. Who knows. Hoping for the best, I held my tongue.

We'd been booked to play between sets of a typical Long Island dance band whose name I can't remember, and were watching from the wings while the patrons danced around to a frenetic version of the Isley Brothers' "Twist and Shout," which closed the first set. As the crowd caught its breath, out onstage loped four long-haired guys who looked like they'd just walked off the corner of Bleecker and MacDougal (they had), and they set up their little amps and prepared to do God knows what. I peered out at the audience and was met with a collective look of "Who the fuck are these guys?" It hadn't even been a year since I'd been a member of The Kingsmen, when I would have strode onstage in this setting with the confidence of an emperor. Now I felt like a stranger in a strange land.

I turned to Joe, and he was already staring straight back at me. We both knew it was going to be a long night. John took out his autoharp, and it was like the denizens of Manhasset had been visited by a group of Martians wielding rayguns.

We launched into John's original "Younger Girl," played at piddling volume, and were greeted by vacant stares. We ended the set to those same vacant stares. Hey, at least they didn't throw bottles. Though we did have some kids come up to us afterward and say nice things, mostly about John's harmonica playing and Zalman's guitar work, we also encountered some audible whispers of "faggot" and other barely restrained hostility. A year from now, the suburbs would be ready for folk-rock and mop tops. In the late spring of 1965, at least at My Father's Place, they were not. We piled all the equipment and amps back in the cars and sulked back to the Village, where our pride was repaired with several rounds of tequila and beers at Googie's.

This was rather distressing. Forget playing in Peoria; were we going to be able to play outside of the Night Owl Cafe? Because up to this point, that was the only place we'd proven ourselves.

We knew we'd need to figure it out outside of the Village, to repair our flagging confidence as much as anything else. It was while we drowned our sorrows at Googie's that Fritz Richmond suggested a venue that made us stand up and take notice. Now, we always listened to Fritz, whom we loved personally and revered as a musician. He was the first guy we knew to wear round granny glasses (his were cobalt-blue-tinted), which were later adopted by John Sebastian and eventually appropriated from our John by another John — Lennon. As mentioned, Fritz was the one who'd first floated the name "Lovin' Spoonful." He was a big, lanky beanpole like me but was considered an arbiter of great taste by all of the folkies and our band. We were several drinks in when Fritz blurted out, "Why don't you guys go up and play Club 47?"

"Club 47 . . . Fritz, are you fucking nuts?" Zally shot back.

Situated in the heart of Cambridge, Massachusetts, right near Harvard University, Club 47 was then considered the shining emblem of folk purity. It had started out as a blues and jazz club in its original incarnation at 47 Mount Auburn Street, but since moving to its new locale on Palmer Street in 1963 it had become very much a folkie's paradise. Bob Dylan, Joan Baez and Pete Seeger had all played there. John and Zally had visited Club 47, and had even played the venue as folkies earlier in their careers. Cambridge folkies were so snobby that many of them even looked down on the New York folkies — how in God's name where they going to accept a group of New York rock 'n' rollers in their club?

But Fritz, who had played Club 47 a bunch with The Kweskin Jug Band, was persuasive. He convinced us that Dylan's forays into folk-rock and The Byrds' folk bona fides were beginning to open minds, albeit slowly. Fritz said he'd lobby to get us a gig and would help fill the club with friendly faces. It would be exposure and give us more experience, at a minimum.

After another week of successful shows at the Night Owl to get our confidence back following the disaster in Manhasset, we ventured up to Cambridge and gave it a shot.

Although Fritz did deliver us some fans — including him and other members of The Kweskins like Geoff Muldaur and his wife, vocalist Maria Muldaur — a few minutes into our first set it looked like we'd incited a local chapter meeting of FUASE — Folkies United Against Stupid Electricity. As soon as Zally played his first chord, a girl in the front row — an ultra-hip folkie chick with ironed hair — stuck fingers in both her ears, which was greeted by Zally with a huge smile. He walked over to his amp and turned it up to 10. Before the end of the first set, over half of the FUASEs had bolted.

For the second set we turned it down a little bit, which tamed the remaining crowd enough to win us some respectable if not rousing applause. The gig wasn't an unqualified success, but it had gone better than expected. And Fritz was right — you could see that many folk fans were ready to embrace these new louder sounds, but there had to be at least token resistance to it from the diehards. The drive back to Greenwich Village this time was definitely not the voyage of shame we'd taken after My Father's Place. We'd made our music work in a tough venue, and as a bonus had made some new fans outside the Village.

Back in New York, as our management began setting up farther-flung dates for us, Koppelman-Rubin tried to iron out another perceived rough spot, which was the vocal abilities of me and Zally — or lack thereof. All four guys in The Beatles sang, and our management was also looking at Roger McGuinn, Gene Clark and David Crosby from The Byrds, all of whom were capable of taking vocals. Word came down from on high that Boone and Yanovsky had to sing more and better. Now, Zally actually did sing — he just had a raspy and occasionally out-of-tune voice — but I hadn't sung since *H.M.S. Pinafore* in junior high and wasn't too keen on starting back up now. I still admire bass players like Paul McCartney or Sting who can sing when they play, because to me playing bass in a rock combo requires full concentration. I was worried that singing would take my focus away from playing the bass well and helping ground the rhythm section.

But to keep everyone happy we agreed to go see this established vocal teacher just down Broadway from the Brill Building and Koppelman-Rubin Associates. It was apparent to this teacher early on that our hearts were not in it. We were walked through the notes of the scale and taught some breathing exercises that would give us more power to sing, but between our cracking bad jokes or flirting with every skirt that walked by, you could tell Koppelman-Rubin were wasting their money (or more likely our money, since we'd eventually find out that every dollar spent was billed back to the band). We made it to a few lessons, but I'm sure the teacher was none too upset when we stopped showing up. I don't think my quitting deprived the world of the next Mario Lanza.

This behavior from Zally and me would become an increasing part of our schtick. We would fuck up every photo shoot, derail interviews with our antics and generally be a handful. Bob Cavallo tried to get us to tone it down, but that wasn't getting through. Bob was a constant target of Zally's abuse-couched-as-humor, as was our later publicist Dan Moriarty. I'm sure the routine was annoying to many, but we were young, restless guys who even from the start couldn't resist calling bullshit on all the showbiz nonsense like interviews and photo shoots. It broke up the monotony, though I'm positive our usual photographer and Zally's roommate, Henry Diltz — an eventually famous rock photographer who had been a member of The Modern Folk Quartet and got his break in photography by taking pictures of us — thinks I'm a knucklehead to this day. (Henry also played clarinet on the *Hums* album and was responsible for encouraging me to take up photography, a hobby I still enjoy today.)

Soon after the adventures in vocalizing, I made another decision that would live in infamy, when I decided I needed a new bass guitar. Actually I have to blame Felix Pappalardi for some of the decision, since it was Felix who recommended trading in my beloved white Fender Precision Bass for a Guild Starfire II with custom electrics. The Fender was a great bass, but in the era before quality bass amps, it just couldn't produce the kind of tone I needed to rock out Spoonful-style.

To this day, I don't lament my lost loves as much as lost musical instruments. The Goldtop Les Paul guitar I traded when I switched to playing bass as a member of The Kingsmen now commands five figures among collectors. I regretted giving up the Fender Precision Bass for more musical reasons. Even though the Guild was lighter, easier on the fingers and might have looked cool for TV appearances, I could never make it sound as good as Felix said it was supposed to. I should have waited it out with the fretted Fender bass. Once bass amps and PAs got better, the Fender produced a punchier sound that was far superior to the Guild's. It wasn't the last mistake I'd ever make, but it was one that would endure.

Soon after I'd made the switch to the Guild, we were informed by management that we'd been booked to do what would be our first TV show, down in Miami — an appearance that would be made almost in tandem with the release of the "Do You Believe in Magic" single. It was a local Saturday morning program on Channel 10 out of Miami, run by a disc jockey named Rick Shaw. Koppelman-Rubin had a relationship with Shaw, who was an institution in South Florida (he'd been one of many of the U.S.'s many self-appointed "fifth Beatles" when the Fab Four made their first trek through Miami in February 1964). This would allow us to get some experience in front of a TV audience, and that feather in our cap would be helpful once we went out to the West Coast, where most of the big music shows like *American Bandstand* and *Where The Action Is* originated.

We'd also get a chance to play before some new audiences in Daytona Beach and Jacksonville while we were down in my old home state of Florida.

We were nervous for the show, which was a typical groovy *Bandstand* type of program with kids dancing while we played. Rick's show was set in outdoor locales around Miami, and was very low budget, with homemade props and the like. As it turned out, it was ideal for Zally's brand of cut-up comedy, and he shone throughout, looking every bit the star he was becoming. The rest of us were just glad to get through it uneventfully. We raced through "Do You Believe in Magic," but the audience responded favorably and apparently the switchboard at Channel 10 did not light up with calls from horrified viewers.

The next morning, as we were leaving the hotel to drive to our next gig, like something out of a movie, a newspaper truck drove up, the back flew open and a few stacks of out-of-town newspapers were dropped right at my feet. To my great surprise, right there on the cover of the New York *Daily News* was a half-page mugshot of my brother Skip with an accompanying headline that read "Hundreds Arrested in East Hampton Drug Raid." Well, *that* caught my attention. I got the feeling I had just gone from budding TV star to brother of busted drug dealer.

For reasons unknown to me, Skip and some friends had rented a summer house in East Hampton that happened to be right across from the local police station. We knew some of those cops, but these were still the days of "Why don't ya get a haircut, girlie," and the sight of a bunch of long-haired musicians attracted immediate attention among the locals and the cops. Inevitably, the first major party at the house provoked police attention, including a warrant to search the house on the basis of purported drug activity. Skip and everyone else at the party were busted after a large jar of powder was found under one of the bathroom sinks. Of course, by the time the *Daily News* hit the sidewalk in Miami, the local Barney Fifes had determined that the jar contained soap powder left there by the house's previous tenant.

It wouldn't be until my return to New York that I'd discover that my brother was not, in fact, a drug felon. I was fairly mortified there for a few days, though. This event wouldn't derail my career, but did offer a glimpse of the future.

In the beginning of August, with the single beginning to take off in certain markets, it was time to hit the West Coast. Just after the sound of record company gunfire had ceased ringing in my ears, I found myself sitting alongside Zal Yanovsky, preparing for takeoff on a 707 bound for San Francisco. In the belly of the plane sat the new Samsonite suitcases the band had been given by Charley

Koppelman and Don Rubin to accompany the 21-gun sendoff from the Kama Sutra guys.

Airlines had just started providing headsets for passenger entertainment, and as the plane taxied for the trip to the West Coast, Zally and I heard the unmistakable first notes of The Beach Boys' latest opus, "California Girls," ringing in our ears. That might sound clichéd and unlikely, but it happened. ("California Girls" was released as a single on July 12, 1965, about three weeks before our California trip.) Zally and I gave each other a knowing look, and I watched him lean back in his airplane seat and close his eyes. Nothing needed to be said. We were on our way.

The Disneyland-like aura surrounding this trip would continue upon our arrival in San Francisco.

We were picked up at the airport by the record promo man whom the distributor had hired to take us around to the various radio stations, meet the key jocks and plug our record. He rented a big ol' Cadillac convertible on the way to our first stop, DJ Tom "Big Daddy" Donahue's station, KYA. Tom was very influential locally, as he managed groups (he had discovered a band of guys who would become our friends, The Beau Brummels) and also owned a nightclub, Mother's, where we'd play our first West Coast gigs.

Donahue had also been part of the payola scandal that ensnared Alan Freed and other DJs in the early '60s, and he moved from the East Coast to the high ground of San Francisco because of it. Koppelman and Rubin knew Donahue from those payola days and got us hooked up with him for our sojourn out west.

Immediately upon jumping in the Cadillac, the promo guy tuned the radio station to Donahue and KYA. And then we heard it. Almost as if he'd pressed play on a tape recorder, I heard the easily identifiable opening drum fill of "Do You Believe in Magic." Whether it had been set up beforehand for Donahue to play our song at a certain time coinciding with our arrival, I have no idea, but this was before cell phones, so it would have been fairly difficult to pull it off with this level of precision. We were hearing our song on the radio for the first time, and yeah, all the things you hear about that moment are true. Not to be corny about it, but it truly was magic. After freezing our asses off at the Bull's Head, after dodging cat-sized cockroaches at the Albert, after nearly starving to death at the Café Bizarre and after having our demo rejected by 30 record labels, we had proof via the loud, clear signal of a major AM radio station that the hard work was paying off.

We got more proof throughout our couple of weeks in California, when more people began showing up at the shows and singing John's lyrics right back at the band.

It wasn't until we got inside the doors at Mother's that we discovered we'd be sharing the bill with none other than Maria D . . . the stripper. A folk-rock band and a stripper, who'da thunk it? Tom Donahue thunk it. Apparently Tom was trying to steal some of the business from another club down the street called the Condor, featuring legendary topless dancer Carol Doda, whose bust size had gone from 36 to 44 inches in the past year via then-unheard-of silicone injections. Donahue invited us over to the club to see the setup and meet Maria, who was beautiful, with rather obvious physical assets as well. However unusual the arrangement, we didn't even have to be talked into playing this gig. We'd later find out The Beatles had played behind strippers too, during their Hamburg apprenticeship.

There were a few technical glitches that first night at Mother's, but the shows progressively got better, and more packed, throughout the week. By the second night, even Maria said she liked our act. (Joe Butler would get separate, private shows from both Maria D and Carol Doda before the week ended. Ahem.)

A couple of key people came to see us that week, including Billy Hearst, the 15-year-old grandson of media magnate William Randolph Hearst (first cousin of Patty), who came up to us after a show and told us what a fan he was. (I guess having Hearst connections helped you get around underage drinking laws in San Francisco.) Zally looked right at him and whispered, "Rosebud." I had no idea what he was talking about. The kid just smiled, knowing

Zally was alluding to *Citizen Kane*, the legendary film Orson Welles based loosely on young Hearst's grandfather.

While at Mother's we also got a nice write-up from the *San Francisco Chronicle*'s revered music critic Ralph Gleason (later the co-founder of *Rolling Stone*), at a time when good reviews for pop acts were hardly commonplace. "The best group in the U.S.!" Gleason gushed. "I'm glad to be alive at a time when I can hear them." Our place in Ralph Gleason's good graces would serve us well down the line.

From San Francisco it was on to L.A., where we played a string of the fading old-showbiz venues on the Sunset Strip, like Ciro's, the Crescendo and the Trip, as well as taping some TV appearances for *American Bandstand*, *The Merv Griffin Show* and *The Lloyd Thaxton Show*, among others. Thaxton had this staircase in the middle of the set that The Spoonful was asked to descend before playing our song. We made a plan beforehand to tumble down the stairs like bowling pins, a plan we didn't let the producers in on. We just wanted to see how Thaxton, this old, plastic variety-show square, would react. He was obviously a bit taken aback when we crumpled in a heap at the bottom of the stairs, so we'd achieved our goal.

But really the highlight of the West Coast trip for me, and I'm sure the others, was playing the Rose Bowl. Sure, we were bottom of a bill that included headliner Herman's Hermits and others like The Turtles and The Bobby Fuller Four. Just the chance to play at a stadium in front of that many people was a thrill. The Rose Bowl was set up so the stage would face out to half of the seating bowl. Even with half the seats closed off, there were still 35,000 people packed into one end of the venue, which was probably a good 34,000 more than any of us had ever performed in front of. We were unsure how we'd be received, but the roar that went up from the crowd when we launched into "Do You Believe in Magic" was deafening, and not soon forgotten by The Lovin' Spoonful or those in our circle. Kind of like hearing your song on the radio for the first time, it was a high that is impossible to describe. And like a powerful narcotic, the lure of getting out there to do it again was irresistible.

There were other, less positive indications during that Rose Bowl experience that proved we had arrived in the world of show business.

One was in the dressing room area, which in this case was the stadium locker rooms where the bands were changing and getting ready for the show. The Bobby Fuller Four, a group of rockers from Texas, were riding the wave of a song called "I Fought the Law," which had been a regional hit in L.A. but was beginning to take off in other markets. I liked the song — which had been written five years earlier by Sonny Curtis from Buddy Holly's band, The Crickets — but knew nothing about the band. I saw the guys go into their dressing area and noted to someone, maybe John, that they looked a lot older than us, or at least a lot more at home in this setting. Anyway, not even 10 minutes later I heard a shriek and looked toward their dressing room, from which three teenyboppers emerged crying and screaming. I was standing together with John, Zally and Joe, and all of us instinctively took a step in the direction of the girls to see whether somebody needed help. We thought there was a fire or an injury or something, which shows you the level of naïve newbie we were at this stage of our careers. Just then, out the dressing room door came the members of the Bobby Fuller Four, led by Fuller himself, laughing while they were zipping and buttoning up street clothes and obviously taking great delight in whatever had just happened. If someone had snapped a picture of the four of us at that moment, they would have noted a reaction of "Oh. OK."

Not that The Lovin' Spoonful were Boy Scouts, but compared to some of our contemporaries we always handled the groupie thing with discretion, if not always chivalry. Joe Butler was the best-looking guy in the group and got a lot of girls, as did the charismatic Zally (who I was told also had a liaison with Maria D during the Mother's run). As the frontman, John Sebastian was never going to be hurting in that realm either. Despite being relatively shy and inexperienced with girls (and being the bass player) I certainly had my opportunities throughout the life of the band. But (sorry, folks), there were no orgies or assembly line sex with groupies or underage girls that I ever witnessed. We weren't the world's most wholesome guys, but I like to think we were decent human beings even at the height of our fame, and we never subjected any female to anything she wasn't a willing participant in.

Anyway, less than a year after the Rose Bowl show, Bobby Fuller was found dead in his car in Hollywood, about 15 miles from the Rose Bowl. The case remains unsolved, but the unsubstantiated legend says Fuller was murdered by a well-known L.A. mob figure to avenge Fuller's involvement with his girlfriend.

The other Rose Bowl incident that was mildly unsettling happened after we had finished our show and were riding out of the venue in an open convertible. We had stayed after the show and were one of the last acts to leave, so the level of security had dropped off considerably. As we pulled out of the parking area beneath the facility, a swarm of teenage girls overwhelmed the few security guards on duty and surrounded our car in a mad, frenzied rush. I'm not even sure these girls had time to process who we were, or even cared; they just saw the long hair, assumed we were musicians and made their move. A couple of girls dove right into the car and just started grabbing. I managed to duck down out of the way, but poor John, who had been sitting up on the folded convertible top, was grabbed around the neck by a screaming teenager. As he tried to wriggle free, the girl managed to grab onto his collar and started pulling. I was scrambling to help him, but this girl had a death grip on the collar, and I watched as John's expression went from concern to horror to what looked to me like suffocation. Finally our road manager, Rich Chiaro, pried her arms apart and was able to free John from her grasp. With that, we plowed our way through the crowd before speeding off to our hotel, with John four sheets whiter than just a few minutes before. The incident would make a lasting impression on John, and helped make his relationship with our fans, especially when they were in big groups, somewhat less than enthusiastic. We flew back to New York the next day, having just survived our first episode of Spoonfulmania.

During the California trip, the momentum really began to gather behind "Magic," which steadily rose from No. 96 to its eventual peak at No. 9 in October. We had a hit single, and that meant Kama Sutra had a need for more Lovin' Spoonful product that we could go out and promote via TV shows and live appearances.

By this point we were suitably impressed with Koppelman-Rubin, who had delivered everything they had said they would and more. They got our single on the radio, and via the MGM distribution deal they got the record into stores where it would sell. Their influence and connections had gotten us some big-time gigs and appearances on television shows that had a lot of reach with the groups of people inclined to buy our records and concert tickets. To this day, I don't think Elektra or Phil Spector could have done what Charley and Don did to launch us into pop stardom during the second half of 1965. If we had signed with Spector, we might have still been in our third month of autoharp overdubs on the first single. With every success, we trusted Charley and Don more, and were willing to put our careers — and ultimately our fate — in their hands.

A follow-up single to "Magic" and then a full-length album were our next orders of business. We were booked for a handful of late-summer and early-fall dates at Bell Sound, where we'd cut the demo sides, sessions that we'd have to squeeze in around some upcoming dates at Brooklyn's Fox Theatre. The emphasis during the album sessions would be speed, not craft, though Erik Jacobsen's production work and the great sonics of Bell Sound ensured the material we recorded for the first album turned out pretty well. Most of what we recorded for the album, which would also be called *Do You Believe in Magic*, we'd been playing night after night as part of our live act since the early days at the Night Owl.

The jug band and blues-sounding numbers in our repertoire would take center stage, including tunes John and Zally had first learned from The Holy Modal Rounders ("Blues in the Bottle"), The

Jim Kweskin Jug Band ("My Gal") and a long-dead 1920s bluesman named Henry Thomas ("Fishin' Blues"). We paid tribute to Phil Spector with Joe's vocal on The Ronettes' "You Baby," and to our friend Fred Neil with his "The Other Side of This Life" (which Joe nailed in a mere 27 vocal takes, as Fred Neil himself looked on!). We ripped off Lonnie Johnson with our "Sportin' Life" and did a representative take of our live staple "Wild About My Lovin'." But John Sebastian's originals were the most distinctive thing on the album.

In addition to the title song and our setlist standard "Younger Girl," there was a cut we thought had single potential called "Did You Ever Have to Make Up Your Mind," based on an experience John had at summer camp when he was a kid, when he fell in love with twin sisters. The song was an attempt to evoke a '50s band out of New Orleans we all loved called Huey "Piano" Smith & His Clowns, with John and Zally simultaneously finger-picking on two guitars to mirror the sound of Huey's rockin' piano. It was a hell of a cool-sounding song.

But the song on this album that brings back the best and worst personal memories for me was our instrumental rave-up "Night Owl Blues." The song had been a crowd favorite from the very beginning, and showed the instrumental chops of the group better than any other piece in our repertoire. It was a collection of solos, with John blowing a mean harp for the first verse, Zally coming in with a blistering verse of guitar work, and me taking a rare bass solo before we all came back together at the end of the piece. Unfortunately, on the night of the session, we were having trouble getting it together. I had recently been reintroduced to the amphetamines known as "black beauties," and at least Zally and I were using them to get through the session amid a weeks-long stretch that included lots of work, too much play and not enough sleep. I didn't really think the drugs were affecting my playing, but for whatever reason, we were having lots of trouble getting a definitive take on one of our signature pieces. Someone would miss a cue, Joe or Zally would speed up, one of us would miss a note

. . . whatever. Finally, after about four hours of tinkering, we had it. John and Zally aced their parts. Joe was keeping perfect time, and we were holding down the bottom expertly. Then it was time for my bass solo, and goddamn it if my fingers didn't freeze up on the spot. I'm not sure whether it was the black beauties, or if I was just transfixed by how well the others were playing and got a case of nerves, but I plumb stopped.

"Stephen," Erik said incredulously, before pausing for what seemed like minutes. "You stopped . . . why did you stop?"

I honestly wasn't sure, but we were already overtime on the session we booked, so that was it. Nowadays they would just take my solo from a different take and slap it on the track Pro Tools–style, or I could have come back in and overdubbed the solo the next day, but with other commitments lined up and the clock ticking on getting this album into the marketplace, Erik just faded the track during Zally's guitar solo, and that was it. (The "alternate take" released on the 2002 remaster of the album includes my bass solo but sounds to me like a Frankenstein creation that was indeed spliced together from different takes.) If we'd had any notion that people would still be talking about these recordings almost 50 years later, maybe we would have kept plugging away, but this was 1965 and getting everything perfect was seen as an unattainable goal and a waste of time. Just pop music, right? Extremely disappointing, though whatever my musical missteps during that session, I was beginning to contribute in other ways.

I didn't really think of myself as a songwriter, but I liked to sit at the piano during idle times backstage or at sessions and noodle on pieces. One day we were bumming around with Leslie Vega, the girl who'd recently become Joe's girlfriend (and would later become his first wife), at her parents' house on King Street in the Village. I sat down at her parents' piano and began futzing around with this melodic little figure, which everyone there thought had some potential.

"What's that called, Boone?" Joe asked.

It didn't really have a name or lyrics, but I had this girl Nurit Wilde on my mind. Nurit was a friend of John and Zally's — Zally knew her from Toronto — and the guys thought we were perfect for each other so they'd fixed us up on a date at some point during our first flashes of fame. Nurit had a lovely personality, but we were both sort of tiptoeing around each other, kind of faking it, not being real. At some point I told her, in a way designed to ease the tension, that she didn't have to be so nice.

"It's called 'You Didn't Have to Be So Nice, I Would Have Liked You Anyway,'" I replied to Joe.

And a song was born. I started to flesh out the lyrics that would accompany the music, but at some point got stuck so I turned to John to help me finish some lines and verses. To this day I'm not totally sure what lines he wrote and what lines I wrote, but at the end we had collaborated, for the first time, on a really great song. (For you rock folklorists, Nurit Wilde ended up dating and having a child with Mike Nesmith of The Monkees. Our own romantic entanglement ended after that one date, though we are still in contact via email.) Again, Erik Jacobsen's beautiful production and the vocal arrangement put together by our friend Jerry Yester brings out the best in the tune. Though we were mindful not to produce songs that were a carbon copy of our other songs, the presence of John's autoharp, the drum fill that kicks off the song and the shuffling tempo were all concessions to the hit formula we'd found with "Magic." But added to that mix was the distinctive presence of chimes, which were rented from the legendary Carroll Music Instrument Studio in Manhattan, as well as a gorgeous, unmistakable Pete Drake–like guitar overdub from Zally. The vocals, both John's lead and Joe's backing vocal, perfectly represent the melancholy of the lyrics. Both John and Joe play drums on the track too.

The track came out incredibly well, and although it wouldn't make it onto the album, we slated "Nice" to become our second single in December 1965. I was extremely proud of that song, which I still believe holds up well after all these years.

The time in which those first recordings were made remains a blur almost 50 years later. I look back at our calendar from those days and see that we did album and single sessions, a bunch of TV shows (*Where the Action Is*, *Shindig!*, *Hullabaloo*) where we either mimed or actually played our first single, as well as a slew of live dates in the New York area.

Apparently we were visible enough that someone thought we'd make pretty good Monkees. As in The Monkees, the made-for-TV band patterned after The Beatles that was set up by a couple of Hollywood producers named Bob Rafelson and Bert Schneider. One day in the early fall, Bob Cavallo called us together for a band meeting. Bob had been doing a great job for us as manager — it would not be until much later that I would appreciate how much thought and work goes into managing this type of act, especially with the particular personalities in The Lovin' Spoonful. Bob came into the studio to the usual ribbing from Zally, which he brushed aside before saying, "You guys are being asked to meet with some producers who are putting together a show about a band trying to make it to the big time." There were immediate questions from all of us about the nature of the show, who the producers were, where the show would be seen etc.

"Do I get to be the star?" Zally asked with his usual wide grin. We were curious enough to take the meeting — then as now, the letters "TV" got everyone's attention.

The next day, at an office on Madison Avenue in Manhattan, we were introduced to Bob Rafelson and Bert Schneider. They laid out the general idea they had in mind, telling us the show would be a *Hard Day's Night*–type comedy called *The Monkees* and that NBC had interest in airing the show nationally. They were looking for four distinct personalities who would look good on camera and could handle playing music and some comedic acting, mainly improv. They said the TV band would perform new songs (they didn't say who would write them) that would be packaged and distributed to radio and shops. I looked over at John Sebastian during their spiel, and he seemed to be somewhere else. Zally and Joe were asking questions that weren't getting particularly direct answers from Rafelson and Schneider — the concept and the operation still seemed to be somewhat in flux. I mainly remained quiet.

After the producers left, we talked in private with Cavallo.

"What do you think, Bob?" I asked.

"Well," he said, "if it blossomed into a full-blown hit on network television, it would be huge for all of us."

"And what if it flopped?" Zally said.

"That's the sticking point in the whole deal," Bob responded. "I guess it would depend on how big the radio hits were, to try to carry on after the TV show is canceled."

John spoke up, and right away you could tell he wasn't feeling it. "They're going to make us change the name of the band, you know. We'd be known as The Monkees."

I could look around the room and see very little enthusiasm for changing our name. That said, the concept seemed worth exploring in my mind. It sounded like these guys had a good idea and if it made it to the tube, it would probably be accompanied by hit records as well. The four of us fit the bill for the four distinct personalities they were looking for. Joe and Zally would be perfect for what they wanted, Joe for his chick magnet good looks and Zally for his zaniness and over-the-top personality. As it turned out, Joe and Zally would both be working actors later on down the line. John and I were less likely to fit in. Me because I still did not like looking at the camera or even into the audience when I was high on pot, which by this point was almost all of the time. And I was still self-conscious about my scarecrow looks — I hated every picture taken of me, including the ones that had been on the single and album sleeves. John could have pulled it off as the John Lennon dry-witted intellectual-type, but I don't think there was any fiber in his being that had an interest in being a TV actor. The guy was the son of a classically trained musician and had played behind Mississippi John Hurt and Fred Neil. He wanted to be successful in pop music and was willing to put up with a certain amount of promotion to get there, but goofing around on TV was not really why John Sebastian got into this business.

"It looks to me like this show is going to be a rerun of *A Hard Day's Night*, and I doubt that they'll be able to one-up The Beatles," John said. "They're going to end up looking like copycats." The tide began to turn with that comment. We'd come by our early successes the hard way, and had stayed true to the vision to get there. With our career looking up, there was no real reason to alter course based on someone else's vision. Though it was never presented to us as "you have the job if you want it," we took our names out of the running to be The Monkees. (As it happened, Jerry Yester would be close to taking one of the roles too, but eventually turned it down when the producers refused to consider his bandmates in The Modern Folk Quartet.)

Was it the right move, knowing what we know now? I think so. Davy Jones, Mike Nesmith, Peter Tork (my old Greenwich Village pal) and Micky Dolenz were better suited for that job than we were, and I think the problems The Monkees had when they tried to break from the formula to write and play their own music would have come up a lot faster for us since we'd already been working as a band and writing our own material. There's no chance they would have let us play "Blues in the Bottle" or "Night Owl Blues" on that show.

We might have made more money, or been able to trade off our name a bit longer due to the visibility of the show, but we probably would have sacrificed some self-respect and critical respect too. A similar argument came up later on when we turned down the opportunity to do what would have been a very lucrative, very high-visibility commercial for Coca-Cola. The Monkees were talented guys and better musicians and writers than most people give them credit for, but they still encounter a residue of prejudice (for example, they've yet to be voted into the Rock and Roll Hall of Fame) that we haven't faced to such a degree.

Right around the time of the *Monkees* flirtation came my happiest memory during this era, the unbelievable run of concerts we did as part of an ensemble put on by legendary New York DJ Murray the K at the Fox Theatre in Brooklyn from September 3 to 12, 1965. We were one of two white acts, along with The McCoys of "Hang On Sloopy" fame, sharing a bill with The Four Tops, Smokey Robinson and The Miracles, The Supremes, Patti LaBelle and The Bluebelles, Stevie Wonder, The Marvelettes, and Martha and the Vandellas. Wow, what a lineup. I'm not sure what we had to do with these acts, beyond the very tenuous link we had on AM radio — maybe Murray was doing Koppelman and Rubin a favor — but there was no way we were turning it down. Frankly we probably would have gone to these shows as fans if we weren't on the bill.

I was stunned by Patti LaBelle, who was all of 21 at the time, completely mesmerizing the audience, and other performers looking on, with her a capella version of "Danny Boy." I'll never forget the good vibes of the mostly black audiences, who were a little skeptical of The Lovin' Spoonful at times but always showed respect for our act. We even got a couple of standing ovations for "Night Owl Blues" — and I nailed all the bass solos. It felt like the Motown groups wanted to impress us too, and we had several people come up and offer praise and encouragement for what we were doing, which knocked us right out.

One of these meetings of the mutual admiration society occurred at the pool hall right across the street from the theater, during a break in the action. We were hanging out with members of The Four Tops and The Temptations — the classic lineup of David Ruffin, Eddie Kendricks, Melvin Franklin, Paul Williams and Otis Williams, who were riding the wave of their first big hits "The Way You Do the Things You Do" and "My Girl." As we compared notes and had a couple of drinks, a member of The Temptations produced a folded tinfoil packet containing some white powder I was unfamiliar with. This was my first introduction to cocaine. I watched some of the other guys snort lines, and when I was offered one, I didn't say no. It didn't really change my life — I enjoyed the mild lift I got from cocaine but still preferred pot — but it was an eye-opener and moreover was an interesting bonding experience with some artists for whom we had unending respect.

I'll never forget the end of each show, when all the performers would come out onstage and do a final number together. Standing alongside a young Stevie Wonder, I could feel the emotion generated by the musicians on that stage. It was an unbelievable experience with musicians we really respected, and with audiences we wanted to work hard to impress.

The acceptance and good fortune of The Lovin' Spoonful was growing in the fall of 1965. Which meant it was time to double down.

Chapter 5

...IT'S A DIFFERENT WORLD

Bum-ba-ba-bum, ba-ba-ba-bum-ba-ba-bum. Over and over, I sat at the back of the bus and tried to make my fingers reach the right bass frets, with the proper timing and rhythm, until I was finally convinced I had it down and it sounded like the record. The song was "I Can't Help Myself," and I'd been fixated on figuring out the part since I'd heard The Funk Brothers' Tony Newton, accompanying The Four Tops, playing it onstage at the Fox Theatre.

I proudly sidled up to James Jamerson, the Motown legend who'd played on the record and was making a rare appearance on the road, playing bass for The Supremes on the dual Supremes/Spoonful tour we'd embarked on a week earlier. I played him the fruits of my labor. His eyes never strayed from the open bus window. We were somewhere near Oklahoma City. "You're playing it the white boy's way," he laughed.

James reached into the seat behind him and picked up his own bass. His long fingers effortlessly stretched across the octaves in perfect time. Bum-ba-ba-bum, ba-ba-ba-bum-ba-ba-bum. Well, fuck.

The two and a half weeks The Lovin' Spoonful spent touring the southern U.S. by bus with The Supremes in November 1965 were a master class in several different subjects, including music, the entertainment business and the attitudes of the South at a time when the Civil Rights Act of 1964 was not even a year and a half old.

The idea for the tour had been devised by a promoter who'd apparently heard about the successes of the Murray the K shows. For The Spoonful, the twin billing along with a hit act like The Supremes would give us some cachet within the industry and among radio listeners and record buyers. For Motown, the idea was that The Supremes would get a chance to work in front of different types of audiences. A lot of the material Diana Ross and co. would be doing on this tour would be of the supper club variety featured on the *Supremes at the Copa* album, which had been climbing the Billboard charts since its release earlier that month.

When we first found out we were going to do a tour with The Supremes, I was flummoxed. Why would they want us as their opening act? What would their fans think of a bunch of uppity white boys coming into their house? Forget liking us, would they even listen to us? Then I found out it was going to be a bus tour of the Deep South.

"Do the agents know what the Deep South is like?" I asked Bob Cavallo. "They don't like blacks, and they probably dislike long hair even more."

"You guys made it work at the Fox Theatre, you can make it work in the South," he said.

Despite his reassurances, I was nervous for us on a couple of fronts.

I was the only one in our group who'd had any experience with rednecks and the Deep South, from my time living in North Florida as a kid. I knew we were going to be sitting ducks, this touring troupe of black folks and hippies. John and Zally were socially conscious and knew plenty about the Civil Rights issues of the day, but I didn't think they had any clue what it was going to be like to experience it firsthand.

But I was psyched to work with The Supremes, as we all were. The idea of going on tour with three of the hottest girls in show business was irresistible to us. Diana Ross, Mary Wilson and Flo Ballard were all great singers and performers, and they were all really attractive. They'd also been cranking out hit after hit, and we were eager to see if we could get some of that stardust sprinkled on us.

We all flew to the first date in Lafayette, Louisiana, playing before a group of mainly college students at the local university. The show itself went fine. The kids sang along with "Magic" and were polite, not surprisingly saving their biggest cheers for The Supremes and their backing band, billed as The Earl Van Dyke Orchestra. The review in the next day's paper (at a time when concert reviews for pop music were not standard, and when they did appear often had the dismissive tone that "real music" reviewers seemed to reserve for anything with a beat) was a little more reserved. The male reviewer dismissed The Supremes' R&B-flavored hits: "The lyrics are monotonously similar to the hundreds of others that dwell on the agony and ecstasy of pre- and post-adolescent love, usually unrequited. Constantly recurring throughout is the appellation 'baby,' another indication of the trend toward Momism underscored by Philip Wylie years ago and the femininization of today's society. Rock Around The Clock because we're heading for a matriarchy, baby, baby, and the hand that rocks the cradle is a swinging chick." See, folks, there were conservative fearmongers around in 1965 too.

The reviewer from Lafayette liked their "adult music" — "The Supremes' real talent, however lies away from the dreary 3-chord R&R field into the more legitimate musical pastures of pop and Broadway showtunes."

Oh, and even we were acknowledged, in 35 crisp words: "The Lovin' Spoonful was there, too. They are four young fellers with long beautiful hair. They have three very loud electric guitars, one drum, and oodles of energy, really they do. They sang some songs."

They sang some songs. Hey, at least our long beautiful hair wasn't offered up as further evidence of the feminization of today's society.

After the show we got our first taste of the eye-opening nature of the 1960s South. We were still in our stage clothes and looking for something to eat when the bus pulled up to a diner in Lafayette that was segregated in the sense that blacks had to order from the carry-out window, while we white folks were expected to have our meals in the dining room. We didn't like it, and I'm sure The Supremes didn't like it, but we were all hungry and no one was in the mood to make a stand against what was recognized as obvious, naked racism. After the waitress came to the table and took our order, John got up to make a phone call to this girl he'd started dating back in New York named Lorey Kaye. As he was talking we heard some raised voices from the bar area.

"Hey, look at that long-haired faggot with the peppermint-striped shirt." The comment was directed at John, but if he heard it, he wasn't letting on. The voices got louder, and everybody in the crowded restaurant had taken notice.

"Hey faggot, look at us, faggot." One of the rednecks started to make his way toward where John was standing, and me, Joe and Zally jumped up to intervene. We weren't the only ones. A couple of the college kids, big guys who looked like athletes, who had been at the concert that night, bravely spoke up.

"Hey, leave these guys alone. They're musicians. We just saw them play a show over at the Coliseum." The rednecks looked like they were trying to process this information through brains damaged by the night's alcohol intake, and possibly generations of inbreeding. As they were deciding whether to advance or retreat, the door to the diner swung open, and in walked all 12 members of The Earl Van Dyke Orchestra, alerted by one of The Supremes (I think it was Diana) who had heard the altercation from the carryout window. The place fell stone silent.

This O.K. Corral–type scenario was nearing a climax when the clown prince of defusing tension got to work. Zally went running toward the door and jumped right into the arms of the enormous EVD bandleader. The EVD guys filed out and we followed right behind them onto the bus, from which we promptly got the hell out of there. When I looked at John, his eyes were as big as saucers.

"Only 15 dates left," I reminded him.

We wended our way from Lafayette to Memphis and on to Tulsa, Oklahoma City and Dallas before heading east. In 1965, tour buses were little more than conventional buses like Greyhound and Trailways used, and if the air conditioning worked it was just enough to keep you from sweating. Between the singers and the bands, there were more than 20 pieces, so we had to tow a trailer to carry the band gear.

The tour bus was a moving party, though the tour manager, Big John, was a tough SOB and nobody gave him any shit. It was on the longer drives that we would really mingle. The girls were kept under tight surveillance by their minder from Motown, and Diana in particular was kept almost in isolation. I couldn't tell whether she was stuck up or just shy, but the fact that she was apart from the rest of the group definitely struck me as strange. The Supremes had only been major hitmakers for about a year and a half by this point, but she had already emerged as the star of the group, both in public and private. Mary and Flo, on the other hand, were very personable and willing to play poker and tell jokes and fraternize with all the boys — up to a point. From everything I saw, things were kept above board. These were 21- and 22-year-old women, and The Earl Van Dyke Orchestra had some hardcore touring players who I got the sense had seen it all and then some. Had everyone not been kept on a tight leash, including the red-blooded young guys in The Spoonful, there could have been real difficulties.

I mostly sat in the back of the bus with the EVD guys, who were content to take my money in poker with an occasional musical tip thrown in. I'm sure I looked out of place in this environment, but it didn't feel that way. Having played with King Charles in the house band at the Cottage Inn, I'd socialized with plenty of black folks and had enough of a musical lexicon to keep up.

I don't know if the other guys were as comfortable socially, but I know all four of us were inspired musically on that tour. On what qualified as the second leg, which started in Georgia and wound its way through the Carolinas and eventually up through Virginia and into Baltimore, John Sebastian wrote two of our best-loved songs.

On a sticky day somewhere in Northeast Georgia, he came up with the line "I was down in Savannah eating cream and bananas when the heat just made me faint." From there he was off and running, writing words that evoked some of Dylan's psychedelic-vision songs ("I was told a little tale about a skinny-as-a-rail eight-foot cowboy with a headache").

He played the beginnings of the song for Zally, who loved the irreverence of the lyric and threw in a classic Zally line, in a section of the song that dealt with surfing, about "trying to mooch a towel from the hoi polloi." Then John married the whole thing to a line he'd had kicking around him for a while, which he'd used in a cartoon he wrote for Mississippi John Hurt and ended up being the song's refrain: "The doctor said give him jug band music, it seems to make him feel just fine." The song made no literal or linear sense, which was why it was brilliant. "Jug Band Music" would also end up being one of our most important songs to me musically, since when we got to Bell Sound the next month, the song included an opening bass riff that would become one of my signature recorded moments.

But the bigger piece of writing history in the career arc of The Lovin' Spoonful occurred near the end of the tour. On a miserable rainy day, traveling to Greensboro, North Carolina, John was trying to snap himself out of a funk. The tour, while fun, was becoming a little bit of a physical grind, and John found himself alternately worn out and pining for his new love, Lorey.

Looking to cheer himself up, he was plucking his guitar in the "straight eight" Motown style that we'd heard so much on this tour, from "Baby Love" and "Where Did Our Love Go" and beyond. As he peered out the window, feeling like he'd rather be anywhere in the world on this rainy day, the line came out: "What a day for a daydream . . ." Maybe 20 minutes later, he'd finished the song, though recording it would prove to be considerably more difficult.

There were two guitar figures in the song, with John playing the oompah part on his '58 Les Paul and Zally playing the backbeat figure on John's Heritage Gibson acoustic. But the staccato kind of rhythm of the song prevented John and Zal from getting the guitars in sync, and the track kept breaking down when one guy would get ahead of the other. Just as had happened with "Night Owl Blues," at some point the song was temporarily abandoned, at which point Erik Jacobsen started painstakingly piecing together takes with scissors and tape. Eventually he came up with a complete guitar track, after which I overdubbed a tack piano part, Joe Butler added spoons and Zally appended his Thunderbird electric guitar. With John's vocal, harmonica and whistling helping carry the catchy tune, we had a song in "Daydream" that John would later admit was "in fact, a splicing wonder."

It wasn't until we had a master take that Zally said to John, "Oh by the way, good job ripping off 'Got a Date with an Angel,'" referring to the Hal Kemp song from the '30s which, upon reflection, did bear some resemblance to "Daydream" in the vocal melody. Oh, well — imitation is the sincerest form of flattery, and all that jazz.

Aside from the similarity to the Kemp standard, I have to admit I didn't particularly love "Daydream" at the time. I was OK with it as an album track, but I didn't think it had commercial potential — instincts that were, in this case, way off.

All in all, we'd remember the tour with The Supremes as a high-water mark in our experience as a band. Our playing had gotten tighter and we'd won some new friends and fans, but there was no opportunity for such reflection at the time. We worked like dogs for the rest for 1965 as the demand for performances and product began to multiply.

We went straight from The Supremes tour to Los Angeles, where we'd been invited by Phil Spector to appear in a concert movie called *The Big T.N.T. Show*, which was a kind of sequel to a successful and later legendary film shot the previous year called *The T.A.M.I. Show*. Along with The Spoonful, Spector had invited luminaries like The Byrds, Donovan, Ray Charles, Bo Diddley, Roger Miller,

Petula Clark, Joan Baez and, naturally, Ike & Tina Turner and The Ronettes from his own stable. Our friend Jerry Yester and his group The Modern Folk Quartet, also produced by Phil, were there too. It was quite the assemblage of talent. It was hard to believe, walking around backstage alongside all these stars who were now considered peers, that a year ago The Lovin' Spoonful hadn't even existed.

We played a rough version of "Do You Believe in Magic." Joe messed up the opening beat, to Zally's public announcement of "Joe's fault!" before we restarted the song. Any embarrassment from that incident (which made it into the final cut of the film) was washed away by the performance of our upcoming single "You Didn't Have to Be So Nice," which went over really well with the audience at the Moulin Rouge club, where the show was filmed.

After *The Big T.N.T. Show* we stayed out in L.A. for a couple of weeks to do a residency at a short-lived nightclub on Sunset Boulevard, right next to the Playboy Club, called the Trip. By the time we took the stage for our first show there, we were considered the hottest new act on the scene, especially in Los Angeles, where our records were in heavy rotation. When I came off the stage after the first set on our first night at the club, I began chatting with David Crosby from The Byrds. David shared my interest in sailing and sports cars, and as we talked he said, "Let's go for a ride in my new Porsche, I just got it. I'll get you back onstage just in time for the next set." Sounded OK to me. Once we were in David's car, he broke out some potent hash-laced pot, which we smoked as we raced around L.A. in his fine new vehicle. True to his word, David had me back on time, but I was so high on the smoke that I could barely see my feet, which was always where I looked whenever I went onstage high. Somehow I muddled through the set.

At the end of our first night at The Trip, one of the waitresses approached me. I'd noticed her from the stage early on, as she was a great-looking gal with dramatic makeup and a nice body. We talked and flirted, which led to getting a bite to eat at Ben Frank's, a nearby diner and Hollywood institution where on any given night you could find all manner of stars chowing down. On this particular night I was considered a star, and the waitress — Jeannie Franklyn — and I would begin a casual relationship that would go on for quite a while. I spent the night with her that night — once the makeup came off she looked entirely different, and far less predatory. On that trip Jeannie also showed me some of her homemade clothes and offered to make me some custom pants, using the wide wale corduroy that was just then becoming the material of choice for hipsters. I got her to make me a custom turtleneck leather motorcycle shirt, which was the coolest piece of clothing I had ever had. She also showed some of her clothes to Zally, who just had to have some, and once he was wearing her stuff, everyone noticed. Soon everybody from the rock world who came through L.A. had to have "Genie the Tailor" make them some clothes, and she became a star in her own right. Within a year she had rock star clients from the U.S. and England, and by 1968 she had her own boutique in L.A.

Tragically Jeannie was the victim of her own success. In May 1969, while she was traveling on an English tour with her boyfriend, Richard Thompson of Fairport Convention, the roadie who was driving the band's van fell asleep at the wheel, the van crashed, and Jeannie was killed at the age of 27 along with Fairport Convention's drummer, Martin Lamble. There was a great outpouring of grief in the rock community, and Cream bass player Jack Bruce named his first solo album *Songs for a Tailor* as a tribute to Jeannie.

After the Trip gig we did a couple of dates in the Midwest and then came back home to chilly New York City for four mid-December days at Bell Sound, where we were to record a brand new album. An album!? It had only been 10 weeks since we'd finished off the *Do You Believe in Magic* album, 10 weeks that had been jam-packed with live dates and TV appearances. While we were really tight as a band by this point, we hadn't had much time to write or rehearse new material, and these sessions were going to be hurried. They would start on December 13, and we were due in Cleveland for a string of TV appearances and live dates on December 17. Four weary guys and their producer, four days, and the expectation of a brand new album. But that's the way it went in those days, so we got to work.

We already had the finished master of "You Didn't Have to Be So Nice," which hadn't gone on the last album but we already knew would be one of the cornerstones of the new one.

We had the aforementioned "Daydream" and "Jug Band Music," which we managed to get down on tape. We had one of John's older songs, the really pretty Burt Bacharach–like "Didn't Want to Have to Do It," and we got down a good take of our live staple, a cover of Dr. Feelgood's "Bald Headed Lena." On the latter, Zally was doing his vocal take and didn't know how to vamp through one of the vocal breaks, so he picked up his glass of water and gargled his way through the last verse. Only Zal Yanovsky could have come up with that part, which everyone thought was hilarious and pure Zally, and made it into the final mix.

John and Erik dusted off another older Sebastian song, the Robert Johnson–influenced "Warm Baby," which had just missed the cut for the last album but passed muster for this one.

Added to that handful of songs were some things I have to believe were little more than fragments of ideas when we walked through the door at Bell Sound. A couple, admittedly, were filler. We had an instrumental called "Big Noise from Speonk" (Speonk being the easternmost commuter stop on the Long Island Rail Road, not far from the Bull's Head Inn), which was a jam that incorporated elements of John's harmonica work from Fred Neil's "Candyman." We had a distortion-driven Beatles knockoff called "There She Is," written by John and sung by Joe, which was brief but pleasant and remains a favorite among some of our fans.

Better was "Let the Boy Rock and Roll," where you'll hear some of the best playing to be found on a Lovin' Spoonful record. A Chuck Berry–inspired co-write between John and Joe, the song is grounded by the rhythm section, with Joe playing the shuffle style that was really his strength as a drummer, and me locked in with Joe's bass drum, holding down the back end. Then you have Zally's fantastic and distinctive playing on the Guild Thunderbird, and an impassioned vocal by John, whose love for the song showed. "Let the Boy Rock and Roll" was very nearly a single, and I think it should have been, if only to show that The Lovin' Spoonful could rock out.

It's here that I should probably admit I didn't always see eye to eye with Erik Jacobsen in the studio, in particular with how he recorded and mixed the rhythm section. Erik was a brilliant producer, sharp as a tack in the studio and single-minded in his pursuit to get things right, but you can barely hear the bass and drums on some of our records, and I think that's partially down to the substandard equipment of the day and partially down to Erik's approach. His background was as a folkie — I think he heard the voices and guitars just fine but didn't have as much time or need for the bass and drums. It kind of bugs me when I hear or read things suggesting Joe and I were incidental to the band's sound, or that we were some kind of a wimpy rhythm section. It's the mix! I'm not saying we were Entwistle and Moon in the power department, but we were better than some of those mixes would lead you to believe. I bring this up here to say "Let the Boy Rock and Roll" was one where I was happy with the way things sounded — that track rocks.

Two more from the *Daydream* album that showed John's development as a songwriter were "Day Blues" and "It's Not Time Now."

"Day Blues" was written by John for and about Zally, who had a habit, like many musicians who had become accustomed to a nocturnal lifestyle, of staying up until the morning light. The song was recorded late in the evening with the lights in the studio turned way down, and I think we did a good job capturing the mood John was looking to find. I also think John had Fred Neil's style in mind when he wrote the song — it definitely sounds like something Fred could have sung.

But the composition of John's on this album (with help from Zally) that blew me away was "It's Not Time Now," which is the song in the Lovin' Spoonful canon that not nearly enough people know. But many who do know it tell me it's their favorite Lovin' Spoonful song.

On top of a finger-picking guitar part that was a tribute to Johnny Cash's guitar player, Luther Perkins, and another steady country shuffle from Joe on the drums, John wrote a wonderful, honest lyric about the very familiar pop song territory of relationships and arguments, one that manages to avoid all the usual rock 'n' roll clichés. It's hard to believe a guy who was 21 years old could write a lyric as heavy as "But we've taken sides in anger and we can't back down/ Now we're fighting just to bring the other down." I already knew John had talent as a writer before he brought in this song, but "It's Not Time Now" showed a level of growth and depth that told me the sky was the limit for our group. It was inspiring. So I wrote my own song.

The experience of the previous few months, and the heady work currently being done in the studio, made me realize how far we'd come since those first few weeks of starving in the Village, wondering whether we'd make it. In addition to feeling like my own adolescence had reached an end, there was now a palpable sense that things had changed and that the past and our youth were only going to get smaller in the rearview mirror, whether we liked it or not. The reality was that with a couple of hit songs on the charts ("You Didn't Have to Be So Nice" had entered the chart in early December and was climbing), the old friends you bumped into in the Village started treating you a little differently. It was exhilarating to feel like we were headed somewhere, but there was a definite sense of melancholy at the same time over the good times and people we were leaving.

I tried to frame this sort of inevitability when I wrote "Butchie's Tune," which used our old No. 1 fan Butchie as a symbol representing what we stood to gain, and what we were about to lose: "Please don't you cry when the time to part has come/ It's not for what you've said or anything that you've done/ I've got to go anywhere anytime/ And I'm leaving, gone today/ On my way."

All the guys were really encouraging when I brought the song in the next day. John helped me polish up a couple of lines while we rode over to the session, and Zally took my melody and worked out a lovely Floyd Cramer slipnote-style guitar part for it. Joe, who had just one lead vocal on the album so far, volunteered to sing it. I can admit all these years later that this made me slightly nervous. Joe got attacked by some of our fans and even members of our band for his propensity toward crooning, which did not always jibe with our folk-rock musical style and in my opinion was intentional to maintain his ladies' man image. He thought that Tom Jones schtick was what the girls wanted to hear, though he had (and has) a perfectly nice natural voice. Even John Sebastian would admit that Joe was probably the best pure singer in the group, and I always thought he should have left that showbiz crooner voice where it belonged, in the Holiday Inn lounge.

But to his credit, Joe's restrained vocal on "Butchie's Tune" was free of affectation and spot-on perfect for what the song needed. The track came out great, and is another one of those songs that might not be our best known but seems to be beloved by everyone who calls themselves a true Spoonful fan. I always thought it could be a great country hit in the hands of the right artist, and though that hasn't happened (yet!), "Butchie's Tune" has been used in two cinematic settings. The first was Michelangelo Antonioni's influential and critically acclaimed 1966 film *Blow-Up*, when the backing track is heard over a surrealistic scene featuring models posing. The second, more recent usage was in a 2012 episode of the hit 1960s-set drama *Mad Men*, in the final scene of that episode, featuring two characters reflecting on a particularly bad day. I sure am happy to see the song live on, and especially for it to be used in a classy context on what is considered one of the best television shows ever made.

After four days in the studio, we had enough for an album and it was "hello, Cleveland" for a couple of days, before we returned home for a few weeks of R&R during the Christmas season of 1965.

Being back home on Long Island for the holidays was kind of strange. I don't think my parents and brothers knew quite what to make of Steve the rock star, and frankly neither did I. My two younger brothers, Charlie and Mike, were both thrilled to have seen me on television. I think Skip, who'd been a working musician a lot longer than me, was a little puzzled about how fast we'd taken off and how little effort it seemed to take to get there. My mom and dad seemed proud in their way, though my dad was still in line with most of his generation when it came to rock 'n' roll. Even though it had been 10 years since Elvis burst on the scene, guys like my dad still thought this was all just a fad that would soon be gone. It was only recently that I'd become certain he was wrong.

Right before we'd done The Supremes tour, I'd left a deposit with a real estate agent with instructions to find me a house, and just before Christmas he rang back with some good news. He had found a small but unique house for me, and at $325 a month it was right in my price range. It was located at 343 West 12th Street in the meat packing district at the heart of the West Village. It was an actual carriage house that had been converted to a one-bedroom apartment with the bedroom/bath upstairs and the kitchen/living area downstairs. I had a relatively private entrance down an alley from West 12th Street, with a small patio between the main building and the carriage house. The fireplace had been boarded over, I suppose to keep the squirrels and rodents out, and the place needed some paint and putty but had a great location and was a diamond in the rough. After talking with my brothers and friends, I found a Jamaican national to come in and re-plaster the surrounding stonework and put down a nice brick hearth. My friend Terry Jackson, who had found me the Jamaican mason, built me a great little bar and kitchen-counter-type console, and with four bar stools I was in business. With a little love and care I was able to get the apartment in shape, and soon after the calendar had flipped to 1966 I was living on my own for the first time ever. But I wouldn't get to enjoy it long before we were back out on the road for some dates out west.

We had a job in Honolulu that I was excited about. I kind of considered myself an East Coast surfer guy, even though there were not too many East Coast guys into surfing in the mid-1960s. I loved The

Beach Boys and Jan and Dean, and I even liked those uncool Beach Blanket movies, and now here I was getting to go to the Mecca of it all. For one day. Yes that's right, we were going to be in Hawaii for one 24-hour day. We had bookings back in the mainland, so there was no time for a mini-vacation. But I was determined to make the most of the trip, so after we got to Hawaii I rented my own Mustang from Hertz, and with about 12 hours between the gig at the Honolulu Convention Center and our flight to California, I got into that Mustang with a map and a bottle of rum and saw as much as I could see. I went to Diamond Head and drove up to the fabled North Shore, where I was able to see a few actual surfers but no big waves. This was a minor disappointment, as I had expected to see nothing but 25-foot waves, but that is just not how it is, even in Hawaii. At least I got lei'd.

The rest of the winter was spent doing a number of package shows, where we were billed alongside acts including The Yardbirds, The Turtles, The Beau Brummels, Sonny & Cher, Chad & Jeremy and The Beach Boys. In February, in the midst of this run, the "Daydream" single was released and began climbing the charts, where it eventually became our third single out of three to reach the Top 10. Once that happened, the crowds we played before got more enthusiastic, and battles over billing began between our management and that of our fellow performers. One such quarrel occurred with The Beach Boys, with whom we played almost a month of shows in March and April 1966.

We loved The Beach Boys' music and got along great with just about every member of the band. Brian Wilson was by then out of the picture when it came to touring, but I loved talking about hot rods with his brother Carl, and Dennis Wilson was a life-of-the-party guy with a lot of charisma about whom no one could say a bad word.

The Beach Boys had a bigger fan base and more hits than we did, but by the winter of 1966, their image, and their relatively short haircuts, had become a little dated with some of the kids. I don't know if The Lovin' Spoonful were the cutting edge of hip, but we were pretty hot with audiences and there was a definite question about who was the biggest drawing card on this tour.

I don't think any of us in The Spoonful really cared whether we went on first or second — again, we really respected The Beach Boys — but at one concert we showed up and were met with an itinerary that had us going on last, headlining the bill.

Apparently Mike Love saw this and flipped out — which should not have surprised me, since Love was the one guy in The Beach Boys who was a total dick and I could not stand. He was (and by most accounts remains) an obnoxious, boorish braggart, whose high and whiny singing voice would have been consigned to the karaoke circuit were it not for the fact that he happened to be the cousin of a musical genius named Brian Wilson. Love was born on third base, but based on his ungracious behavior I guess he thinks he hit a triple.

Anyway, once Mike Love dug in his heels about the billing, we suddenly cared. I didn't want to fight with The Beach Boys, but no one wanted this marginally talented hack to get his way. The managers and promoters duked it out, and ultimately it was decided that we would alternate top billing for the remainder of the tour, which was by all accounts a big success.

Another interesting confrontation around this time occurred with our record company, which decided to take out a full-page ad in *Billboard* to promote the "Daydream" single. That was great, but what wasn't was the configuration of the ad, which said "Lovin' . . . Spoonful . . . Daydream" stacked on separate lines with the first letters of each of those words illustrated so the eye was drawn to "L . . . S . . . D."

This made the band's blood boil. Since day one, some in the press and public had made a continuous effort to link the name "Lovin' Spoonful" with drug use, specifically the spoon used in shooting heroin. We weren't anti-drug in either rhetoric or practice, but John hadn't been thinking of heroin spoons when he named the band, and the thought of people mistaking the band name as a drug reference had crossed our minds for all of three seconds before we'd dismissed it as a silly notion. After working hard to distance our name from this association, here it was looking like we were trying to trade off the drug connection in the pages of *Billboard*. We protested mightily to the boys at Kama Sutra, but the hay was already out of the barn and I don't think our protests would have mattered anyway. After they'd pushed most of the right buttons for the past year, this was the first time we would question whether the Kama Sutra/Koppelman-Rubin axis really had our best interests at heart.

"Daydream" would eventually just miss the No. 1 spot on Billboard (peaking at No. 2) and hit No. 1 on Cashbox. Sometime before the *Daydream* album was released in March, we got word that the single was taking off in Britain as well. "Magic" and "Nice" hadn't done much in England, so this was surprising news, and though many American groups had received a chilly welcome in the post-Beatles U.K., we knew it was time to capitalize on the single's success (it would end up being our biggest hit in England, where Paul McCartney heard it and wrote a song he later admitted was an homage, called "Good Day Sunshine"). Our management set up a few live and TV dates in England and Sweden for April that we were looking forward to in a big way.

These were heady times, but luckily there was always something to humble us. It was around this time that we were engaging in an increasingly common part of the band's routine — getting on an airplane to fly to a string of live dates — when who did we see seated in the first-class cabin but Miles Davis. Musical deities didn't come any more godlike in 1966 than Davis, and we all kind of nudged each other and whispered and discussed whether to approach him. John, who was the pedigreed muso and resident encyclopedia of musical knowledge in the group, decided he couldn't let this moment slip away. Also, we were reasonably famous by this time and it seemed like all manner of great musicians, artists and entertainers were telling us how much they dug us too.

So John went up to Davis, and the gushing began: "Mr. Davis, I just wanted to tell you how much we love your music. *Kind of*

Blue, Sketches of Spain . . . just amazing work." He went on and on, nervously speed-talking and telling Davis how much our band loved his music and respected his contributions to jazz specifically and American art in general.

When he was finally done, Miles Davis just looked John Sebastian square in the face and said, "I don't talk to honkies."

When John recounted this, the rest of us just fell apart in hysterics. We could not control ourselves. For the rest of that trip John couldn't initiate a conversation with any of us that wasn't met with a reply of "I don't talk to honkies."

We weren't due back in a recording studio until June, but just before we were to depart to Europe, an interesting offer came in that was too good to pass up. A young director named Woody Allen had made a bizarre comedy film, which was basically an already existing Japanese spy movie with comedic dialogue dubbed in English overtop of it. The film, which was to be called *What's Up, Tiger Lily?*, needed a soundtrack and some musical sequences to help pad the length, and as a hot young group we were approached for the job. The timing was not good — we'd basically have two days to record the soundtrack before we left for an important tour overseas — but we were used to working fast in the studio, we were going to get to appear in some new musical sequences shot specifically for the film and we (particularly Zally) loved the goofball concept, so we agreed.

These sessions would be different in the respect that the producer calling the shots wasn't Erik Jacobsen but a guy named Jack Lewis, and the studio would not be our familiar Bell Sound but a movie soundstage, National Recording Studios. Basically our orders were to watch the movie and record some "appropriate" music on top of it, which didn't prove to be all that daunting.

We had a couple of new songs that seemed to fit the outlandish concept, including our goofy "Pow!" which was a sort of lyrical cousin to "Jug Band Music" and on which my brother Skip was given a writing credit along with all four members of the band. I get asked a lot what John is singing in the chorus, and the answer (drumroll please) is "wee until pow." What it means I have no idea — probably nothing.

The only other proper new song on the soundtrack was John's "Respoken," which was the best song on the record and featured some out-there guitar work from Zally. I thought it should have been a single.

We also cut a "live" version of "Fishin' Blues" from our first album, which sounded awfully strange when offset against a Japanese spy film, but everything about the movie was intentionally incongruous, so I guess it made some perverse sense.

All the other music we made was of the incidental-soundtrack variety, and Jack Lewis, a wonderful guy who had also produced the music for *Lawrence of Arabia*, gave us a lot of tips on what was needed for the score. He also gave us freedom to do what we wanted sonically — we could record ourselves dropping plates on the floor if we wanted — and that really helped us along creatively and made the process fun. I don't remember much about the filming of our musical sequences, but the film shows me wearing all black against the all-black backdrop of the studio, so I guess I was there.

So I'm in a Woody Allen movie, although apparently Woody didn't really like the results of the film — or The Lovin' Spoonful. I heard he sued the production company over our addition to the movie, claiming that our presence meant they'd tampered with his work. Whatever. I'm not sure I ever got paid for *What's Up, Tiger Lily?*, but I had a good time helping to create it.

Just after our initial foray into film music making, it was off to England for a trip that would prove to be among the most memorable events in the history of the group. It had only been about a year and a half since I'd gone on the motorcycle tour around the continent with Peter. I'd had such a blast that I knew I'd be back before long; I just never expected to have a professional reason to be back so soon. Nor could I have envisioned having a hit on the English charts, or rubbing elbows with The Beatles and The Rolling Stones. Again, I'm sure my 22-year-old self wasn't really reflecting on any of this at the time, since by April 1966 all this stuff that would have seemed unbelievable in my past life was now becoming old hat. The only thing that was normal was the surreal, so we just kept on moving.

That said, we were a little nervous about England. The American groups who sprang up as would-be challengers to The Beatles and the rest of the British Invasion had been basically ignored in Britain. Our friends The Byrds had been treated roughly by the press and audiences when they'd gone to England in the summer of 1965, so we knew, chart hit or not, it was going to take some work for us to be fully accepted there. Though we were already growing weary of some of the American press and teenybopper magazines, with their inane questions, we knew we'd need to put our best foot forward if this trip was to be a success.

Our entourage for the trip consisted of Bob Cavallo, who went ahead of us to work out some logistics; Erik Jacobsen; our PR guy, Dan Moriarty; road manager Rich Chiaro and a photographer we knew named Don Paulsen. We were staying at the May Fair Hotel in Piccadilly, which is where a lot of the American acts, including Dylan, had stayed on their journeys there.

The VC10 jetliner touched down at Heathrow, and right on the tarmac we had our first audience with the British media, who were waiting in advance of a champagne press reception (paid for by us, we'd later find out). We were all tired from the intercontinental flight but the adrenaline was flowing, so we answered all the questions cordially and seemed to charm the media throng. So far, so good.

Once the official duties were over, we set out in pursuit of some London nightlife. I should have warned the guys that pubs in Britain closed at 11 p.m., because we found ourselves on the street and searching for options soon after our usual dinnertime. Trying to figure out what to do, Joe remembered an invitation he'd been extended at the press reception, to a party given by this guy named Tara Browne. An Irishman who turned out to be an heir to the Guinness fortune, Browne had a house in the Belgravia section of London, and we were invited to stop by.

Not quite knowing what to expect but possessing few options, we instructed the driver of the vintage 1932 Rolls-Royce shuttling us around London (also at our expense, unbeknownst to us) to take us over to Browne's. When we got there, it became clear this guy was pretty well connected to the swinging London community. A bunch of local scenemakers were in attendance, as well as American actor Ben Carruthers. We were greeted warmly by Tara, who handed each of us a big lump of hash as a welcome gift. Hey, this guy was all right. We mingled well into the early morning hours — I met a British girl there whom I became obsessed with and was holed up with for a big portion of our trip — and Tara insisted that we travel to his estate in Dublin the next week to play his 21st birthday party. He said he'd pay the freight to get us there and we'd be compensated for our performance, but beyond that it would be a great party with lots of cool people to meet. It just so happened we had that day off before we returned to the States, so we agreed.

In the meantime, there was important business to attend to. Our management had set up appearances throughout the next week on local TV staples *Top of the Pops*, *Ready Steady Go!* and *Thank Your Lucky Stars*, in addition to an appearance on BBC Radio.

The *Top of the Pops* appearance was interesting for a couple of reasons, not the least of which was the fact that multiple members of the group were high as a kite off the potent hash we'd been given at Tara's party the night before. We were stoned out of our minds for that appearance — John had to be woken up just before we got our cue to perform "Daydream."

I also have a hazy memory of our management arguing with the lead singer of the other band playing the show that day — Mick Jagger of The Rolling Stones — over who was to get top billing on the performance. Jagger struck some in our party as a bit petulant, an impression that would be reinforced when we saw him in action in a social setting later in the trip. The rest of The Stones, particularly Brian Jones, could not have been cooler.

Later in the week we played *Ready Steady Go!*, as part of a show that also featured British acts Dusty Springfield and Manfred Mann, before traveling north and playing a couple of less-than-memorable gigs up in Birmingham and Manchester. Our first week in Europe had been entertaining and enjoyable, but the second was where the real adventures were had.

A by-invitation-only concert was being given for us at a venue called the Marquee Club, a joint in central London where The Rolling Stones had played their first show in 1962 and which we were told was currently the terrain for a lot of the happening musical acts in the area. But when I'd gone by the venue on April 18, 1966, the night before we were to play, some cat named David Bowie was playing. Never heard of him. I guess we'd have to wait to see whether this place would live up to its reputation. When I walked out onstage and scanned an audience that included John Lennon, George Harrison, Brian Jones, Steve Winwood, Spencer Davis and Eric Clapton, among others, I became convinced. I'd already played lots of bigger venues and before TV audiences of millions, but to say I was extremely nervous for this show would be an understatement. All the screaming girls, radio play and record sales in the world are a pale substitute for the acceptance of your peers, and a lot of people we really respected were in that room. There was definitely a feeling that much was at stake here.

The show went well, but only after we narrowly sidestepped disaster.

Near the end of our show, as we were playing "Fishin' Blues," our power suddenly went out and we lost the use of our amplifiers. It took a second to figure out what was happening, during which time Joe just kept soldiering on with the beat. Not quite knowing what to do, Zally and I kept plucking the strings and strumming as if they were still amplified, and since the microphones still worked, John continued to sing. As we came to the end of the tune, standing before a lot of musicians who undoubtedly empathized with our plight, the house went nuts with cheers. It turned out that the AC converter that we needed to change the power in our amps from U.S. standard to Euro had failed, thus taking out our amps. But by gutting it out and continuing with the show, we won over the crowd in spades.

The warm reception continued after the show, when we were visited at the May Fair by many of the famous musical dignitaries we'd seen at the Marquee. Lennon and Harrison, who history tells us had recorded the rhythm track to "Doctor Robert" that very night, hung out well into the wee morning hours, drinking and smoking hash provided by George. (George and John Sebastian later snuck off to play the sitar after the party got too rowdy.) Zally was in typical form, throwing liquor bottles out the fourth-story window, to the chagrin of the hotel management, while our John talked to The Beatles' John about our experience making *What's Up, Tiger Lily?*. Although there are conflicting tales about what Lennon was like in "real life," our band found him to be very humble, friendly and interesting to talk to on that night in 1966. The Beatles narrative says that by this point John was going through a bit of a personal crisis as a cloistered suburbanite with a young family he was struggling to commit to, but none of that was apparent when he visited us at the May Fair. I don't know if he thought of us as peers, but he sure treated us like it. Before they left, we made plans to see each other again when The Beatles came back to America that summer.

The next night we played a proper gig at a club called Blaises in Kensington, where Jimi Hendrix and Pink Floyd would soon cut their teeth. Brian Jones was there that night and invited us to a wild party at his house afterward.

Then it was on to Stockholm, where we played Sweden's version of *Ready Steady Go!* on a show that also included a hit Swedish act called The Hep Stars. The Hep Stars' piano player was a guy named Benny Andersson, who revealed himself to be a big Spoonful fan and later found fame and fortune as a member of ABBA.

But for all the exhilarating highs of that trip, it was the grand finale — the massive birthday party for Tara Browne — that remains seared into my memory all these years later.

The formal invitation read: "A party in honour of the honourable Tara Browne on his 21st birthday at Lugalla in County Wicklow, the country residence of his parents, Lord Oranmore and Browne, and Oonagh (Guinness) Lady Oranmore and Browne."

When we got there in the early twilight, we encountered quite the party, and quite the mix of partygoers. Counts and countesses, barons and baronesses and lords-a-leaping were joined by high-fashion models, members of The Rolling Stones and pounds of hashish. Mick and Keith Richards were there, as was Brian Jones with his girlfriend, Anita Pallenberg, later to be stolen away by Keith. American philanthropist John Paul Getty was there, as was Paul McCartney's brother Mike and probably lots of other famous folks I can't remember.

We played a set and partied all night before being invited to stay over at this country estate, which sat at the junction separating two mountain ranges.

I remember waking up the next day and having a cup of coffee with Tara as we looked out over the Irish countryside. I really enjoyed talking to him — he was a bright, gregarious guy who loved The Spoonful and actually looked a little bit like me.

"So where does this property begin and end?" I asked Tara as we looked out onto the fields. He pointed to his left.

"See those peaks way out there beyond the horizon?"

I nodded. He pointed to his right.

"OK, see those peaks way out on that side?"

"Yep."

"Everything in between is our property."

I was impressed. Having grown up around wealthy families in the Hamptons, I was fairly used to seeing extravagance, but this was a cut far above anything I had ever experienced. Yet for all his family's wealth and taste, this guy Tara Browne was just a humble 21-year-old kid with very few airs about him. I was stunned when I heard about eight months later that he had been killed in a car crash in London. His 21st would be the last birthday Tara would ever celebrate, and our private show for him would be his last birthday present.

His friend John Lennon immortalized the crash in the song "A Day in the Life," with the line "He blew his mind out in a car/ He didn't notice that the lights had changed," though that's not what really happened — Tara swerved to avoid a turning Volkswagen, and his Lotus Elan hit a parked van, killing him instantly. He was buried at the foot of the Wicklow mountain range he had pointed out to me on our trip there. Who knows what Tara Browne could have become, but I'm glad to say I got to know him for a few days during a trip that remains a high point of my personal and professional life.

As The Lovin' Spoonful and our entourage flew back from London on that last week in April, it was a top-of-the-world type of feeling. We'd successfully promoted our band and its records to a brand new audience, been encouraged and treated as equals by artists who were considered tops in their field, and done some world-class sightseeing along the way. The morale of the band, and the sense of collegiality we felt with each other, would never be higher than it was after the England/Sweden/Ireland trip. The inspiration even spilled over to our creative process, where we began writing and experimenting with new sounds to help keep us in the upper echelon to which we now, by all indications, belonged.

As that VC10 soared five miles above the earth and headed back to New York, the sun came beaming through the airplane windows. Soon, The Lovin' Spoonful would find out what happens when you fly too close to the sun.

Chapter 6
POW!

The events of May 20, 1966, have haunted me for just about every day that has followed.

I'm really not trying to be melodramatic about this, just honest.

The marijuana arrest that landed me and Zal Yanovsky in a San Francisco jail cell in the spring of '66 was the touchstone for a series of events that affected my job, my career and my relationships with friends, colleagues and loved ones, and would eventually cause me to leave the country and change my general outlook — for better or for worse — from that day forward. It's an episode I've found difficult to talk or write about over all these years, though internally I've Monday-morning-quarterbacked it to death. I've felt shame, resentment and anger over what took place, and I've directed a sizable and maybe unhealthy amount of those feelings toward myself.

Meanwhile, writing and talking about my life and career before that date feels like discussing a stranger. The guy rehearsing with his buddies in the Albert Hotel may have occupied my body, but was otherwise just some naïve kid blissfully unaware of the carnage that lay ahead. There's a line of demarcation there that is impossible for me to ignore, like the divide between BC and AD in my life. In that

121

respect, I guess those police department booking papers were the start of my New Testament.

I feel the need to say all this because in the nearly half-century since, there has been quite a lot of misinformation and questionable interpretation over what occurred that night and how it impacted the related parties in its aftermath. My friend John Sebastian, for one, has never publicly assigned much meaning to the bust and its relationship to the downfall of The Lovin' Spoonful. And though I love John like a brother, and I'll always respect his work and his role in shaping mine, John didn't live this chapter in nearly the same way I did. He was there, but he wasn't. He may have been the leader of our band during its peak, but he's not qualified to be the voice of authority on this one, nor is Joe Butler or anyone else. There were two people arrested that night, and one is dead. I'm the only one still here to set the record straight about what happened, painful though it may be to talk about.

Returning to the States after our triumphant trip to Europe, we finished up the final mixes for a song called "Summer in the City," which everyone in our organization was convinced was a No. 1 hit. We had a scheduled West Coast tour and were going to base out of L.A., but the tour was to begin with a show at the Greek Theatre in Berkeley on May 21. The plan was for the band to fly to San Francisco, spend a couple of days doing record and radio promotion, play the gig at the Greek and then head down to Los Angeles, where Zally, Joe and I were staying at a rented house in the Hollywood Hills amid some concert and recording dates. John and his girlfriend Lorey had their own house down closer to Hollywood.

By this point, Zally and I spent almost all our time on the road together. We ate together and went out to the clubs together, and if possible would rent our own car and travel separately from the rest of the group. When the band flew somewhere together, Zally and I would end up as seatmates. This trip reflected that setup. On the limo ride to the airport I asked him what his plans were after we got to San Francisco.

"Well, these guys I know from [a local comedy troupe called] The Committee are having a party tonight, you wanna go?"

"Ahh. I'm still running on empty, I might just get to the hotel and crash," I said.

"Yeah, I'm wiped out too," Zally said, "but there's a friend of mine from Toronto who's going to be in town, and I wanna see if he's going to be at the party. Plus there are bound to be some 'sweet things' there. Let's make a call after we land." Sounded good to me.

I had a few drinks after takeoff and fell asleep, only to be awoken by an elbow in the ribs.

"Look out the window, Stebun," Zally said, using his favorite nickname for me.

Groggy from sleep and booze, I peered out the plane's window to the incredible sight of the Rocky Mountains' peaks glistening in the afternoon sun. It was May, so most of the mountaintops were still covered with snow. I can still remember looking at that beautiful vision and feeling like I was literally on top of the world.

By the time the flight had landed, it was mid-afternoon and instead of riding in the limo to the hotel, I stepped up to the Hertz window. The Spoonful had Hertz as their official rental car agency, and I hoped to be able to get one of the just-released Shelby GT350H Mustangs that they were renting to their best customers. Unfortunately there were none available at the airport location, so I settled for a nice little red Mustang coupe. (I would eventually rent — and promptly crash — one of those GT road rockets in Los Angeles.) The decision to rent a car would be costly in more ways than one, as it turned out.

About a half-hour after we checked into the hotel, Zally called my room.

"My buddy from Toronto is here and he's planning on going up to the party tonight. You wanna go?"

I did not know the people who were going to be at the party — Zalman knew some of them from his days in Toronto. Going to a party where I didn't know anyone except my bandmate did not seem all that exciting to me, but I knew Zally was looking forward to seeing his friends, and what else was there to do anyway — watch TV?

"Yeah, let's go," I said. "Do you think we should ask the guys?"

"I already did," Zally said. "Rich [Chiaro, our road manager] doesn't want to go and neither do John or Joe, although they said we should pick up a bag of weed if there's any to be had."

"How are we going to do that?" I asked.

"Oh, I already mentioned it to my friend, he said he could probably work out a lid for us," Zally answered. (A lid is a West Coast term for roughly an ounce of pot. I think it originated in the use of a tobacco pouch to hold an ounce, the amount a consumer usually wanted to buy. You could measure it without a scale — possession of a scale could constitute "intent to sell" to the authorities — so having a way to do so was very common.)

It took us about a half-hour to get to the party, which was in the Pacific Heights area of San Francisco — strictly a middle-class residential area with single-family homes. We drove by the house and Zally said, "There's the number, this is it!" You could tell there was a party going on, as there were people out on the porch and the lights were on in every room of the house.

Zally's friend was already on the porch as we walked up and he called out to him, "Zalman, what it is!"

He and Zally hugged, we were introduced and in the three of us went.

The house was pretty full and the smell of pot was strong in the air. In 1966, pot use was very illegal. While San Francisco had a liberal reputation both socially and politically, and the police in San Francisco did not have the bad reputation of the L.A. black-and-whites, anti-marijuana laws were still ruthlessly enforced there.

Once at the party, in typical fashion, Zally became the center of attention. This was a stoner party among the arts and theater crowd, with pretty girls all around, and soon we were drinking beer, smoking dope and having a great time. I was introduced around to many of the partygoers, including Howard Hesseman, a well-known member of The Committee who would later become famous on the TV shows *WKRP in Cincinnati* and *Head of the Class*. After a few beers and passed-around joints, I was starting to get tired and found Zalman.

"Did you get that bag of weed to take back with us?" I asked.

He shook his head no; he'd been busy talking and drinking. "Right, Boonie. Let me see about that." He then headed back into the kitchen, out of my sight. About 10 minutes later he came back, patted his pocket and said, "We're in shape, let's head out." After a whole bunch of "see ya laters" and "good luck at the show tomorrow nights," we headed down the steps and out to the car.

I had not driven the Mustang two blocks down this quiet street when out of nowhere came the red lights of a police car behind us. Panic! Though Zal and I were both stoned and probably drunk, I was completely surprised, because we weren't speeding nor from my perspective driving unusually. As I slowed down to stop, Zally, who was carrying the pot, pulled it out of his jacket and stuffed it under his seat. We pulled to a stop and the officer — I only saw one at first — came up to the driver's window with a flashlight and asked for the usual ID and registration, and then almost immediately asked if he could search the car. By now I was totally shaken up, and then I noticed another officer standing behind the car on Zally's side, also with a flashlight. Before I could even say yes or no to the search, they asked us to step out of the car and went right to the passenger seat and pulled out the bag of pot. We said nothing about where we'd gotten the weed or who it belonged to, but because of the panic we were both feeling, instead of denying everything we started to ask the cops for a break. I told them we were in town to do a show the next night at the Greek . . . couldn't they just drop the whole thing? Or maybe it could be worked out somehow? Bad mistake, among many we would make.

The next thing you know, we were in the patrol car headed for the downtown jail, scared to death and with no idea what was coming next. I do remember the palpable feeling that the air going out of The Lovin' Spoonful balloon was a real possibility. I looked over at

Zally, and the contrast between the on-top-of-the-world rock star of a few minutes ago and what now looked like a ghost with long hair and a jacket sitting beside me, will stay with me forever. (In fact, "Forever," the only song I would write for the final Lovin' Spoonful album I'd play on, is based on that memory. I hear it today and can still feel the melancholy.) Little did I know how badly this was going to turn out. Remembering that look on Zally's face, I am pretty sure he knew.

On this particular Friday night the booking desk was loud and scary. I had never been arrested before, and trying to get a grip on what was happening was difficult if not plain impossible. Zally kept shaking his head and muttering, "Not good, not good," and then in typical Zalman fashion would make a joke about his run-ins with the Toronto police, back when he was living on the street up there. But it was no joke when it came time for me to step up to the window and get booked into jail.

The desk sergeant asked me to put everything in my pockets on the counter. As I started to go through mine I remembered that I had a block of black hashish that a friend of mine had smuggled back from Afghanistan and given to me as a gift. It was about a one-ounce block of the very best opiated hash you could find in those days, and when I realized it had to come out, I removed it and put it on the counter. The sergeant asked me what it was, and in a rare moment of clarity, I said I was a bass player and it was rosin for my bow. He looked at it and just shrugged and wrote down "bass rosin" and put it in my property envelope. I was astonished, but in those days hashish was very rare and I'm sure he had probably never seen a block like that before.

We were put in a holding cell with about 10 other guys, mostly drunks and petty criminals. Long hair still being pretty new, even among criminals, we did not look like the rest of our fellow detainees, and they let us know.

"Hey man, where you guys from? What's up with the hair?" they asked.

Another guy came up to Zally and said, "Didn't I see you on TV?"

"Aren't you guys in a rock band?" said another. We just tried to play it as quiet as we could.

"Yeah, we're in a band," I said. "But nobody you ever heard of."

After about an hour, another one of our cellmates said, "Aren't you guys in The Lovin' Spoonful?" By this time we didn't care if they got pissed, we just didn't answer them. There was something about that question, though, that freaked me. There was nothing to be gained by trying to make friends with these guys, so ignoring them was no big deal, but that sentence hung in the air. *Aren't you guys in The Lovin' Spoonful?* Standing together in that cell, we both realized that this was real.

"I can't believe they put the hash in my property bag," I said to Zally, trying to lighten up the horrible sinking feeling.

"If they give it back, I'm smoking half of it as soon as we get out," Zally replied with a forced laugh.

As the beer and pot we'd ingested wore off, and the reality of actually being in a cell sank in, it kinda felt like coming down with the flu. "When the fuck are we going to get our call?" Zally said almost to no one, but obviously to me. I can only speculate as to why it took so long for us to get our phone call — maybe what to do about the two guys from the rock band was being discussed behind the scenes.

"I don't know, you're the one who's been arrested before."

One of our cellmates came up and started up again with "Didn't you guys play that song 'What a Day for a Daydream' on the *Hullabaloo* show?" Ignoring him was difficult, since he had us pegged — we had done that show just a couple of months before.

"They *are* The Lovin' Spoonful, man," another one chimed in. It was like one of those echoes that slowly gets quieter and quieter as it fades into time. To paraphrase The Animals, we had to get out of this place.

We spent the rest of the night in the holding tank, and at around nine or 10 in the morning, Rich came down to the jail and bailed us out, but not before another count was added to my possession charge. As my "bass rosin" was being handed back to me, a narcotics officer happened to walk by the booking desk and was able to identify the hashish block.

"What the fuck happened?" Rich asked as we walked out into the blinding sun of an early morning in San Francisco. Adjusting my eyes to the bright light, I looked at Zally and Rich and said, "I fucked up, man, I shouldn't have said nothing to the cops when they stopped us."

Zally just muttered, "My visa, man, my visa." He had said something to me when we had a private moment about how "this bust could really fuck up my visa status." I didn't know anything about his immigration situation. It had been barely brought up in the past.

By now I was reviewing all of the events of the night before and was starting to think a little more clearly about what had happened and why. First of all, I could think of no good reason why we were stopped in the first place. I was driving normally, and although drugs were found, this was a rental car that had just been picked up earlier that night. For all the cops knew, anything could have been under the seat when we got the car. Also, I had not given permission for the police to search; they just went ahead and did it illegally. I was starting to think that given those circumstances, if we toughed this out we just might be able to walk on the charges.

I was also growing skeptical about whether this had been a routine stoppage of a vehicle by police on local patrol, or whether something more sinister was afoot. As soon as we were booked, officers began asking us if we knew the name Chip Monck. I'd heard the name — he was a guy who'd worked at a few of the Greenwich Village clubs and as a lighting director at the Newport Folk Festival — but I didn't really know him and wasn't sure why we were being asked about him. To this day, I have no idea, though I'd find out much later that Chip Monck was being linked (for reasons unknown) by police to the local drug trade via his relationships with San Francisco–based music figures. It's possible the cops saw a connection between The

Lovin' Spoonful and Chip Monck, and it's possible that someone inside the party we'd attended had informed them of our presence in the neighborhood. Again, to be stopped without any discernible cause on a quiet suburban street seemed a little fishy. But once the questions stopped and we were freed, the whys and wherefores were placed on the back burner and the focus became making all of this go away.

Before we got back to the motel, a story had to be concocted to tell the others where we had been. We knew John and Joe needed an explanation for our absence, but in addition to being embarrassed over what had happened, we didn't want to cause any unnecessary panic within the group. And even though John and Joe were our trusted friends, the more people knew we'd been busted for pot, the greater the likelihood of the story getting into the press and becoming a PR problem.

"Let's just tell them the party got raided, and we got locked up with a bunch of people from the party," Zally said.

"Do they do that out here?" I wondered.

"We have to be careful what's made public about this until it is resolved," Rich said.

"Gets resolved?" I said hopefully, thinking that Rich may already know something about what the outcome might be.

Rich shot back in a defeated-sounding voice, "This is going to be difficult to handle. Bob [Cavallo] and Charley Koppelman are flying out as we speak. I think we should stick with Zally's story for now."

I was too burnt out by the last 12 hours to resist that plan. All I wanted to do at that point was go to sleep and wake up realizing it had all been a terrible dream.

We got to the motel and spun the story. It seemed to satisfy them, at least for the time being. I went to sleep and woke up to the nightmare, while trying to get ready for the show at the Greek. I picked up the motel phone and dialed Zally's room.

"How ya doin'?"

"Fucking great," Zally said, sarcasm dripping from the other end of the receiver. "What about you?"

I thought for a second and said, "We did get busted, didn't we?"

Gallows humor would become our secret language, and while it may not have been all that funny, it helped Zally and me from coming unglued completely. As bad as this was, at least we were in it together.

We got ourselves ready to go over to Berkeley and headed across the Bay to begin life after the bust. We did the show that night as planned. Despite the fact that neither Zalman nor myself were feeling very well, the show seemed to go over fine with the audience, though in my paranoia I swore they must have known everything. Every time I looked over at Zally that night, he looked like I felt: bummed out.

Afterward, we went back to our motel and John and Joe were told Zally and I were going to stick around San Francisco and do some radio promotion for the band rather than immediately going on to L.A. This seemed to satisfy them, although I suspect they had an inkling something wasn't right — this was not the way we usually operated. The next day, Zally and I were scheduled for what I thought was going to be a meeting between us and our new attorney. When I was told the name of the lawyer that our management had hired for us — attorney to the stars Melvin Belli — I was relieved. Belli's name was one I had heard before, and his résumé, which included his defense of Jack Ruby against the Lee Harvey Oswald murder charge, was exceptional. I was starting to feel a little better about this whole mess, until we walked into Belli's office.

There in this typically wood-paneled and expensive-looking office, surrounded by a wall of legal books and many overstuffed chairs, were our manager, Bob Cavallo; our road manager, Rich; our executive producer, Charley Koppelman; and some other guys in suits who did not look friendly at all. The first thing our lawyer did after the cursory introductions was to introduce Zally and me to these men — the San Francisco chief of police and district attorney. Really, for this piddling case of pot possession? What were these people doing here? Belli then opened a big legal-looking book and began to read aloud the statute that we were being charged under and then moved to another section that dealt with the commission of this crime by an alien visitor, referring to Zally, who was a Canadian citizen.

He proceeded to basically say that Zalman could be deported immediately — even though he'd been found guilty of nothing — and could be barred from returning to the U.S., potentially forever. I looked around the room for some comforting words in our defense, or at least some protestations about the arrest, but they were not forthcoming. Even Belli, for all his well-known savvy as a litigator, made no mention of what type of conditions would have made the case defensible. Silence was our defense.

Finally, the district attorney spoke up.

"Perhaps there's some way this can be worked out," he said, as if he'd been rehearsing the line. It did not take a brain surgeon to know what was coming next. "If you gentlemen are willing to work with our friends here from the SFPD, introduce them around at one of your parties, maybe we can make all this go away and you can go about your business."

I recoiled at the suggestion. Zally squirmed in his seat.

What they were saying was a deal could be struck if we'd be willing to fink out some of our associates in the drug trade, not that we really had any. It's not like we had a pot dealer on the payroll, or were hooked up with some marijuana syndicate in major U.S. cities, but clearly these guys thought we were something more than recreational pot users.

We listened to the whole spiel, and when we left the room with Bob and Charley and Rich without committing to anything, it was made clear to me that we were not going to be presented with any choices other than cooperate or do the time.

"What about the stop-and-search?" I demanded. "They just went ahead and searched the car, we weren't doing anything wrong."

"They said you told them they could search the car," Charley blurted out.

"I did not, that's bullshit," I argued.

"Well the cops feel pretty strongly about this," someone added.

It was made to sound like failing to cooperate would essentially spell the end of The Lovin' Spoonful as we knew it. Belli and the rest made it seem so cut-and-dried. And we believed it.

I could not imagine in any way giving up anyone for smoking dope. I came from the honor-above-all environment of a military family. My dad had used political influence to get into the Marine Corps during World War II when he was too old to enlist, and had always taught me to be true to myself. Zally came from a family of political activists — his dad, Avrom, was a political cartoonist and well-known communist around Toronto — and Zally himself had lived on a kibbutz in Israel. We both believed in the emerging ideals of the counterculture, including the sense of community and communal enlightenment that came from indulging in the benevolent substance of marijuana. The very idea of deserting one of our fellow travelers on that path by turning them over to the authorities was as repugnant as I could imagine. There wasn't a strand in our DNA that was comfortable with finking, but with hardly any time to decide, what were we to do? Zally and I only had, according to Belli, very little time before Zally would be deported and the band would grind to a halt.

I didn't care if I had to go to jail for a while for a lid of pot. I'm sure Zally felt the same way, but when you're in a band as big as The Spoonful were at that time, we didn't have the luxury of thinking only about ourselves in this situation. We had the rest of the band, our road crew, managers and label people — the lives of whom were tied to our existence and success — to think about. We had friends, families and loved ones who would have been impacted negatively by what was sure to become a scandal if our bust became public, and would have had to help carry around the shame that accompanied the scandal. We had fans, the ones who bought our records and concert tickets, who would be let down. Yes, we were worried for ourselves and our individual careers, but to suggest that we cooperated only out of self-preservation for Steve Boone and Zal Yanovsky is a gross oversimplification. This was far bigger than us. And the clock was ticking.

Half a century later, it's easy to second-guess the naïveté of all involved, but remember that this was May 1966 and it would be another year before the drug culture, both in San Francisco and elsewhere, was in full flower. This was before Keith Moon was busted in Michigan, or The Stones and Beatles were arrested in England on drug charges. There were plenty of jazz players who'd had problems with heroin and other drugs, but no mainstream pop musician had faced a situation like this. The closest proxy in the music business up to this point was probably Johnny Cash's arrest in 1965 for trying to smuggle pills across the border from Mexico, but prescription narcotics did not carry nearly the same stigma in 1966 as an illicit and still not widely understood substance like marijuana.

Thus, law enforcement in San Francisco at this time had no real playbook. Had this happened a year later, at the height of Haight-Ashbury, the discovery of two young guys with pot would not have been nearly as novel, the unlawful search and seizure may not have happened and in all likelihood the "plea bargain" scenario would not have been floated, given the proliferation of the local drug culture and the fact that the gains the cops could make from such an introduction to drug culture would have been like two sandbags in the path of a tsunami.

There was also no precedent for our management or label on how to deal with this type of crisis. Had this happened after The Stones or The Beatles got busted, management and the band (and even Belli, who would eventually represent The Stones) would have had a strategy in place before the cops even visited our car window that night.

All this seems obvious in hindsight, but at that moment Zally and I were two scared-shitless early-20-somethings faced with losing our careers at the height of our abilities and fame, and the threat was very real due to the specter of deportation for Zally, and the absence of information in that place and time about what a drug indictment could mean. I guess since my immigration status wasn't on the line, I could have turned down the deal and gone to jail, leaving Zally twisting in the wind and deciding whether to be deported, but I never would have done that. We were in this together. Zally and I got pretty drunk and tried to find some light at the end of the tunnel, but there wasn't any. John and Joe were eventually told, but they still didn't know the whole story. They thought we'd been busted with a whole bunch of people and would just be fined, or something minor. Looking back, I don't remember why we did not sit down with the other band members and discuss what we were about to do. Maybe if we had, there would have been a "one for all and all for one" moment in which we would have been convinced to reject the deal. I believe now that had we turned down the offer by the DA and fought the arrest, it would have been ugly for a while, and Zally would have been deported temporarily but returned to the U.S. after the arrest was declared illegal, either for no probable cause or for improper search.

Though we were both sickened by it, with all the information we had at our disposal at that moment, we made what we believed was the only decision we could make. The district attorney wanted us to introduce an undercover officer into the group of friends that were at the party we went to that night. In exchange, all charges were to be dropped, our arrest records expunged and in the event of further legal action derived from this operation, we would not be required to appear in court in the future. Also, there was to be no publicity released about the bust. This was the only way we could make all this go away.

With terrible sadness, we agreed to introduce an undercover agent around at a party as a friend of ours in the music business.

Zally and I were left in San Francisco and needed not only to get our heads around this, but to hope that someone would have a party that we could invite ourselves to. As we sat in the motel room and talked through the scenarios, I offered up this idea: "Let's just invite ourselves to this party and tell the host what is going to happen and swear them to secrecy but at least they will know that our 'friend' is a narc and let the word out not to sell him anything."

"Boone," Zally said, using my last name, something he never did. "Do you really believe anyone would keep this a secret? And if the cops find out we did that, they would really throw the book at us and I would never be allowed back in this country."

Zally's understanding of international politics based on his father's communist background was obviously occupying his thoughts. At this point he was far less naïve than I was in thinking we could somehow weasel out of this.

Either way, I was on the verge of losing it. I thought back to Tara Browne's birthday party in Ireland just a month earlier, mingling with and being lauded by not only the royalty of rock but the royalty of the new generation as well. And now Zalman and I were thrown to the mercy of cooperation with the agents of the status quo.

In my heart I knew this was going to turn out badly, but I had to find a way to convince myself that cooperation was not capitulation, and that maybe, just maybe, no one would notice what we were about to do.

"Zally, do you think they will give us a badge?" I cracked.

"Well I will make certain they do," he said, his voice rising like a narrator in one of those comic book radio serials, "And from that day on we will forever be superheroes: 'The Death Duo.'" From that day on, whether on the road or in the studio, Zally and I called ourselves The Death Duo.

The next day, word came down that a party was going on that night in town, and we were invited to come by whenever. Life was becoming a nonstop party in San Francisco in 1966, and while the party objectives were mostly indulgent and hedonistic, a lot of the party conversation was political in nature. The war in Vietnam was turning uglier by the day, and despite having just turned the corner in the Civil Rights Movement, the underlying organizations of protest and confrontation were still in place. So almost all these "parties" were also gatherings of leaders and lieutenants of the coming anti-war movement. As members of a popular group, albeit one that had been apolitical in both our music and public discourse, we were seen as figures to potentially carry the flag for the movement. There was also the potential for excommunication for those who betrayed the movement. I was somewhat aware of this possibility when we agreed to introduce this guy into the circle, but I was also wildly naïve in believing that the police department would hold up their end of the deal.

The next day, the SFPD gave us a time and place to appear before the party setup, and for the whole day leading up to our date with destiny, I sat like a zombie and stared at a darkened TV in my room. There was no one to talk to about this. Family and close friends were a coast away, and what could I tell them, anyway? We had agreed to do this, and there was no cheering squad for that anywhere in my world. Finally, The Death Duo got in the rental car on the way to our fate, or what felt to us like a one-car motorcade of shame.

The drive from our motel to the police department where we would meet the agent and narcotics squad was one of the most uncomfortable car rides I had ever taken. Zally and I tried to make light of it in the arrogant style we had adopted while on the road, but levity wasn't really working here. Just before we went into the office, as we parked the car, I can still remember turning to Zalman, and without a word being said both of us broke down in tears and hugged each other. Then, without looking back, we walked into the evening that would ultimately succeed in dismantling the very thing we were trying to save.

In the police squad room we met our "friend" and went over the guidelines we were supposed to follow. I could sense that even among frontline cops there is little respect for finks, though the people we had to deal with were polite and businesslike, and tried to make the experience less humiliating than it was. I guess I wanted to believe this was all going to turn out OK. The agent whom we were to introduce was nice enough I suppose, but did not look like anybody in the music business. He looked like a cop and talked like a cop, and I didn't think anyone was going to believe he was a friend of ours. I remember thinking that was good, because if anyone smelled a rat maybe it would help avoid any transactions being made that would send someone to jail. When we got to the party house and went inside, it was like an out-of-body experience. It was like Zally and I were in a play and the other actors all knew each others' lines. We went through the motions of introducing this guy who visually didn't fit in, and trying to explain why he was hanging around with us. I'm sure Zally and I appeared, if not nervous, at least apprehensive. Small talk was made and I even think some weed was passed around. I don't think the agent smoked anything except maybe cigarettes, as undercover narcs try to avoid getting high with targets for security reasons.

It was all pretty uneventful and anticlimactic, and I could not wait to get out of there. After we went back to the station to be debriefed, it was all supposed to be over.

The next day, Zally and I got on a plane and flew to LAX, where we both attempted to step back into life as we knew it in The Lovin' Spoonful. (We probably should have returned that infamous red Mustang first, since it sat in an impound lot for months and eventually cost me $800 once Hertz tracked it down.) For a while, the reality of what had happened up in San Francisco was put away into the back of our brains by the relentless work schedule and ongoing successes of the band. The rest of the tour went fine, and we did TV shows like *Where the Action Is* and *The Lloyd Thaxton Show*, which were perfect for the type of shtick The Spoonful did. "Summer in the City" was soon to be released, and we were literally the hit of the L.A. music scene. As the days went on, what happened in San Francisco became like a dream that hadn't really happened — but as with a dream, I would wake up sweating and feeling a sense of doom that someday, somewhere, it was all going to come out and bring us down.

As it turned out, I had good reason to feel that way. I was soon to discover that the nightmare had only just begun.

Chapter 7
IT'S NOT TIME NOW

You could look into the eyes of The Beatles and see a group of guys who were tired. It was August 23, 1966, and we were commiserating in the home locker room at Shea Stadium, which was also The Beatles' dressing room (the Mets were away in Chicago, playing the Cubs). We'd made good on our promise to catch up with the guys when they came through the U.S. again, though we hadn't quite planned for it to happen in this setting.

The plan had been to go to the show as Beatles fans. John and Lorey, Zally and his girlfriend, the great Canadian actress Jackie Burroughs (the two of them dressed as monks as an attempted disguise) and Joe and I all got general admission tickets, probably through The Beatles' booking agent Sid Bernstein, who was friendly with our management. Joe and I had just sat down in great seats behind third base when we noticed a buzz in the crowd. It was like that Dylan lyric — "Something's happening but you don't know what it is . . ."

All of a sudden a chorus of screams could be heard from behind us. I wheeled around, and between us and the screams, I could see two uniformed police officers looking down at us. It looked like all the color had drained from the cops' faces. I didn't know if someone had a bomb or what. I could literally feel the swell of the crowd, as they moved forward in their seats to see what the commotion was about. It was about us. Some teenyboppers had spotted Joe Butler, and were spreading the word.

I'm not quite sure why we thought we'd just be able to roam Shea Stadium anonymously, given that "Summer in the City" had been released the month before and was currently residing at No. 1 on the Billboard charts. It was our fifth Top 10 single out of five, and third straight to reach the Top 2 after "Daydream" and "Did You Ever Have to Make Up Your Mind," which had been revived from the first album and repurposed as a single.

Apparently we were a little too well known by now to be left alone in the crowd. The surge of excitement was scary, because as we'd experienced the previous year at the Rose Bowl, with that many people and so little security, things can get out of hand quickly.

I could see the two cops get on their radios and move toward us. Already fans were up in their seats and surging forward. In about a minute or so Joe and I had two cops close to us, and the word came down on the radio to round us up and take us out of the seating area. Soon our entire group was taken down through the stands and out onto the field between the stage and the dugout, where one of the opening acts was waiting to go on. The next thing I knew, we'd been whisked through the dugout and back into the locker rooms, where we stood face to face with our rescue squad — The Beatles. Evidently security had called Beatles management, and to avoid any further fan activity they'd been told to take us back into the locker room.

I felt a little bad about imposing on them in this setting. I know from personal experience that in the hour or so before a big show like this, the artist usually likes to be left alone to get ready for the performance. But just as they'd been when we saw them in the spring, The Beatles could not have been nicer to us. We talked and joked for about 45 minutes, during which Paul and I had an extensive talk about music. Paul and Ringo hadn't come to the Marquee Club show, so this was my first experience with both of them, and Paul was great. (Ringo was quiet.) We compared notes on electric basses — I told him I admired his Höfner violin bass, which he proceeded to hand to me. It was a left-handed model, so although I was able to crudely play it, I told him I couldn't tell if I liked it.

He said, "I tell you what, when I get back to England I will send you a right-handed model, on me." (Dear Sir Paul: I am still awaiting receipt of one right-handed Höfner bass.)

As wonderful and friendly as they were, we noticed the guys seemed a little more uptight than they had in England. We attributed that to pre-show nerves, but as we now know this was a bit of a Waterloo for the group.

They had just released *Revolver* but couldn't play any songs from it live because of the album's complex arrangements. The tour had started under a cloud of controversy because of John Lennon's "bigger than Jesus" comments, which were taken out of context, infuriating the religious right and causing stress for the group (especially Lennon) and their associates. Perhaps related was the fact that their show the previous year at Shea had been a sold-out spectacle, but this time about 20 percent of the tickets went unsold.

As it turned out, this would be The Beatles' final tour. Their show six days later at Candlestick Park in San Francisco would mark the end of The Fab Four as a touring unit. I look at backstage pictures from the Shea Stadium show and I see what I saw that day — a group that was growing weary. They were beginning to quietly take on water.

So were The Lovin' Spoonful. The bust was never far from my mind nor Zally's during this period, and the demoralizing nature of it was beginning to infiltrate the fabric of the band, however slowly. By all appearances, however, we were at the height of our powers.

The night after we hung out with The Beatles at Shea, we played the brand new Rheingold Central Park Music Festival (later to become the Schaefer Music Festival), where a reporter from

Newsweek came out and did a profile of the band. The *New York Times* and *Time* magazine also did features on the group around the same time. All commented on the popularity and quality of "Summer in the City," which we'd released during the appropriate season, on July 4, 1966, but had actually been written and recorded before we left for England in the spring.

You hear a lot about songs that become mega-hits despite being conceived in 20 minutes with lyrics scrawled on the back of matchbooks. Well, "Summer in the City" was not that song. A number of people both inside and outside the band played a role in the writing and recording of the song, including yours truly, and it's hard to imagine it turning out as well as it did if you take out any one of those contributions.

The germ of the song started with Mark Sebastian, John's younger brother by seven years, who had been doing some writing, maybe with a notion that songwriting could become a family business. Mark handed John a tape of a song he'd written called "It's a Different World," which was like a bossa nova tune, with some decent lyrics and some that Mark would probably admit sounded like the work of the 14-year-old he was. (There's been some misinformation about this over the years, but Mark had written a completed song intended for commercial consideration — not a poem for school, as some have suggested!)

John cherry-picked the best parts of the "It's a Different World" lyric and melody, and tried to marry them to this variation on a riff he'd heard a session piano player named Artie Schroeck play when we were making the *What's Up, Tiger Lily?* soundtrack. The tension in the Artie Schroeck riff and the more straightforward feel of what had been Mark's chorus sounded incredible when fused together, creating a huge release when you got to the chorus. John wrote some new lyrics for the verses that perfectly reflected that tension, using a hot summer day as the subject matter. Except that unlike most summer songs, which idealized the warm weather, John got real about what Manhattan felt like in July and August. These were not the lazy hazy crazy days of summer — it was fucking hot out. But when the sun went down and it cooled off a few degrees, you could go out and dance, get wasted, try to get laid and maybe find a reason to brave the next day's heat. It was the kind of thing a lot of people could relate to.

When John brought the song in, even in its then-crude state, I thought it was incredible. I loved that it sounded unlike anything we'd ever done. Truth be told, I was glad it had some balls, because as much as I'd appreciated our previous material, I was tired of hearing my male friends outside the music business ask when the "Fag Rock Quartet" was coming out with a new record. I'd heard our lyrics parodied by these same people as "What a gay for a gaydream" and similar sophomoric insults. Those guys didn't know shit, but I liked the idea of proving them wrong nonetheless.

As we were working up the song at Columbia Studio B, it was decided that something more was needed, a middle-eight or bridge or something to offset the tense part and the free-swinging part. I had this thing I'd been noodling with at the piano during breaks in the sessions, this kind of jazzy figure that had a weird time signature and sounded a little bit like George Gershwin. It never seemed like we were going to have any place for this within the context of a rock song, but it was fun to play and it was infectious enough that I guess it got into people's heads.

As we were deciding how to complete the song, John said, "Hey, what about Steven's piano thing?" We tried it, it worked. There's a term used in drag racing called "the racer's edge," that little extra something that one competitor with equal equipment has over another that allows them to prevail. At the risk of sounding immodest, I think my unique contribution to "Summer in the City" was what allowed an already spectacular piece of work to achieve its iconic status.

The song was really shaping up as something special, and everyone recognized it. Subsequently the idea of putting "city" noises — traffic, maybe a construction crew — over my piano part was floated. This was a fairly unusual component for a pop song, but Zally in particular was completely tickled by the idea. So we brought in this little old radio soundman who sat crossed-leg on the floor with a portable reel-to-reel and boxes and tapes of car horns and pneumatic drills, and overdubbed some city noises that really complemented my faux-Gershwin part.

Other contributions included the vocal arrangements and harmonies, which 14-year-old Mark Sebastian had some say in (and did a great job), and a guitar part from Zally that he described as "some of my best chakka-chakkas."

But the unsung hero in this whole two-minute, 45-second opera had to be Roy Halee.

Roy was a studio engineer at Columbia who was working with us for the first time and we'd quickly grown to admire, as he had a number of innovative ideas. When it came time to do the drum overdubs, Roy devised the notion of putting a mic at the top of the eighth floor stairwell, the Voice of the Theatre loud speaker at the bottom, then "wowing" the volume to give the sound extra punch. The reason the drums sound so powerful on that song is because of Roy Halee, whom we would later unsuccessfully try to steal as our exclusive engineer. Roy would go on to replicate the sound when recording the drums for the Simon & Garfunkel hit "The Boxer."

The magazine *Hit Parader* actually came in to do a first-person feature and captured some other details about the session:

> Steve Boone did the arranging. He added another instrumental figure, and, together with the other guys, selected the instruments to be played. The instrumental background was recorded in 4 steps. The first take had drums, organ, electric piano and rhythm guitar. Next a bass and autoharp were dubbed on the soundtrack and the third time around a guitar. The final overdub added more percussion, including a big wastebasket that Zal kept hitting with a drumstick . . . Everyone is dying to hear the vocal . . . even just once . . . but

John is too tired. He sings it the following night. Donovan drops in and listens for a while.

I don't remember what Donovan thought of the song, but I know what I thought — it was a smash. When it was released in July, "Summer in the City" caught fire, as we knew it would. It knocked "Wild Thing" by The Troggs out of the top spot and spent three weeks there before our pal Donovan knocked it out with "Sunshine Superman."

Going on 50 years since its release, I am grateful to report that I continue to receive a steady income from my one-third royalty on "Summer in the City." It's been featured in scores of TV shows and movies and commercials and has been covered by a number of artists, including acts as diverse as B.B. King, Joe Jackson, Joe Cocker, The Stranglers, Styx and Butthole Surfers. The Quincy Jones version from the '70s has been sampled by a number of hip-hop artists, and I get a writing credit every time it does. The indie band Eels did a spooky and cool dirge-like version on the deluxe edition of their 2013 album *Wonderful, Glorious*. (They didn't use my piano interlude, though they'll be pleased to know I still get paid!)

But beyond the royalties, what makes me happy about "Summer in the City" is how it has endured. *Billboard* named it as their No. 1 summer song of all time in a poll a while back, and Elton John played it at Sting's Rainforest benefit at Carnegie Hall in 2010, with John Sebastian on guitar. I'm confident it's one of those songs that'll be around long after everyone involved in making it is gone, and that's something that motivates everyone who calls themselves an artist.

We were proud of the song, and knew it would be one of the foundational elements of the next album, which Kama Sutra and our management began demanding almost as soon as *Daydream* had cracked the Top 10, maybe even before.

It's important to note how things were changing in 1966 when it came to the concept of recordings. This was the year of *Pet Sounds* and *Revolver*, two definitive album statements in a field that had been dominated by singles. Dylan had always been considered more of an albums artist, but when *Blonde on Blonde* came out in mid-1966, it was greeted as an event unlike anything that had occurred when his previous albums came out.

The paradigm was shifting. More experimentation was welcomed, and albums were being conceived as cohesive statements of artistic expression.

I'd like to think this shift among our contemporaries was recognized by The Spoonful, but we were on the treadmill of live dates and appearances and perhaps didn't see the rising tide until it was waist-deep. Had we been recording for Capitol or Columbia — hell, even Elektra — I think we would have been made to see it.

But we were the only major act on Kama Sutra, which was a label run by a group of guys whose background was singles, and was distributed by MGM, another label with no interest or foresight in the emerging medium of the rock album. Again, I don't think we would have bolted out of the gate with such success on the singles charts or radio were it not for Kama Sutra and MGM — they did a great job of breaking us in the only way rock 'n' roll acts really got broken at that time. In my opinion they just didn't have their antennae up for what was coming next. The success of the *Daydream* album had pleased everybody, but there was little consideration given to the construction of that album, or the next one, beyond its being a collection of songs.

That's not to say the album that would become *Hums of Lovin' Spoonful* was bad — it wasn't. Many people, me included, think *Hums* is our best album. It just wasn't groundbreaking at a time when you either charted new musical territory or risked being perceived as losing ground.

In fact, though the different-sounding (for us) "Summer in the City" is the song most associated with *Hums*, really the record accentuates what you might consider our roots. There were no cover songs on this album, but plenty of our influences were present.

The lead track, John's "Lovin' You," had evolved out of John and Zally riffing on some Mississippi John Hurt tunes. "Henry Thomas" was pure jug band. "Voodoo in My Basement" was a nod to Howlin' Wolf, and "4 Eyes" — John's autobiographical rocker about growing up wearing glasses — owed musically to Robert Johnson. "Darlin' Companion," which would later be covered by Johnny Cash on his live album *At San Quentin*, is country-flavored, while "Nashville Cats" is flat-out country.

John had some pointed lyrics directed at the drummer in our group on the second song on *Hums*, the old-timey-sounding "Bes' Friends." As mentioned, Joe Butler was the legendary skirt chaser in our group, with the qualifier that good-looking young guys in successful rock bands don't have to do all that much chasing. When I lived with Joe briefly on Bedford Street in the Village, he was bringing multiple girls a day back to our cramped and decidedly non-soundproof apartment, and his behavior on the road with our growing legion of groupies was neither discreet nor abashed. Early in our career, we were confronted after one show by an irate father of a teenaged fan Joe had allegedly impregnated, and whom our management had to pay off to make the whole crisis disappear. So it wasn't a great mystery which person John — in the throes of what he thought was domestic bliss with Lorey — was singing about when he wrote: "Well I've heard your dirty stories about your last affair/ And how you got in houses when you knew no one was there/ If you want to find a lover gonna love 'til the end/ Go on and find yourself a lover that can be your best friend."

Other notables on the album included a rare and pretty writing collaboration between John and Zally called "Coconut Grove," named after the hip bohemian enclave south of Miami where friends of ours like Fred Neil were wintertime fixtures. John wrote the words lying on his back in the sunshine while on a boat ride on Biscayne Bay with Freddie. The track, from which evolved from an instrumental tune on *What's Up, Tiger Lily?* called "Lookin' to Spy," includes some of the best guitar work you'll hear on a Lovin' Spoonful recording (which is saying something) and includes a beautiful, almost whispered vocal by John. David Lee Roth, of all people, did an atypically understated version of it on his first solo album in 1985, and artists like Sandie Shaw and Paul Weller have also done perfect justice to what is a great and underrated song.

My biggest contribution to the album, in addition to "Summer in the City," was a song called "Full Measure," which took its title from a story I'd read in the paper about GIs who'd been killed in Vietnam and which referenced the Gettysburg Address ("that cause for which they gave the last full measure of devotion"). I also liked the double musical meaning, as a measure is a term used in musical notation. At first I wanted the song to be a dedication to the soldiers who go and fight for their country, but The Spoonful were not an outwardly political band and I never could get into a comfort zone using that kind of theme. Either it would sound too smarmy and exploitative or it would resemble a "Green Beret" pseudo-patriotic anthem, which I doubted would pass muster.

So I switched the context to be of the more familiar "relationship" variety. I started thinking about how when you're truly in a dedicated relationship and you want it to last, you need to give everything you can and hold back nothing to make it work. Though I don't think I had a particular girl in mind when I wrote it, I thought about the fleeting nature of most youthful relationships and came up with the line "the full measure of your giving, you don't yet understand." I was off and running on the lyrics, which John later helped me finish.

For the music, I had another of those "musical riffs" that I'd play on piano when no one was one around, and I tried out the lyric and it fit.

The recording of "Full Measure" was a blast, and the crash/bass slide at the beginning of the fade-out was a masterpiece production by Erik and Roy, a moment that has been pointed out as one of the great sounds on any Spoonful record. Again, Joe was given a vocal on a song I'd co-written. He suppressed his instinct to croon and instead tried to get a strong vocal performance.

The song nearly became the single, but that idea was later abandoned, to my chagrin. It ended up as the b-side of "Nashville Cats," which I suppose was not the worst parting gift, but had

"Full Measure" been pushed, I believe it could have been a Top 20, perhaps even Top 10, record. It actually did chart as a b-side hit in several markets, including L.A., which is why it went to No. 87 despite being on the flip side. It would also be the last time John and I would work together on writing a Lovin' Spoonful song — a little strange, since all the songs we'd written together had enjoyed some type of success, be it on the charts or in a film. You would think the publishers would have been leaning on us to produce as a duo, but for whatever reason, they weren't.

And then, there is "Rain on the Roof." There is probably not a song in our catalog that inspired so much contentiousness among the members of The Lovin' Spoonful, at least not one that we released. And the disagreement wasn't even about the song itself.

The song is a medieval-sounding, "new love" kind of tune about two lovers listening to the rain. It was written by John while holed up with Lorey in his West 11th Street apartment in the Village during a summer storm.

The recording we got was fine, and the arrangement and production by Erik was typically well done. Originally John and Joe and Zally sang the vocal in a round, but that approach was abandoned. The instrumental track featured an antique 12-string guitar made by Ditson — a pedal steel that John played — and Zally's Thunderbird guitar, which was manipulated to sound like a French horn. Added to that was the Irish harp that John played, which he'd acquired during our trip to Dublin for Tara Browne's party. I thought the guitar work on the song was spectacular, and you can find me saying, for the record, in the liner notes to the *Hums* CD reissue that "I thought it sounded like music from heaven."

Which I did. I just thought it was a horrible choice as the single that would follow "Summer in the City," and so did Joe. I honestly don't remember what Zally's opinion was — this was after the bust, and he was beginning to retreat from band decisions — but in this case it may have been the ex-rockers (me and Joe) against the ex-folkies (John, Zally and Erik).

As popular as we'd been previously, there was no denying that "Summer in the City" was a song that won us favor with a new group of fans. It went well beyond the teenyboppers and resonated with general music fans and, yes, those who'd been inclined to think of us as the "Fag Rock Quartet." It wasn't that I wanted to pander to the lowest common denominator; I just felt strongly that "Rain on the Roof" went too far the other way and would alienate some of the new converts.

John, noting that we'd been conscious about not releasing consecutive singles that sounded too much alike, thought this choice would show another dimension to our sound. I'm sure the fact that it was an autobiographical song about his relationship with Lorey played into his forcefulness on the issue. Why Kama Sutra didn't step in and demand a more natural follow-up, I really don't know, but by this point John Sebastian walked on water with the label, so they were probably inclined to step aside and give him his way.

The complaints fell on deaf ears. "Rain on the Roof" was released as the next single. It's not like it bombed — the song went to No. 10, making us six-for-six in singles to reach the Top 10, and was a bigger hit in parts of Europe — but I have to believe anything we had released in the wake of "Summer in the City" would have had a really good chance to hit the Top 10. The short-term losses may have been minor when it came to the charts, but I still believe there were broader implications for a band that was getting close to reaching a Beatles-like level of universal acceptance for everything we did musically. I wonder how many people heard "Rain on the Roof" on their radios in the early fall of 1966 and said, "Oh, they're back to the wimpy shit," and disregarded us all over again. And it's a shame, because it's a really lovely little song; I just think its release was badly timed.

What should we have released as a single instead? John's "4 Eyes" was probably the closest thing other than "Summer in the City" to a rocker, but it's fair to say it wasn't single material. People seem to like the up-tempo "Lovin' You," which was a hit for Bobby Darin.

"Respoken" wasn't on *Hums*, but I liked it a lot. We never released "Darlin' Companion" or "Coconut Grove" as singles ("Darlin' Companion" was later used as a b-side), but the fact that both were admired enough to inspire covers by top artists tells me the Spoonful versions could have been contenders. Honestly, the simplest thing to do would have been to move our next single, "Nashville Cats/Full Measure" up to follow "Summer in the City" in the batting order. It was very different from "Summer," and people liked it enough to send "Nashville Cats" to No. 8 and "Full Measure" into the Top 100 when it was released later on. If "Rain on the Roof" had come out after "Nashville Cats," maybe the contrast wouldn't have been so stark. Who knows, and at this point who cares? But at the time, that decision was considerably more than trivial, and exposed some feelings among band members that had been lingering below the surface for some time.

For one, John and Lorey were becoming annoying as shit.

For you fans of the show *Seinfeld*, you know the episode where Jerry and his new girlfriend gross out all their friends with their constant public displays of affection and calling each other by the pet name "Schmoopie" in baby talk? This was John and Lorey. Which was fine; I mean, John was 22 years old and in the first serious relationship of his life. People have different levels of tolerance for it, but it's OK to show affection for someone you love. I think we all got that part.

The problem was, no one besides John liked Lorey. The whole band, including John, had met her when we were playing this gig early in our career at a venue in Hell's Kitchen called Steve Paul's The Scene, which would soon be a very famous rock club. Lorey was a waitress there, and she sidled up to us immediately, as we'd later find out she did with all musicians. The discussion among the members of The Lovin' Spoonful was that Lorey Kaye was going to be the first girl to have sex with every member of the band. I don't exactly remember the order, but Joe and Zally both slept with her soon thereafter. I did not partake. Once she slept with John, she became his steady girlfriend.

Me (middle) with my brother Mike (right) and a friend on D'Allyon Avenue, St. Augustine, Florida.
[COURTESY STEVE BOONE]

High school yearbook picture, Westhampton Beach High School.
[COURTESY STEVE BOONE]

Before I played the bass, I strummed a Les Paul Goldtop guitar with The Kingsmen at the Cottage Inn, East Hampton, New York, 1963.
[COURTESY STEVE BOONE]

In Spain on my G-80 Matchless with new friend Judy Gunn.
[COURTESY CAROLYN PURDY]

Snowed in at the Night Owl Café in Greenwich Village, 1968.
[COURTESY STEVE BOONE]

Me in 1966. [© HENRY DILTZ]

Mom and Dad are
obviously thrilled with
meeting Ed Sullivan
after the show.
[ED SULLIVAN STAFF PHOTO]

PHOTO BY HENRY DILTZ

Poor Henry Diltz —
every time he took a picture he had to deal with Zally or me!

[© HENRY DILTZ]

The Death Duo.

[COURTESY STEVE BOONE]

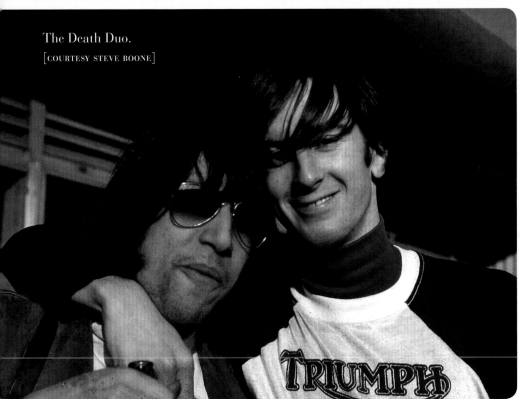

THE LOVIN' SPOONFUL in an alleyway behind the Minetta Tavern, Greenwich Village. (L to R: Joe Butler, John Sebastian, me, Zal Yanovsky) [© HENRY DILTZ]

Tuning up for our *Esquire* magazine photo shoot. [© HENRY DILTZ]

MR. BASSMAN.

[© HENRY DILTZ]

The Lovin' Spoonful live! [© HENRY DILTZ]

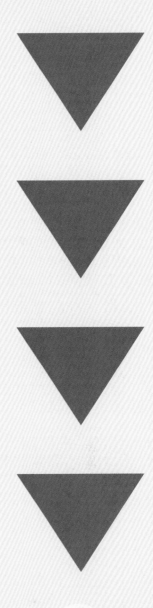

The Death Duo work on "The Dance of Pain and Pleasure." [© HENRY DILTZ]

The Spoonful doing promo at a radio station. [© HENRY DILTZ]

Lovin' Spoonful's 1967 line up with Jerry Yester. Note that Zally still lurks in the background.
[© HENRY DILTZ]

Blanche Ltd. at the Latin Casino, White Marsh, Maryland, with me on my Fender jazz bass.
[COURTESY STEVE BOONE]

Steve Boone, "butt head."
[COURTESY STEVE BOONE]

My Ferrari 250 GT Lusso was
my most beautiful ride.
[COURTESY STEVE BOONE]

The houseboat that became the Blue
Seas Studio, Inner Harbor, Baltimore.
[COURTESY STEVE BOONE]

Cygnus in Virgin Gorda Sound,
1970, before "bareboats and
umbrella drinks." Idyllic!
[COURTESY STEVE BOONE]

Sailing off a fair trade wind in the eastern Caribbean.
[COURTESY STEVE BOONE]

Cold-weather sailing with my Chesapeake Bay Retriever, Gruff, headed for Annapolis on the *Carolina Garnet*.
[COURTESY STEVE BOONE]

Mr. Bassman
at Disney's
Flower Power.
[© HANNAH YESTER]

Today's Lovin' Spoonful line up with the fabulous photographer Henry Diltz in front. In the back, from left to right: Phil Smith, Joe Butler, me, Jerry Yester and Mike Arturi. [© LAURI NEUBERT]

It was not long before John and Lorey were spending every waking (and sleeping) minute together, except when we were on tour. He called her constantly from the road, and soon they began talking about marriage. It was only then that we received a window into the character of Lorey Kaye.

You see, John had a small legal matter preventing him from marrying Lorey: though no one in the press or beyond our closest circle knew it, he was already married. And his wife was Butchie, of "Butchie's Tune" fame, who had been our close friend, supporter and surrogate mother at the Albert Hotel. It was not a real marriage — to this day I don't know whether there was a single moment of romance between John and Butchie — but a way to help prevent John from being drafted. I was unfit for service in Vietnam because of my injuries in the auto accident in 1960; Joe had served in the Air Force and was exempt from future service; Zally was Canadian. But John was American, of age and able-bodied, so if his number got called there was a very real possibility that the main creative force in our band could be sent to wield an M16 in Southeast Asia. Being married wasn't a complete safeguard against his being drafted, but we'd heard it would help, so early in the Night Owl days, Butchie — God bless her — agreed to go down to the courthouse and become Mrs. John Sebastian.

So, fast forward to the summer of 1966, and Lorey finds out state laws against polygamy are preventing her and John from getting married, and she freaks the fuck out. Now, if John had kept this little fact from a woman he was living with and intended to marry, then shame on him. But once that difficult conversation is out of the way, what do you do? It's not like he was carrying on a secret relationship with Butchie, or Lorey was going to be labeled a homewrecker or something. Hardly anyone even knew about the marriage. Instead, Lorey demanded John divorce Butchie right away, increasing the possibility that he would be draft material and maybe even arousing suspicion among the draft board that he'd broken the law in a conscious attempt to avoid service. And

John, head over heels in love and willing to give Lorey whatever she wanted, agreed to it. When I heard about this, I was livid; it just seemed so selfish to me. Whenever the new Mrs. John Sebastian came around after that, I could feel my skin crawl, while the distance between me and John grew.

Bringing this all back to "Rain on the Roof," I was growing just a bit weary of playing on cloying love songs about a woman for whom I had barely concealed disdain. And — though this probably wasn't fair, because his musical instincts were almost always impeccable — I was starting to wonder just a bit about John's judgment being clouded by the relationship. When you combine that with the fact that he was necessarily taking a major leadership role in group decisions, you could see a divide beginning to grow in the band. The divide was soon to become more pronounced.

In the meantime, my own group of friends was changing, and my interests in things not related to music were growing. From March 1966 onward, a couple of guys named Pinhead and Dennis were a near-constant presence in my life.

One night in March, I walked into my carriage house expecting to find my friend from East Hampton, Billy Harvey, who'd been my sometimes-roommate since I'd begun renting the place. Billy was in my high school class when I moved to Long Island in 1958, and though he was the product of a strong-willed single mother and was basically a good guy, Billy seemed to be a magnet for trouble. He was somebody my parents would have preferred I not hang out with, but we had a mutual love for motor racing that bonded us, and our friendship had endured over the years. His mom also knew a lot of stock car racers somehow, and I liked to hear his firsthand stories about them. On this particular week in 1966, Billy had already been beaten up and thrown down a flight of stairs by some mysterious characters from elsewhere in New York. He claimed it was over a girl, but I doubted his story and was anxious for him to go back to the Island.

Anyway, I did find Billy when I walked into the house that night, and I also found another guy — who was holding a knife to Billy's throat in my living room. This was a new one. I wasn't quite sure what to say or do.

"What's going on?" I said.

"I'm gonna kill your friend," the intruder returned.

"Well I don't know why you wanna kill him, but you can't do it in my house." (I think they call that a compromise.)

The knife wielder smiled. He was about my age, but looked like a football player, six-foot-four and maybe 225 pounds, and was handsome in a tough-guy way. He started talking in quiet but measured tones, and presented himself confidently.

"Your friend here would probably find it best to get out of New York . . . permanently," he said. He did not threaten me or offer consequences for a failure to act, but I got the impression that he did not make threats lightly.

He had made his point, and soon lowered the knife and released Billy. As he was leaving my apartment I followed him out from a safe distance and watched him and two other guys, who looked like they had walked right off a construction site in Queens, get into a beat-up red Ford pickup. As they drove away, I walked back into the house and tried to get my blood pressure under control.

"Billy, what the fuck was that about?" I demanded.

This time it wasn't over a girl. Billy explained that this guy, who called himself Willy but whom everyone knew as Pinhead, was a fixture at a storefront motorcycle shop downtown. In addition to being a body shop with a mechanic, the store allowed customers to keep their bikes there for storage or long-term repair. One day when Billy was walking by the storefront, he looked in, as any motorcycle enthusiast would, and thought he saw a bike that looked exactly like the one his friend, stock car racer Reynaldo Herrera (who usually raced at Riverhead under the name Ronnie Herra), had reported stolen just weeks before. Without attempting to get any kind of confirmation of the bike's ownership, Billy called the cops and reported having seen the bike in this store.

How word got to Pinhead and led him to my house was unclear at this time, but I would find out later. I put Billy on a bus to L.A. that night, and he didn't come back to New York for 20 years.

Once Billy was out of the picture, I for some reason decided to go up to the shop and check things out for myself. I was immediately welcomed in and subsequently invited to the clubhouse these guys maintained on East 88th Street in Manhattan. I probably should not have accepted the offer at that time in my life, with The Spoonful going strong, but as it happened, Chris Dewey, a friend of mine from a prominent New York family, had also made acquaintance with these guys and said I should come hang out next time he was up there.

"You will like these guys," Dewey said.

Stopping by the apartment, I was greeted by another real tough-looking guy, named Dennis. Dennis Caras was his full name, and the apartment was his. He was pure Damon Runyon — swarthy, beady-eyed, thick Queens accent and roughly good-looking. He appeared to be more or less the ringleader of this crew. The apartment itself was the typical railroad flat, with a large living/dining area and a hall down one side leading to bedrooms, baths and kitchen. A motorcycle was up on milk crates in the dining area. At the time of my first visit, there were about 10 guys hanging out in addition to Chris and myself. White T-shirts with the sleeves rolled up and long hair slicked back in ducktails. They were everything the Fonz and Potsie on *Happy Days* wanted to be, and much more. These were the kind of people who were hanging on the front stoops when I first went to Skip's apartment in late 1964. The names of the other guys were pure New Yawk — Jimmy the Mop and Fortuna, whose first name was Bobby but no one called him that. Ligsy and Rico had a shop in Queens, and I guess the glue that brought them all together was motorcycles — racing, riding and ripping them off — although I did not know about the ripping-them-off part for a while.

Then, as if to top it all off, just after a big fat doobie had started going around, without even knocking, in through the front door comes another big guy — but this one was in a police uniform. Andrew Ditmar had made his appearance. He was a beat cop from a nearby precinct and a very good friend of Dennis'. I did not know this, though, and for a second the thought of my entire career going down the tubes flashed through my brain. I guess everyone could see me react with horror, as all the laughter in the room was aimed at me. The cop was one of the gang, and the mystery of how Pinhead had found out who had ratted out his shop became clearer.

I liked these guys, and while they did not present the wholesome image my career demanded, I found myself spending more and more time up at Dennis', getting to know this crew. Why would I start hanging with such characters? It has to do with the kind of friends I grew up with. Nearly all of my life, with the exception of the five years I lived in St. Augustine, had been spent in the environs of the wealthy class. Nearly everyone I knew as a friend came from wealthier circumstances than I did. I have always been able to make friends easily, so the only way I knew that this was not how everyone lived was to compare lifestyles. In the background was always the influence of my older brother, Skip. His being six years older than me made him practically like an uncle. For reasons I can't explain, he seemed to gravitate toward the wild side with his friends. The influence of several movies, most notably James Dean's two biggest hits, *Rebel Without a Cause* and *East of Eden*, presented an image that Skip liked, and from a distance I liked it too. Also, the post-war years in America were very conservative and the conformity among young people was stifling.

Seeing how Skip would dress and act made a deep impression on me, though I was still too young to emulate him. Once the military was out of the picture, I became freer to adopt some of the anti-social behavior that Skip and his friends were exhibiting. Moving to East Hampton was the beginning of the change. In East Hampton I was not accepted easily by the preppie kids in my class, so for reasons that could probably be expanded upon by a psychiatrist, I picked my friends from the lower-middle class and adopted their habits.

Once I got to living in New York, my friends, with the exception of a few, were mostly kids without direction or motivation and were all from the Island.

Meeting the 88th Street crew was a revelation. With the success that The Spoonful was bringing me, I felt free to make friends with whomever I wanted. These guys reminded me of the types that would come out to the Westhampton drag strip on weekends and race their hot rods. This was the kind of friend I now wanted to hang out with. Oddly enough, many of the hangers-on at 88th St. were preppies from the Upper East Side and were probably looking for the same kind of excitement I was. I knew I wasn't being treated so well just because I was a cool guy — the fact that I was in a big-time rock band was my ticket to enter that world. My association with Dennis and Pinhead would be a gateway to a seedier realm that would soon become more pervasive in my life.

So let me introduce you to the main characters from this crew.

Dennis Caras. It was his apartment, and he was from Queens and about five years older than me. He lived by the hustle. The ladies liked him because he was very handsome in that Mediterranean way, and he spoke with the classic New Yawk accent. Actually a very sensitive person but big and gruff, not one to shy away from a fight. I would stay in touch with Dennis throughout the '70s and early '80s, until he fell off a ladder working down in Tampa and ultimately died from those injuries.

Pinhead (Willy Barth). Definitely the leader of the pack. Practically speaking he was the most settled of the bunch. In addition to the bike shop, he had a trucking company on Long Island and ran it himself, which as I found out in my travels with him sometimes meant he had to go and beat the shit out of one of his drivers who'd screwed up. Tough as nails, although he did not have the hard look that Dennis did. Pinhead was also a very attractive guy to the ladies. If you saw him in a business suit, you would think he was a young CEO. If you saw him at the motorcycle races, he looked like a champion. If you went into a crowded bar, he would be the one who stood out from the rest. He was also the one who I thought could be counted on in a real pinch, and the true badass of the bunch. I witnessed a fight at the motorcycle races one day after Pin had heard that someone had threatened to "beat his ass bloody." He immediately searched out this guy and beat the crap out of him so bad in front of the whole crowd at the track — both his friends and the other guys — that a huge guy known as "Tony the Animal" had to go over and get Pinhead to stop beating the guy. He eventually went on the run from the law over some other issues. After he was caught, sensing the hopelessness of his probable lifetime sentence in jail, he committed suicide in a New York jail (the Tombs) by gnawing his veins until he bled to death.

Andrew Ditmar (Ditmar). Andy was a big, gregarious NYC cop who walked on both sides of the tracks. He would come and go from the scene and sometimes acted as a lookout for Pinhead and his activities. I would stay somewhat in touch with Andy over the years. I last saw him in Pompano Beach, Florida, in the 1990s, where he had come with a bunch of the guys from the New York doo-wop scene to hang out for the winter. He may still be around, but I have not seen him since.

Bobby Fortuna (the Kid). Bobby was the youngest of the bunch, and when I first met him he was mostly the gofer. A real easygoing guy who had a deceptively mild personality. Running errands for the older guys was his mission, and he once incurred Pinhead's wrath when he borrowed my rent-a-car out in the Hamptons and wrecked it driving it around. He got beat by Pin with a two-by-four to the point where he almost had to be hospitalized. I would lose track of Bobby until one day in the 1990s, when I ran into him in Fort Lauderdale, where he was running his own paint and body shop. We became close friends again until he passed away from a brain hemorrhage in 2002.

Jimmy the Mop. I never knew Jimmy's last name. He also had a shop in Queens that did car repair and ultimately became a go-to shop for racing motorcycles. He was one of the best riders in the crew — always a winner on the racetrack — and a quiet kind of guy. I did not know or hang out with "the Mop" except to go to the races with him, or to his shop with Dennis or Pin.

Ligsy. Another mystery guy. He would show up at the races and was a boss rider, but I did not know that much about him except that he, like the Mop and Pinhead, was a champion bike rider. He too was from Queens and probably involved in the car/motorcycle repair business. A hot rodder.

These guys were all loosely affiliated with a motorcycle gang from Brooklyn called the Aliens. On one of The Spoonful's appearances on *The Ed Sullivan Show*, I wore a cut-off jean jacket with the Aliens name on the back and all the colors of a then-current outlaw motorcycle gang. I was told that because I'd done this, my back was forever covered by this gang, although I never did have to take them up on that offer, thank God.

Another time, I was just off the airplane from a Spoonful gig and I went straight to Dennis' apartment. A phone call came in shortly after my arrival asking for help; the caller said they were being ripped off by a rival gang. Everybody jumped into action, grabbing whatever tool could be used as a weapon. You did not want to get caught with a gun in New York in those days. The guys told me to stay there, but I wanted to show my willingness to be part of the crew and grabbed a long box wrench, which I stuck in my overcoat pocket. When we got to the apartment, also on the East Side, we went up the stairs and a couple of guys went out on the fire escape while the rest of us stood up against the wall. One of us knocked on the door, and what happened next is still a blur in my memory. The door opened, and the guy in front of me was pulled into the apartment in a flash. As I went to look in, I was lifted off the ground, feet dangling, by a big burly guy, who said, "You are under arrest." He put me down and searched me, and it must have been a sight. Here I was in a camel-hair overcoat with shoulder-length hair and skinny as a bone, trying to act like a tough guy. After about 30 confusing minutes we were let go and immediately headed for the 88th Street house to review what had happened. It turned out that what their friends thought was a rip-off was in fact an undercover buy that had gone bad, but because no one was carrying any illegal weapons, the cops decided that they could not make charges stick and let us go. Several lessons learned here. One: do not stick your neck out unless you know where you are sticking it. Two: you, Steve Boone, are not from the same material that these guys are cut from, and if you know what's good for you, do not do this again.

It was through Dennis and Pinhead's crew that my interest in cars became stoked again, and it was soon after "Summer in the City" began climbing the charts that I became fixated on buying my dream car. I'd already had a couple of nice cars, including an MGA and an Austin-Healey 3000 MKII, both of which are classics and collectibles today. But my personal dream car was always a Ferrari. Way back in 1963, parked outside of Mitty's, one of my favorite nightclubs on Long Island, I laid eyes on a Ferrari coupe that immediately made its way to the top of the I've-gotta-have-this list. It was the beautiful 250 GT Lusso, and though I didn't have any realistic way of being able to buy a car like this, the Lusso was one of the reasons I'd made that special trip to the Ferrari factory in Maranello when I motorcycled through Europe.

So in the early fall of 1966 I was looking through the Sunday *New York Times* automobile classifieds when this ad jumped out at me. "For sale at Foreign Car City in Nyack, New York: a 1964 Ferrari 250 GT Lusso and a 1965 Ferrari 275 GTB." My friend Fudge, the lighting technician for The Lovin' Spoonful, joined me in my rent-a-car as we headed up to Nyack, just above the Palisades along the Hudson River. I'd seen the dealership owner, Bob Grossman, race Ferraris at Bridgehampton Race Circuit.

On the lot were a Lusso in Ferrari racing red, a 275 GTB (now the most collectible car in the world) and a Ford GT40, maybe 10 of which were being sold to the public worldwide. The GT40 was the car I'd watched run at Monza, and I couldn't believe that not only was I seeing one for sale in New York, but that I had a chance to buy it. I went on a test drive with the GT40, which we got up to 140 miles per hour on the New York Thruway before it promptly ran out of gas. (No matter — from that speed we managed to coast the last miles to the dealership exit!) The GT40 would have turned a lot of heads, but it was a little too expensive at $11,500, and it was a race car, which meant it was no-frills on the inside.

Besides, I was still enraptured by the Ferraris, both of which sat in the lot gleaming with the unmistakable color of Ferrari red.

The brand new GTB was an unbelievable car but at $13,500 was out of my comfortable price range. (A GTB sold at auction in March 2013 for $2.365 million dollars.)

Which left the 250 GT Lusso, hardly a consolation prize. This was the car to own for rock stars — I'd later find out that Eric Clapton and George Harrison each owned one too. It was an amazing vehicle, and since it was two years old with 15,000 miles on it, it was available for the princely sum of $8,500, a huge amount of money in 1966. I test-drove it and fell in love. I was going to have this car, and I got it — with help from John Sebastian, who fronted me the money until my first royalty check for "Summer in the City" came in. John came through like the great friend that he was, and within days I was driving off Bob Grossman's lot in my very own Ferrari.

I drove it for about a year until, just before I left on tour, some dumbass mechanic blew the engine trying to fix it. It didn't run at all, so Dennis told me to bring it into his shop and he'd take care of it. That's when the unthinkable happened, though it shouldn't have been so unthinkable looking back. Dennis ran a chop shop, and almost immediately his shop got raided. The cops told Dennis they were going to hold the seized vehicles at the Queens Whitestone Impound Lot, so when I came off tour I took my title and registration up there to find my Ferrari.

I handed my information to the cop who fronted the Whitestone Pound and he went out to his lot, which was just cars for miles and miles. He came back about 10 minutes later.

"It's not here."

"What do you mean it's not here? The cops told my friend all the impounded cars on this case were coming here. See, here's the number."

"Yup, that's the case number," he said. "And those cars did come here. But your car is not here."

I could tell I wasn't getting much further with this guy, and a couple of calls to the detective assigned to the case got me little more than the same run-around.

As it happened, at the time my dad was the manager of the Garden City Golf Club, and the district attorney for Queens was a member there. Desperate, I asked my dad if he could enlist the DA to help me look into what had happened to my Ferrari.

My dad called me about a week later.

"Forget the car," he said.

"What are you talking about? What did the DA say?"

"He said, 'Tell your son to forget the car, and not to associate with those kinds of people.'"

And that was it. My mind often wanders to what cop or more likely mobster in cahoots with the NYPD got his hands on my car after it left Dennis' shop. As of 2014, I am still searching for my Ferrari GT Lusso — VIN number 4237 — and I've never given up. I still have the title and the paperwork for the original order, signed by Bob Grossman himself. There were only 236 ever made, with the VIN numbers from the high 3000s to low 5000s. Most of them sell for a million to $1.5 million, and they go for a minimum of a half-million dollars in unrestored condition. Just the Borrani wheels are now worth $5,000 apiece.

While that story didn't end well for me, having the Ferrari was helpful in allowing me to temporarily forget the shame of the bust and the accompanying fear of the incident being revealed. The new group of friends, the growing number of female conquests, the great music The Spoonful was making that I was contributing to — it was all helping, or I thought it was. The events of May 1966 in San

Francisco were never too far from my mind, but time was healing the wounds, and I'd been lulled into thinking the whole thing had been swept under the carpet as we'd been told it would.

I'd soon learn that no high-performance vehicle can move fast enough to outrace the past.

Chapter 8
DIDN'T WANT TO HAVE TO DO IT

John Sebastian's face was bright red, and he was as angry as I'd ever seen him.

The image people have of John as a blissed-out hippie with a tender heart is almost totally accurate, which is why this tirade was such an event. The object of his scorn was none other than Erik Jacobsen, our producer and John's longtime friend, who stood at the recording console and absorbed the screams.

"You wiped the vocal? Why the fuck would you wipe the vocal?"

"John, the vocal sucked."

"What the fuck are you talking about, Jake?" John shot back. "That was the take. It was fabulous."

"No it wasn't. It was flat. Ask Brooks." John looked over to Brooks Arthur, the engineer, who may have been looking around for a genie to make him invisible. Brooks' silence was all John needed. He stormed out of the studio, but he'd be back. We still needed a vocal track, after all.

Rewind to the previous evening, a tracking session for a new song called "Darling Be Home Soon," which was going on a soundtrack for a film called *You're a Big Boy Now* by an unknown director

163

named Francis Ford Coppola. The film was actually the 27-year-old Coppola's master's thesis for UCLA film school. As with *What's Up, Tiger Lily?*, Jack Lewis was again involved in the process, which was a big reason why we were excited to do it. Jack had been outstanding to work with on the last soundtrack. But unlike that experience, this would not be a collaborative effort. John had met one-on-one with Coppola on the requirements and vision for the project, and wrote the songs by himself before turning them over to Artie Schroeck, who wrote arrangements for an orchestral production. When we showed up to the soundtrack sessions on that week in mid-October 1966, Zally, Joe and I were greeted by charts that told us what parts to play.

"What the fuck is this?" Zally whispered to me. He was being told to play only on the two and the four, with none of his usual improvisation allowed. He felt he was being punished, and he wasn't sure what for. It sure seemed like we were all being treated like session musicians. I just shrugged.

One of the centerpieces of the soundtrack was to be this particular song, which was frankly fantastic and offered more proof that John had stratospheric talent. In addition to the fine melody, the song had a unique theme — it concerned a male subject waiting for a female to return home, whereas most rock songs in that vein were from the perspective of a working man returning to his awaiting lady. John had written the song while waiting one night for Lorey to come home from work.

Yes, it was another Lorey song, but at least it was a really good one.

When John showed up to do the vocal, Lorey happened to be there, as was Zally's girlfriend, Jackie Burroughs. So John started singing directly to Lorey as he cut the track, and at some point got so wrapped up in the emotion of the lyrics that he pretty much started crying. Not enough that we had to abort the take, but apparently there was enough of a tear in his voice to make the vocal fall flat. Of course, John thought he'd nailed it, and walked out with Lorey, hand in hand. Later, when Erik and Brooks played back the tracks, they knew they had a problem. Since Erik needed every available track on what was a fully orchestrated arrangement, he wiped the vocal, thus creating the scene.

John did return to do the vocal, but that would be the last Lovin' Spoonful album session Erik Jacobsen would ever work. Not long after, he was fired. Though we all had input into the decision (at the time, Joe and I were smitten with Roy Halee, who we erroneously thought we'd be able to pry away from Columbia), it's hard to imagine that Erik would have been shown the door had John Sebastian wanted him to stay. And the "Darling Be Home Soon" incident probably played a major role in John wanting Erik to go.

John had been getting his way with more and more frequency, whether it was on musical choices, or with Bob Cavallo, or with Koppelman-Rubin, and during this period he was not at all shy about asserting himself. To be fair, the guy who Zally used to facetiously refer to as "the Leader" had to lead, because by this point no one else in the group was equipped to do it. I and especially Zally had been more or less in la-la land since the bust. Joe certainly had opinions, but he hadn't established himself as a creative force in the band and wouldn't have been accepted in a primary leadership role by the other three. Meanwhile, John was writing and singing lead on the majority of the songs, so the focus was on him, and it's clear he felt he needed to step up. Looking back, I'm sure it had to be an ungodly amount of pressure, but it was hard to see it that way in the moment.

From where we stood in the fall of 1966, it looked like John was beginning to exert total control and trying to dictate the band's every move, which was not going over well at all, especially when we suspected Lorey was in John's ear on a lot of these issues.

And the guy taking it the worst was Zal Yanovsky. Zally did not like being told what to do or what to play. His sense of spontaneity had informed some of his best moments both onstage and in the studio. He didn't get into the business to be John's sideman or a session player, but unfortunately it wasn't Zally's way to step up and actually articulate that. Instead he just acted out, called people names, said and did other cruel things, and otherwise was pretty much impossible to deal with. Communication between him and John became very stilted. These guys were not getting along, and everyone in our orbit knew it.

A song we never recorded, called "The Dance of Pain and Pleasure," provided evidence that, as a band, we weren't seeing eye to eye either personally or musically.

Sometime in the fall, with the bust still resting like a dull ache at the back of my brain, Zally and I came up with a song that provided a sort of catharsis for what we were going through. Zally had this riff that I loved that was pure Zally, which he played on guitar almost every time he picked one up. Noting how some of my own little riffs had developed into full-blown songs like "You Didn't Have to Be So Nice" and "Full Measure," I said, "Why don't we try to make a song out of that riff?"

He was skeptical but said, "If you think we can, I'll give it a try."

Zally and I hadn't written together very much, if at all, but I said, "Let me put some words together with the riff; we can make it about what we've gone through since San Francisco."

As a member of The Death Duo, he knew exactly what I meant and said, "Yeah — 'the dance of pain and pleasure.'" Which said it all, really. All the great things that were happening in our lives since May had been counterbalanced by the lead weight that was our guilt and despair over the bust. We figured it was a fairly relatable subject, as a lot of people feel the polarity of positive and negative forces in their lives. We weren't going to be overt in talking about the bust; in fact we actually devised "The Dance of Pain and Pleasure" as a dance song, almost a throwback to the early Dick Clark or Joey Dee and The Starliters days. We threw together a verse and a chorus that went: "You've heard about the monkey and the boogaloo/ Here's about a dance that you all can do/ old folks, young folks, measure by measure/ are talkin' 'bout the dance of pain and pleasure." OK, so it wasn't Yeats, but the song was still in a crude state — we were just looking for enough of a frame to present it to Erik and the rest of the band for consideration.

On the night we brought it into the studio, I could sense the skepticism before we'd even played a note. It was just one of those times when the vibes were bad. We got set up in the studio with me on bass and Zally on guitar and vocals. We played the one verse we had, including the riff, and I joined in on the chorus.

When we were finished running through it we were met with vacant stares. No one got it.

Erik was still with us then and said, "You're wasting my time," and walked out.

Joe said, "This is a bunch of crap," and followed him out the door.

John tried to seem interested, if only to balance the others' brutality with some diplomacy, but we quickly discerned he was just trying to be nice. The conversation soon moved to other things. "The Dance of Pain and Pleasure" was dead on arrival.

Zally and I just sat there with a "what did we expect" look on our faces, and soon afterward packed up the guitars. Zally went home, and I headed straight for the bar. It was crushing to be rejected like that. I'm sure the song sounded raw, but I thought that was some of its charm. We'd recorded several songs that had started as fragments but through work and collaboration in the studio had been made to work. That wasn't going to happen here. Nothing more was said about the song between me and Zally, but the gauntlet had been laid down.

Not long after that debacle, with tensions running high within the group, Koppelman and Rubin came to us with what was supposed to be a piece of good news. They and Kama Sutra had renegotiated the distribution deal with MGM, and as part of that agreement were offering us a seven-album record deal. The new contract would give us the first real money that had ever come from Kama Sutra or Koppelman-Rubin. Up to that point we had received mostly pocket money, in the form of a weekly salary, to buy the things we wanted or needed, with a promise of more to come once "the accounting was figured out." We'd had six Top 10 singles and three charting albums, including a Top 10 album, but had not really been paid for them. It was an age-old music business story. We weren't shrewd or distrusting enough to demand a detailed accounting of the money coming in from record sales (maybe Bob Cavallo should have been), we were just told the money was all there on paper and would be released to us in due time. I took a lot of these "pocket money" payouts, which, when coupled with a small payout from publishing royalties, kept me in cash. Joe Butler did not do this, preferring to wait to get most of his money in the lump sum that was to come. This choice by Joe, who also had almost nothing coming in from publishing, would ultimately have dire consequences.

Anyway, the new record deal sounded great. Things were not all sunshine and roses among the four of us, but maybe this vote of confidence on the part of Kama Sutra would be the shot in the arm we'd need to move forward both artistically and collaboratively. It's nice to feel like you're wanted, like you're valued by the label and they believe in you enough to lock you up for the foreseeable future.

Unfortunately, when we showed up to sign the contracts, we learned that value was a relative term for the four members of The Lovin' Spoonful. Inserted into the language of the contract was wording that said something to the effect of "The Lovin' Spoonful can consist of any group of persons as long as one of those persons is John Sebastian." The heading on that section of the contract was titled "Key Man Clause." What it really meant was that The Lovin' Spoonful only existed if John Sebastian was a member of the band. If I left or Zally or Joe left, we were replaceable, but if John left, the contract was null and void and the rest of us could hand in our playbooks. The deal effectively turned us into his sidemen, putting us in a position where every decision was ultimately going to be John's. If John decided he didn't like a song choice or an arrangement or really anything else, he could bail and Kama Sutra wouldn't have to pay us or allow us to make another record.

To this day, I don't think John himself was behind that contract language, nor do I think he had any idea how it would be perceived by the rest of the band. I've known him almost 50 years, and I know he's not a cutthroat businessman — he just doesn't think that way. I think our "business interests" presented it to him as a standard deal, with the key man clause portrayed as a mostly inconsequential safeguard for the guy who was, after all, writing most of the songs and calling most of the musical shots. An outsider might look at the deal and say, "Yeah, but John Sebastian *was* the key man in The Lovin' Spoonful," and maybe that was also the attitude of those who were part of our management or worked at our label. But inside the band we'd always operated democratically, with everyone's input always welcomed and heard. Now, from my perspective, and I'm sure that of the other guys, the discussions we'd had over things like "Rain on the Roof" weren't even going to be discussions anymore. If John wanted to go off with Coppola and work on a movie soundtrack that we had little input into, or if he wanted to do a whole album of love songs to Lorey or fire a producer, we could either accept it or live in fear of his leaving the group to do what he wanted while we went out looking for other jobs.

I say this mostly in hindsight, because the day the deal was signed we weren't given too much time to reflect on the nature of the contract, although I knew it seemed kind of fishy. First of all, our lawyer was David Braun, from the firm Prior, Braun, Cashman, Sherman and Ward, and later the CEO of Polygram Records. The lawyer there to represent the record company was Peter Prior from . . . Prior, Braun, Cashman, Sherman and Ward. That's right, the person representing our interests was partners with the lawyer for the record company! I'm sure that when it came down to enforcing the details of the contract, Braun wasn't really going to go hard after Prior, who had the office right next to his. It was comical, but as with the agreement with the SFPD, I wasn't made to feel like there was much of an alternative. It's not like Cavallo said, "Hey guys, if you don't like the Kama Sutra deal I'll go shop you over here to Capitol or Warner Brothers." Do you think Joe Smith at Warners would have liked to get another crack at what he passed up in 1965?

Knowing that the signature on the page would mean some immediate and greatly desired cash flow, we signed. At the end of the day it all came down to "You want the money, kid?" If anyone raised any objections that day, I don't remember it. Zally was a smart guy and I bet he had some inkling of what was going on, but his soon-to-be-wife Jackie was now living with him in New York and pregnant, and without health insurance I'm sure he needed that advance money.

Once it dawned on us that the only one operating from a position of strength in the new contract was John Sebastian, it was too late to do anything about it. We were all naïve to the max, and even though we were greenhorns in the world of business, the bottom line is we were adults and had no one to blame but ourselves. Once we'd signed, it set into motion the longest collection process that has probably ever ensued from a record contract. We would not see another cent of royalty income for 24 years.

For the moment, a potential morale booster was actually a morale killer, and Zal Yanovsky started to go even further off the rails.

The real beginning of the end came during our January 1967 appearance on *The Ed Sullivan Show*. We were to perform the newly released single "Darling Be Home Soon," a song Zally had come to resent for the reasons stated above. Ed Sullivan loved us so much that he allowed us to bring in a large orchestra to participate in the performance. Just as John was to start the second verse of a serious, earnest love song, Zally — with a rubber toad figurine bouncing up and down from the neck of his guitar — jumped in front of the main camera that was focused on John and started mugging, bouncing up and down, miming the lyrics in a way that sure looked like he was mocking them. On footage of the show, you can clearly make out the audience's laughter at Zally's antics. Not the emotion we were going for out of this song. John was furious. The single stalled on the charts at No. 15, well below expectations, and was our first single to miss the Top 10. I wondered, and I'm sure John did too, whether the bizarre performance during a prime promotional opportunity on *Ed Sullivan* hurt the chances of the single.

By the spring of 1967, it felt like we were putting out these little blazes almost daily with Zally. Then the bust was made public, and the brushfire became an inferno.

First, word filtered back to us that one of the attendees at the party where we'd introduced the narc had been busted, and had been telling people about our connection with the guy we'd introduced around that night in May 1966. Up until that point we had held out a faint, probably naïve hope that our introduction would fail to lead to an arrest. It now looked like that hope was gone. The fuse had been lit.

The San Francisco counterculture at that time was still a small group, and word traveled fast. Apparently the manager of the comedy troupe The Committee, with whom we'd hung out at both San Francisco parties in May '66 and who was associated with the person who got arrested, delivered word about the bust and our possible role in it to a San Francisco author and journalist named Chester Anderson, who specialized in writing angry, bitter anti-establishment leaflets for a group called the Communication Company, the voice of the local counterculture. Anderson was also friends with Paul Williams, who had founded the influential rock music magazine *Crawdaddy!* in early 1966.

Anderson in turn wrote a leaflet detailing our sins and distributing it to all the underground papers, including the *Los Angeles Free Press*, the *East Village Other* in New York and the *Berkeley Barb*. At first, only the *Barb* picked up the story, but the public mention was enough to sound alarm bells for our camp. When I found out not only that the bust was public, but that it was public because someone had been arrested, my heart dropped. Zally acted like he knew it had been coming all along.

Freaked out, Bob Cavallo and Koppelman-Rubin sprang into action. In damage control mode, they contacted the lawyer for the defendant and offered a deal to "help his defense," which was code for "buy his silence." I was told the guy never did a day in jail — Joe Butler swears someone from our camp paid off a judge, though I have no evidence to support this — but the payoff did not shut the guy up. Understandably angry at us and I'm sure provoked by local scribes like Chester Anderson who wanted the story, he continued to leak details of the bust throughout the burgeoning underground.

And anyway, it was too late. Once the *Berkeley Barb* story came out, somebody who said he'd been in the cell with us the night of the bust got in touch with Anderson, who did a whole new leaflet campaign including this new information, which got the attention of the *L.A. Free Press*. The paper devoted an entire page to us, telling people The Lovin' Spoonful was part of the establishment and that if you bought our records, attended our concerts or fucked us, you were part of the establishment too. They'd branded us with the hippie scarlet letter.

Of course, no one from any of these publications nor Anderson himself ever contacted us to check their facts, to get our side or to even attempt to understand why Zally and I had done what we'd done. All of that was incidental to them. The whole point of the underground press was hatred of the authorities, and our cooperation with the authorities gave them a shining gold emblem on which to focus their angst. They needed us to be finks and they needed the story to remain one-sided and one-dimensional. Any compassion or understanding for what we'd been through was only going to be counterproductive to the broader point they were attempting to reinforce to their already converted readership. Nowadays, having witnessed the exploits of Fox News and MSNBC, I understand much better than I did in 1967 what it looks like when a political group does business as a journalistic entity, with a complete lack of nuance.

The humiliation and shame Zally and I had been feeling since May 1966 now had another dimension, since it was other people and not us doing the humiliating and shaming.

On the West Coast, our records were placed in a few shop windows with big slashes through them. Sometime in the spring, we noticed a few picketers and people with signs, though we didn't play any West Coast dates and it did not seem like our broader fan base or the mainstream press had been clued in to what was going on. That would change.

In the midst of all this, the *You're a Big Boy Now* soundtrack was released and fell like a thud, peaking at No. 160 on the Billboard charts. The fact that Kama Sutra had just released a *Best Of* album in March that would eventually become our biggest seller and hit No. 3 on Billboard probably cannibalized the soundtrack's sales. The movie didn't do very well either, and I'm sure that hurt. There were a couple of nice things on *You're a Big Boy Now*, including "Darling Be Home Soon," the title track, and an instrumental I really liked called "Lonely (Amy's Theme)," but most of the album was incidental soundtrack music and not particularly memorable. As mentioned, the making of the soundtrack brings back bad memories for me. It's always felt like a John Sebastian solo album to me, and the personally tumultuous era in which it was released surely doesn't help.

We were all feeling the strain. I don't think John and Joe had realized the magnitude of what Zally and I had done, or what the fallout could be if it was discovered, until after the *Berkeley Barb* and the *L.A. Free Press* started taking their shots. John and Joe hadn't seemed to think it was that big of a deal previously, but now that the heat was on them by association, I got the sense — whether real or imagined — that they'd decided to be retroactively pissed off at us. Both guys were becoming more involved in the hippie ideals of the day, which included smoking tons of pot, and it had to be hard to know they were being associated in the minds of the movement with finks. We were doing our shows, being professional, but there was a distance between us that seemed to be growing by the day. And Zally, of course, continued to be petulant and hard for everyone to deal with.

In May '67, we canceled several gigs while John recovered from a bout of bronchitis. Soon afterward, I was called to his house for a band meeting, and when I got there it was just Joe and John, no

Zally. I thought that was odd, since Zally lived right across the street, but I'd soon find out why he hadn't been invited.

John started the meeting.

"Zally's behavior has gotten to a point where I cannot take it anymore," he said. "It's not just his behavior out in public, but he seems to be making it personal . . . We need to start behaving like a band that likes itself again. I've tried with Zally, but I don't see how we can go on with him in the band."

John was right — he had tried. Back in February, after the *Ed Sullivan* incident, John had suggested the band get away for a retreat of sorts. He arranged for us to stay up at Camp Apple Hill, the place in New Hampshire where he'd attended summer camp as a kid and later as a counselor. His thinking was sound. If we went somewhere as just the four guys in the group, no wives, girlfriends, friends or other distractions, maybe we could rekindle the creative spark that had faded a bit in the last few months. The idea was that we would jam and rehearse a little bit, get back to liking each other as people and as professional colleagues, in a relaxed setting.

It went pretty well for a day or two, but the important elephants in the room were not acknowledged. Namely the despair Zally and I were feeling over the bust, and the fact that we all hated Lorey and the soft musical direction in which John had been drifting since they got more serious. Maybe we would have gotten around to exploring those issues, but the camp had been stocked with toys like snowmobiles and toboggans, and Joe — who had issues, as most of us did, with smoking pot and concentrating — got hit by a passing pickup truck while out on one of the snowmobiles. He wasn't seriously hurt, but it cut short both our rehearsal time and a trip that might have rekindled some magic.

So here we were a couple of months later, with John laying his cards on the table.

"I have thought this over long and hard and it has come down to this," he said. "I can't think of any way to fix it except for us to change what has gone bad. I've made up my mind that either

Zally or me has to go. We either give Zally notice or I am leaving the band."

Joe was sitting in silence, but I already knew he agreed with John about firing Zally. He'd increasingly become the butt of Zally's crude attempts at humor, including calling Joe — an athletically built ex-amateur-boxer — fat, in front of the press and in front of fans. Joe could have killed Zally if he really wanted to, but instead, flying drumsticks had been launched in Zally's direction with more frequency over the past few months.

I was the dissenting opinion on firing Zally. I was closest to him and knew what he was going through because I was going through it too. I don't think anyone really talked in terms of getting people professional help for emotional trauma in 1967 — what could possibly be bothering a famous 22-year-old rock musician? — but it's clear to me now that's what he needed and I probably needed too. I don't even remember bringing up the bust in the meeting, not that I think providing a glimpse into Zally's state of mind would have mattered. But I still thought Zally could be reformed, that we could have a come-to-Jesus talk with him and at least get him to act like a professional and to stop saying "I hate this band" every time we were around him. I would have preferred a meeting where we discussed the band's direction and asked Zally if he wanted to be in the picture. This would have given him an honorable way out, and maybe he would have quit anyway, who knows.

As much as I understood what a fly in the ointment Zally had become, I suggested we give him one more shot. The others weren't having it. You could tell their minds were made up.

Realizing I had little or no support I said, "Well then, let's take a vote for the record." We did, and it was two to one . . . Zally goes.

With his fate sealed, I insisted we break the news to Zally face to face, with all four of us in the room. We set up a meeting at John's apartment for the next day. Joe and I got there first, but Zally wasn't there yet, so we fired up a joint and made awkward small talk. After a few minutes, in walked Zalman.

We didn't usually have band meetings this way, so I sensed he knew something was up. There were a few seconds of awkward silence that felt like hours, before Zally spoke up and said, "Well guys, what's this meeting all about?" I looked at John and then at Joe, who were squirming in their seats and not really saying anything.

Finally, sensing that either guilty conscience or cowardice was keeping us all quiet, I spoke up.

"Zally, the band has taken a vote and you have been fired." I looked him right in the eyes as I said it. He knew he was not being put on. I didn't bother to tell him I'd voted for him to stay, which didn't really matter at this point.

A long minute went by as Zally processed it before saying, "So, is that it?"

"Yes," John said.

"Fine, if that's all there is, then I'm out of here." And he got up and left.

Oddly enough, I felt a deep sense of relief when it was all over. Even taking into account how humiliating it is to be fired — especially when you know it could become public knowledge — I'm sure a big part of Zally was relieved too. In addition to the creative and personal differences and Zally's own angst, Jackie was five months pregnant with their daughter Zoe and I don't think he relished the thought of being on the road or in the studio in October, when the baby was due.

The Lovin' Spoonful would need to find a new lead guitar player to fill Zally's immense shoes. In the meantime, Zally agreed, as part of his settlement for leaving the group, to play the rest of our scheduled dates through June 24, when we had a hometown gig with Judy Collins at the West Side Tennis Club (later to become Forest Hills Tennis Center). It was about a month's worth of dates, and though I'm sure given the circumstances it was as awkward for him as it was for us, Zally never seemed to give less than his best and did not give anyone in the band the cold shoulder offstage.

Part of that was probably business, since he was to receive a substantial lump sum from Lovin' Spoonful, Inc., when he'd completed his obligations, and he didn't want to screw that up.

But the other part was undoubtedly that once the burden of being in the band was lifted, Zally felt like he could be our friend again. And bizarrely, everyone's relationship with Zal Yanovsky took a turn for the better after we'd fired him. He showed up at our gigs and studio dates and photo shoots, just to hang out. He still contributed musical ideas to The Lovin' Spoonful and had members of the band on the solo album he'd release the next year, *Alive and Well in Argentina*. He helped me produce a demo for my brother Skip's new band, Autosalvage, which helped them land a record deal with RCA Records. Though I'm sure he still harbored scars from the bust, he never displayed any animosity about being kicked out of the band, at least that I ever saw. I still think the firing was at the very least hasty, and handled rather poorly, but there's a good chance all we did in May 1967 was fire Zally just before he was about to quit.

Either way, the refashioned Lovin' Spoonful was looking to the future by the middle of 1967, even as we hearkened back to our humble beginnings in our pursuit of a fourth member — our old friend Jerry Yester was joining the band.

Chapter 9

DAY BLUES

Jerry Yester strode onstage for his first concert with The Lovin' Spoonful, guitar in hand, and heard an unsettling chorus of boos mixed in with the ovation from our fans. For a second, he probably took it personally.

It was June 30, 1967, and the venue was the Memorial Coliseum in Portland. Six days earlier, Jerry had watched from the wings as Zal Yanovsky played his final, triumphant show with the group at West Side Tennis Club in Forest Hills, undoubtedly taking mental notes on what was expected of him.

Right after Zally had left the meeting in which he was fired, we'd begun talking about where to go from here, and John immediately suggested Jerry, whom he must have had on his mind for some time. No other names would be brought up. As mixed as my emotions were about Zally's ouster, I loved Jerry Yester and thought he'd be a perfect fit. He'd been part of our circle from the very beginning, helping to arrange the "Do You Believe in Magic" single along with his friend and partner Erik Jacobsen. Since then, his group, The Modern Folk Quartet, had broken up, and he'd been doing a lot of session work and production in L.A. He'd played on The

Monkees' *Headquarters* album, and had produced the latest album, *Renaissance*, by his brother Jim's group, The Association, as well as the eventually influential *Goodbye and Hello* album for a young folk artist named Tim Buckley. Jerry had also released a couple of solo singles for Dunhill Records that hadn't done much, and as it happened he was between gigs and available. He talked it over with his wife, folk singer Judy Henske, and took the gig. We were relieved.

In early June, Jerry packed up Judy and their daughter, Kate, and drove cross-country all the way to the South Fork of Long Island, where we'd be rehearsing at John's remote house in the pine barrens of East Quogue.

Our rehearsals with Jerry went very well from the start, despite the fresh memory of Zally's awkward firing. Jerry did not have Zally's charisma or zany personality, but no one did. Trying to replace Zally with another "character" would have been futile and contrived. And Jerry did not have Zally's rare natural talents as a lead guitarist, but he was infinitely more versatile as a musician, was light years more patient and professional and understood the big picture sonically better than anyone in the band. As much as we missed Zally — hell, Jerry was his good friend, and I'm sure he missed him too — we clicked with Jerry right away and the musical and personal chemistry was good. Our rehearsals made progress quickly, and word went out to our agents that all was well with the transition and to keep the bookings coming.

And now here we were in Portland, getting booed by the same people we'd seen holding picket signs when we entered the Coliseum. The signs called us finks and traitors, and encouraged our fans (who still greatly outnumbered the detractors) to boycott our shows and stop buying our records. Even though we knew the bust was public, none of us had really seen this coming. There had been no such incidents at our recent shows, including the one we'd played before 14,000 fans in Forest Hills the week before. In this era before the Internet or cable TV or even national rock journalism like *Rolling Stone*, news of the bust hadn't really spread to the bulk of our fan base on the East Coast. Most of the information and indignation was concentrated out west, which was closer to the scene of the crime — a fact we were finding out the hard way. As he heard the boos over a bust that he knew little about and had less of a connection to, Jerry must have wondered what the hell he'd gotten himself into.

The boos died down and otherwise the show went fine, as did most of our early shows with Jerry. We didn't dare set foot back in the Bay Area, but we did some other shows out west with Simon & Garfunkel where, if there were incidents related to the bust, they were minor. We did have a couple of billing-related issues on that tour, with Paul Simon playing the Mike Love role and stomping his feet over his group not being the headliner at one particular show at Red Rocks in Denver. Paul had a point — Simon & Garfunkel wouldn't become a worldwide phenomenon until later, after *The Graduate* came out, but they did have three Top 5 singles to their credit ("The Sound of Silence," "Homeward Bound," "I Am a Rock") by that point and were in their ascendancy, unlike the Beach Boys. I wasn't a big fan of Paul personally — he liked John because they were simpatico ex-folkies, but he projected an air of superiority over Joe and me, us dirty rock 'n' rollers — though, like everyone else in our circle, I thought he was an incredible musician and songwriter. More than a decade later, a then-mega-famous Paul would extend The Lovin' Spoonful a musical lifeline when he put us in a movie he was making, so I guess he didn't hold too much of a grudge over the show billing. If memory serves, we worked out a compromise with Simon & Garfunkel similar to what we'd done with The Beach Boys, where we alternated top billing.

With about six weeks of solid gigs behind us, the new Lovin' Spoonful convened in August to work on what would become our first album with Jerry Yester, *Everything Playing*. By this point, even with news about the bust becoming more widespread, I felt energized by working with Jerry and was looking forward to the sessions. It felt like John, who no longer had to deal with managing Zally's personality in addition to his own job of writing and playing, was benefiting from the collaboration with Jerry as well.

But the band's lineup wasn't the only thing that would be changing for the next album. With Erik Jacobsen out of the picture, we needed to find a new producer who would understand our sound and speak our musical language the way Erik had. Our first choice was Roy Halee, but Roy was still employed by Columbia and was too tied up with their artists, including Simon & Garfunkel, to work with us on the album. So Koppelman-Rubin suggested a guy named Joe Wissert, a Philadelphia native who had been working with our friends The Turtles, another group signed to the Koppelman-Rubin stable. Wissert was fresh off two smash hit singles he'd produced for The Turtles — "Happy Together" and "She'd Rather Be With Me" — and was enlisted to work the same magic on The Spoonful.

We didn't really know Wissert, but in our early meetings with him he seemed like a nice enough guy and understood what we were about. His first suggestion was that we get out of the friendly confines of Columbia Studio B and switch to a new facility on West 57th Street called Mira Sound Studios, which was equipped with what we were told was the industry's first 16-track recorder, an Ampex MM-1000. We had been recording on eight-track at Studio B, a facility still in lockstep with a recording industry focused primarily on monaural (mono) recordings. Even The Beatles' groundbreaking *Sgt. Pepper's Lonely Hearts Club Band*, released two months before we started on *Everything Playing*, had been recorded with mono in mind on four linked four-track recorders at EMI in London.

Mira Sound, on the other hand, was looking to the future of stereo recordings with their 16-track recorder. When I first saw the studio and this wondrous machine, I was astounded. Not only were 16 tracks available on the console, but when we originally walked in, 16 speaker monitors hung from the ceiling! (They were later reconfigured into four subgroups.) Rock music was becoming an arms race, an exercise in how you could outdo your peers in the studio, and The Lovin' Spoonful saw Mira Sound as a way to compete. The possibilities for sonic exploration when you had 16 tracks to work with seemed limitless. We happily got to work.

It had been 10 months since we'd been in the studio to record the *You're a Big Boy Now* soundtrack — an eternity for a band that had been recording a new album every three months — so we had a nice cache of material built up for *Everything Playing*.

One of the linchpins of the new record was already in the can, a song of John's called "Six O'Clock" that we'd recorded at Columbia before Erik and Zally were fired, and had released as a single in April. "Six O'Clock" was another of John's mini-masterpieces, with an inventive melody, well-crafted lyrics and hints of Phil Spector and The Beach Boys in the arrangement. The song only reached No. 18 on the charts — I thought it should have hit the Top 5, and blamed its performance on the darkening skies around the group — but appreciation has grown for it over the years, with artists including Elvis Costello playing it in concert.

My favorite song on the record is what was to be our next single, "She's Still a Mystery," another John song that deserved much better than its eventual chart placing at No. 27. The track showed the dimension that Jerry Yester brought to our band, since he devised the arrangement to include string and woodwind players from the New York Philharmonic and horn players from Ray Charles' touring band. I think he had The Beach Boys' "Wouldn't It Be Nice" in mind when he did that arrangement. Lyrically, the song shows John doing the same reminiscing that had inspired "Did You Ever Have to Make Up Your Mind," but I've always assumed "Mystery" was the first, subtle shot across the bow showing all might not be well between the new Mr. and Mrs. Sebastian. "I thought I'd grow up gracefully/ I'd understand my woman thoroughly/ But the more I see/ The more I see there is to see/ And she's still a mystery to me."

Also brilliant, and another song where John's lyrics inspired interpretation within the band, was the slow-burning "Try a Little Bit," the closest thing to Stax-type soul that you'll find in The Lovin' Spoonful catalog. The tune and unique nature of the arrangement is what gets your attention — it's the one and only Spoonful song that featured female background vocals — but look at those lyrics and wonder whether they might be a defense of the lovey-dovey behavior that fueled the chaotic "Darling Be Home Soon" episode. "You've got to try a little bit/ You might even have to cry a little bit/ When you find someone for you." Someone's getting lectured in that song; I guess only John Sebastian could tell you for sure who it is.

More cynicism from John in "Money," which predated The Beatles' similar-toned "You Never Give Me Your Money" by more than a year but sarcastically reflects the growing suspicion in The Lovin' Spoonful's circle about our representation and who might be looking out for their own interests instead of ours. "And I gave money to Bill/ He pays up my bills and helps me make up my mind/ And I give money to Bill/ And he will be on my side."

"Boredom" is John's painfully honest assessments of what life on the road is like.

The last full-fledged John Sebastian effort on *Everything Playing* is "Younger Generation," which John would make famous at Woodstock more than two years after we'd recorded it, and is the strongest indication on this record of the direction he was headed musically. It's a gentle, finger-picked folk song detailing the worries of a father-to-be, who people erroneously assumed was John (his kids weren't born until the '70s). It's a good tune, though it didn't match up to the outsized hopes Kama Sutra had for it. In the trade ads for the album they said "Younger Generation" was "sure to be the most talked-about track of 1968," but they didn't put their money where their mouths were — it was never released as a single.

Clearly, John was still pulling his weight in this group and was continuing to deliver the goods as a songwriter.

As for the rest of us, well, I guess the jury's out.

Joe's "Old Folks" was never going to be a No. 1 hit, but is an underrated country-tinged tune with some nice harmonica playing from John and a tender lyric about the sadness that comes with growing old. I don't know if it's the first pop song that confronts the emotional issues facing the elderly, but it predates both Simon & Garfunkel's "Old Friends" and John Prine's "Hello in There," both of which would become classics. Joe deserves some credit for beating them to that subject.

Jerry was credited with two writing collaborations on his first Lovin' Spoonful album, one with John ("Close Your Eyes") and one with Joe ("Only Pretty, What a Pity"). The heavily orchestrated closer, "Close Your Eyes," was a Bacharach-sounding song that Jerry was never particularly thrilled with. He thinks the vocal was an octave above his range, and I see his point.

"Only Pretty, What a Pity" had more potential, so much so that we played it on our (extremely drunken) next appearance on *Ed Sullivan*. It was the most experimental song on the album, with a tempo change and vocal effect on the middle eight that got your attention, for better or for worse. John played his ass off when we cut the track, but we'd later learn that he hated the song. I remember us having a lot of trouble rehearsing it for live performance — the song was complicated, and so was the arrangement — and John would throw a tantrum like a little boy in the sandbox because he didn't get the song. I wonder if that key man clause entered his mind while we were trying to get a finished master for "Only Pretty, What a Pity."

I have two major contributions on *Everything Playing*. One that I'm OK with all these years later, and one I wish had gone down much differently.

The one I dig is the instrumental that closes side one, a song called "Forever." This developed from a piano melody I had written while reflecting on the bust and the departure of Zal Yanovsky from the group. It was a melancholy sort of piece, which I played for Jerry and he was immediately enthusiastic about. He set to scoring and arranging it, enlisting a full orchestra and bringing what had been a simple little piece to life. He even allowed me to hire King Charles, my old bandmate in The Kingsmen, to contract the musicians to do the orchestra overdubs. It was a long-overdue payback from me to K.C., who had helped me along and made me believe I could be a professional musician. The members of The Lovin' Spoonful did not play a note on "Forever," and I'm not sure why or how I ended up with a solo writing credit on it, because Jerry probably deserved one too. I always thought it would make good exit music for a film score and I kinda-sorta got my wish sometime in the '80s, when ABC Sports played the song in its entirety as part of a montage for a segment used on *Wide World of Sports*. I had used the name "Forever" as my own private working title based on my reflection about the song's subject, but I wasn't sure about it until Kama Sutra was doing art for the sleeve and Bob Cavallo called me on the phone, in immediate need of a title. That was the first time I had ever spoken the word in connection with the song.

The other major contribution, "Priscilla Millionaira," is the main reason that, despite the overall quality of the album, I'll always have a bad association when I think of *Everything Playing*. It's also the one and only lead vocal I have on a Lovin' Spoonful album, and you can probably listen to it and figure out why that is.

I did not write the song — John did — and it was a funky, up-tempo rocker that I could tell he really believed in. Why he offered it to me to sing, I still have no idea, but this was at a time when we were trying to recapture our past collaborative group spirit, and maybe letting me sing a song was a nod in that direction. I've seen it written that I lobbied to sing "Priscilla Millionaira." That's false, though I will concede that I may not have strenuously objected to taking the vocal. I knew I was not a singer, especially when graded against John Sebastian, Joe Butler and Jerry Yester, but this was a time in rock music when classically trained voices were becoming less important. Ringo certainly had his share of below-average vocals on Beatles records, and The Stones were soon to release an album, *Their Satanic Majesties Request*, on which their bass player, Bill Wyman, sang a song.

With the appearance of the key man clause, I also knew I was going to have to show my versatility in case it ever came time for me to look for another job as a musician. But it backfired, because while I think I was versatile, all I really did with "Priscilla Millionaira" was eliminate any doubt about my being a singer. Jerry and John tried to convince me to develop a "character" voice, to sing it in a vocal range I was comfortable with and not to try to equal John or Joe, but I didn't know what that meant or how to do it. Instead, my genius idea was to get wasted. Nervous, I downed an entire bottle of banana liqueur before the session, using the excuse that it would loosen up my vocal chords. But the song was out of whatever limited vocal range I had, and I just shouted my way through it like a drunk doing karaoke. It was awful, and I really wish someone had shaken some sense into me before it got released.

But that was one of the underlying problems with *Everything Playing*. The person who should have stepped up and taken control of that situation was the producer. Erik Jacobsen had been blunt to the point of almost complete tactlessness, so I'm sure he would not have let that song see the light of day. But Joe Wissert simply did not have the same comfort level with us. I don't know if our personalities overwhelmed him or what, but we all found him very difficult to communicate with. He was barely present for the second half of the sessions, and by the time we got to the mixing stage of the album, he was nowhere to be found. We'd heard — not sure if this is true — that he'd gone back to Philadelphia and been admitted to a mental facility after his experience with The Lovin' Spoonful. If that's true, he should consider himself lucky for not having had to deal with Zally, whose antics might have killed poor Joe. Wissert would go on to produce some great records in the '70s, including Earth, Wind & Fire's platinum *Open Our Eyes* and Boz Scaggs' multi-platinum *Silk Degrees*, but the fact is that *Everything Playing* was not Wissert's finest hour. His absence was a particular problem in this case, since we were dealing with 16-track recording and a 16-track mix, created at the studio Wissert had hand-picked, that none of us knew what the hell to do with. The whole project was basically dumped in the lap of Jerry Yester, who was still a relatively inexperienced producer.

It's to Jerry's credit that *Everything Playing* got released at all. I don't think he's that proud of the end result — he may feel the album is too heavily orchestrated, or that we were too intent on filling up all 16 tracks when simpler arrangements might have better suited the songs — but given the assignment he had, I think he did a masterful job. At a minimum I think it helped him learn what to do and what not to do on future albums he'd produce, including beloved records like Tim Buckley's *Happy Sad* and Tom Waits' *Closing Time*.

Anyway, when the album came out in early 1968, it stiffed, staying in the Billboard charts only seven weeks and peaking at No. 118. Given that we were now fully immersed in the age of the album, that was like a punch to the gut. There are plenty of logical reasons you could give for why *Everything Playing* did so poorly, including the fact that it included no Top 10 singles and that the reviews were lukewarm.

You could also make the argument that our audience had grown up and moved on to music they perceived to be edgier, like The Doors or Jefferson Airplane or The Grateful Dead, all of whom I frankly thought sucked. Friends of ours at Elektra, including Paul Rothchild, were involved with The Doors, and I'll never forget being dragged to see them up at the rock club Ungano's on the East Side of Manhattan by these two way-cool sisters I knew named Pam and Paula. The girls couldn't stop raving about them afterward, but I thought they were boring and a downer. And the lyrics to their big hit "Light My Fire" were saying little more than "come on, baby, suck my dick." If people were going to concerts to see the lead singer proposition them and take his clothes off, how were we going to get them excited about listening to the sound of rain on the roof?

Of course, I attributed most of our dwindling popularity to the bust. Whether it was true or not, I was certain that rock fans had dismissed us as a bunch of square establishment finks, and as the lone remaining member of the group who had been involved in the bust, I was guilt-ridden over that thought.

Back in late November, while the album was being prepared for release, a column had appeared in issue No. 2 of a brand new rock publication called *Rolling Stone*, for the first time cluing in national music fans on details of the bust. The piece, with a headline of "LIKE ZALLY, WE ARE ALL VICTIMS," was written by Ralph Gleason, our old friend from the *San Francisco Chronicle* and *Rolling Stone*'s co-founder along with Jann Wenner (whom Ralph would grow to despise). Gleason was sweet and fair and attempted to rehabilitate The Lovin' Spoonful in the eyes of those who were sullying our name.

Gleason explained what had really happened, and how the fallout against us was worse than us working with a narc. He quoted Cass Elliot's reaction to people telling her not to speak to Zally — "'He's one of my best friends,' she yelled. 'That's ridiculous.'" He reminded readers that Zal was Canadian and his livelihood was at stake, adding, "God knows what other pressures were brought to bear. And I do not condone fingering someone either. It was a terrible, tragic thing and in some ways the ones hurt the most were Steve and Zal." And then he offered his full-on support for us:

> But if the Spoonful makes a new album, I will buy it and I will listen to their songs and I will go to see them and I will hope and do hope that their music grows and flourishes. It has been a very great thing and their contribution has been huge and the pleasure they have given has been immeasurable. Do you believe in the magic? Really? Then it seems to me that the only thing to do is forgive and try to forget.

In what was to me the most meaningful moment of the piece, he asked readers to put themselves in our shoes: "'Shove that hot lead up my ass and I'll name everybody,' Lenny Bruce said once. That's reality. If they put YOU in a cell and belt your head around with saps and third degree you — psychologically or physically, it's the same thing — will YOU hold your mud?"

I was beyond grateful, and remain grateful, that Gleason (who died in 1975 of a heart attack at age 58) had taken up our cause. I'm sure there were people in the counterculture, including people at *Rolling Stone* (maybe even his eventual nemesis Jann Wenner), who gave him shit for defending us. He was fair, and what he wrote about the bust for *Rolling Stone* in 1967 is still the most widely referenced article on the subject. If Gleason had destroyed us or said nothing, who knows what the witch hunt would have been like or how the issue would be perceived today?

But the article came out roughly a month before *Everything Playing* was released, and though Gleason bought our new album, it appears *Rolling Stone*'s readership was not inspired to do the same. We continued to get nice turnouts for our concerts, but in the business of making and selling new records, it looked like we were dead meat.

Our first single of 1968, "Money," stalled at No. 48.

Not long after, as we halfheartedly plotted our next move, John Sebastian broke the news, just before a tour rehearsal: he was leaving the group.

"I've talked it over with Bob [Cavallo]," he said. "And this is it. After this next round of dates, I'm leaving the group. You guys can carry on if you want to, but I'm out."

It was probably inevitable. When both of our first two releases of 1968 had become failures, at least by the lofty standards we'd set with seven straight singles in the Top 10 and three albums (including the *Best Of*) in the Top 15, you could feel the spirit dying, especially in John. Jerry's presence had given us the will to carry on and at least try, and we'd made a noble effort, but we were a runaway train and there was too much momentum to stop it. We were all bored and burnt out, and were sick of each other too.

There was a lot of friction, in particular between John and Joe. John and Zally's deteriorating relationship had hidden the fact that John and Joe had never exactly been soul mates. John clearly did not respect Joe's musical contributions or his abilities as a player, and wasn't making much of an effort to disguise it. Joe thought John was pretentious, had a false sense of superiority and claimed too much credit for the success of the group. Joe felt that John slighted him, and the Irish in Joe makes him carry around resentments like he has a wheelbarrow.

I don't remember any raised voices at this meeting, but once John left there was a natural worry expressed over what would become of our contract. John's departure and the key man clause meant Kama Sutra was under no obligation to allow us to continue, even though we still had albums left on our deal. We had about three months of live dates left with John in the group, so that would at least buy us some time. Should we should try to press on as The Lovin' Spoonful minus John? Even if our management and label were supportive of that, I frankly didn't see an easy path to success. Hell, people had stopped buying our records with John, our primary writer and vocalist, still in the group — did we really think they were going to all of a sudden start buying Spoonful records by Steve, Joe and Jerry? Short of getting John Lennon to agree to join us, I suspected we were done.

But Joe felt differently. For one, Joe had been on the brink of a solo career when he joined The Spoonful as our drummer, and I think he believed he had what it took to be the frontman. To be fair, he absolutely had the looks and a strong enough voice to make that argument, though there was no precedent that we knew of for a band's drummer coming out front and morphing into a full-time vocalist (at least until Phil Collins). The other point — also valid — was that our contemporaries, like The Turtles, were having hits written by songwriters that were already a part of the Koppelman-Rubin stable, guys like Garry Bonner and Alan Gordon. If Bonner and Gordon could start feeding us songs that were as good as "Happy Together," well, maybe our fans could overlook the changed dynamics of the band and see us in a whole new light.

Frankly, I didn't like those suggestions — it felt like it was going to be a totally different band. I would have stayed in The Kingsmen if I'd wanted to play someone else's songs. But when there are bills to pay and you're talking about your livelihood, you're not going to dismiss any suggestion out of hand, so I didn't give a firm no right away, and neither did Jerry. There was a brief glimpse when we even thought seriously about bringing Zally back to the group, but after one meeting, during which Zally exhibited a lot of his old bad habits (i.e., abusing Joe), that idea was quickly abandoned.

We did manage to get a couple of songs recorded in the spring at Sunset Sound Recorders in Hollywood, on a day off after we'd worked some gigs with John at Disneyland. There was a medium-sized earthquake amid this run of shows, which I should have taken as a bad sign. We cut a song called "Never Going Back," written by ex–Kingston Trio member John Stewart, who had also written "Daydream Believer" for The Monkees. Joe sang, Stewart himself played guitar and Red Rhodes accompanied on pedal steel. The producer was Chip Douglas, who'd worked with Jerry in The Modern Folk Quartet and had produced "Daydream Believer." I played the session, though for some reason Douglas erased my bass part, recorded over it and put himself down as the bass player in the session log. I liked the song, but when we released it as a single in July, even before word had leaked out about John's departure, it confirmed my fears by stalling at No. 73. (The other song recorded at Sunset Sound, "Baby I Could Be So Good at Loving You," was never released.)

One of my most prominent memories of those last few months of dates in 1968 was our final New York City show, at Avery Fisher Hall. We looked out into the front row and saw none other than Zal Yanovsky, accompanied by his own one-man admiration society — Eric Clapton. Clapton thought Zally was a genius, which should tell you all you need to know about Zal's abilities. For the past few months, I had been singing "Butchie's Tune" in concert, accompanying myself on acoustic guitar. I thought I sang it pretty well — I felt comfortable with country tunes, for some reason — and audiences always responded favorably. But as my turn came to sing the song on this show, I stepped to the mic with my guitar and could see Zalman, Clapton, an ex-girlfriend of mine named Christine Biddle (who had turned me on to the drug DMT, and to Tina Turner's "River Deep — Mountain High") and many friends from the city looking back at me. I played the first few chords, and when it came time to sing, not one word came into my mind. My brain was frozen, and as the seconds ticked away, it did not thaw. I stopped the song, turned to John and said, "Let's go on to the next song." Humiliating.

The last paid Lovin' Spoonful concert featuring John Sebastian took place on June 20, 1968, in Richmond, Virginia. All I remember about the show is that Tiny Tim was on the bill and there was a power outage at some point. How fitting. By the time "Never Going Back" came out, we'd already fulfilled our touring obligations with John.

Even with my career hanging in the balance, I took the summer of '68 off. I was burnt out — I hadn't taken a real, extended vacation that wasn't interrupted by some kind of band obligation since my Europe trip at the end of 1964. I still had some money from the signing of our new deal, and I rented a bungalow in the Hamptons. I also had a new girl on my arm, reflecting my increasing success and confidence with the ladies.

The sea change for me with women had really happened in the fall of 1967, when I'd started hanging out at Salvation nightclub in Sheridan Square on the Upper East Side. I was not really one to cut a rug as a dancer but had been convinced to go to a Halloween party there by my friend Fudge, who in a triumph of bad taste talked me into wearing body paint and going to Salvation as a half white/half black man. I don't remember much about the party, but it was that night that I met a hot waitress named Denise Mourges. Denise, a native Manhattanite and wild party girl, accompanied me home that night. We were extremely hot and heavy for a period of a few months throughout the fall and winter, and in January had even taken a short trip down to the Bahamas along with my friend Peter Davey and his girlfriend and future wife, Sandy Salter. Things were starting to get serious — I'd had plenty of one-night stands, but Denise was the first girl who showed me the benefits of a steady relationship, primary among them being increasingly better sex.

Shortly after that, I was hanging out at my favorite watering hole, Churchill's, when my friend from the Hamptons, Jody Porter, walked in. Jody, who was about a foot shorter than me but fancied himself a tough guy, came in looking for me based on some perceived slight he thought I'd conferred on him. He was poking his finger in my chest, but I don't really remember what it was about, because I was way more focused on this little blonde sweetie he had on his arm, who spoke with a British accent. Her name was Patsy Smith and she was an English model. Within a week, Patsy was riding with me in the Ferrari out to Westhampton, and we had a very intense affair for probably a couple of weeks. It was during this period that Denise came down to a Lovin' Spoonful rehearsal to talk to me about moving into my West 12th Street house, which I'm sure we'd previously discussed. Given what was going on with Patsy, I told Denise I wasn't sure I wanted to be in a committed relationship. And damn if Denise didn't wind up and smash me square in the jaw, almost hard enough to knock me down, right in front of the whole band, who were just standing there in awestruck silence. I totally deserved it too.

The relationship with Patsy Smith was brief, but it was quite the eye-opener. One afternoon I came home to 12th Street to find Patsy already in bed, and on the phone. She told me she was talking to her lesbian lover and asked me if her phone-a-friend could listen in while I screwed Patsy. Well, OK. In the midst of this, Patsy — who I'd already begun to suspect liked it a bit rough — asked me to smack her in the face while her friend listened. After confirming that I'd heard that request right, I obliged. It didn't turn me on like it did her. I wasn't sure how the friend on the telephone liked it, but this kind of thing was all rather bizarre for a nice Catholic boy like me. It wasn't long before Patsy returned to England permanently — which, given how weird things were getting, was frankly a relief — and I never heard from her after that, though I had occasion to read about her in the tabloids 25 or so years later.

Patsy Smith's daughter Mandy made scandalous headlines in

England when it was revealed she'd been dating Rolling Stones bass player Bill Wyman since the age of 13. Mandy and Wyman would later marry (and divorce) when she came of age, so I guess thanks is due to the Smith family for seeing the underlying sexiness in rock 'n' roll bass players. The story went from the ridiculous to the sublime when Patsy herself married Bill Wyman's son, Stephen, thus making her both the mother-in-law and daughter-in-law of Bill Wyman. I can't say Patsy's life would have been any less complicated if we'd stayed together.

But the girl who would end up making the biggest impact on my life during this period, and the one who'd be accompanying me on my summer vacation in the Hamptons, was Patti Curtis. I'd met Patti, of all places, at Allen's Bar and Grill, where my ex-girlfriend Denise's father, George, was the day manager and bartender. I haven't the foggiest idea what I would have been doing at Allen's after I'd broken up with Denise — George and I had been friends, but he must have wanted to shoot me right there in the bar.

I was sitting at the front table at Allen's with some friends, looking out onto Third Avenue, when I spotted this hot brunette with a camera slung over her shoulder getting ready to cross the street toward us. I asked one of the people at my table if they knew who this babe was, and he said, "That's Patti Curtis. You should meet her, I think you would like her."

At that moment in the door she walked and my friend — it may have been Jody — introduced me to Patti. We struck up a conversation and hit it off right away. As it turned out, Patti and her sister Carol were two hot babes who were apparently well known among the East Side preppies. Carol (who would tragically die in a fire soon after I met Patti) was the wild one, but Patti was quiet and anxious to begin a career as a top fashion model. Before a week had gone by, we had dinner, and were steadies thereafter. She came with me to Richmond for The Spoonful's last concert with John, and of course Joe tried to pick her up right in front of me — or under the table, to be more precise.

I met Patti's mother, Maxine, a few days later at Gino's, a "ladies who lunch" restaurant on Lexington Avenue, and the first thing she said to me, even before hello, was "Do you have any money?" As in, "Are you rich enough for my daughter?" I just laughed. She was a real character. I loved Maxine, and I was in love with Patti. We quickly became inseparable, and after I met her I began spending less and less time with the 88th Street crew.

My mother, who had become a real estate agent, leased us a small house right next to hers in Westhampton, and we had a great summer. Skip was nearby, and we had frequent visitors, including The Mamas and the Papas, who came out for a few days. We'd take a speedboat out and go waterskiing, have wild parties all night, smoke pot and take acid. And with some time and space to clear my head, I even found some time to write new music during the day.

When the dust settled after that great summer of '68, it was time to think about work again. My batteries were recharged after a couple of months of R&R, so I called Bob Cavallo to see what was up. I'd had very little contact with The Spoonful circle since our last show in Richmond, so he gave me the lowdown.

There would be a new Lovin' Spoonful album, but I would not be on it and neither would Jerry. Joe Butler had been given the right to use the Spoonful name, and hadn't asked us to be on the new record. I guess he sensed our lack of enthusiasm for the project — I would not have made that album anyway if it meant I couldn't take the summer off.

As you might imagine, *Revelation: Revolution '69* (which was actually released at the end of '68) sounded almost nothing like a Lovin' Spoonful album. "Never Going Back" was on there, along with three compositions by Bonner/Gordon (including "Me About You," which was released as a single) and three more by another Koppelman-Rubin songwriting team, Ralph Dino and John Sembello. Joe had a hand in writing the three other songs, one of which was a horrific seven-minute anti-war sound collage called "War Games." The title track also expressed anti-war sentiments — a major change, since The Lovin' Spoonful had always been willfully apolitical. The cover of the album, which was supposed to be called *Amazing Air* and packaged with clear vinyl until a last-second change by Kama Sutra, bore the words *Revelation: Revolution '69 — The Lovin' Spoonful Featuring Joe Butler*. The image on the cover depicts a naked Joe running ahead of an unidentified naked woman (with nipples airbrushed out, naturally) and a lion (also naked). John Sebastian still seethes over that cover, and the fact that the album exists at all.

Revelation: Revolution '69 is generally dismissed by critics and is often left unmentioned in Spoonful discographies, though it's been reissued on CD a couple of times. I think Joe is embarrassed about it today, which is probably the appropriate emotion. Frankly the album is not as bad as its reputation, but I think it would have been better respected had Joe not used The Lovin' Spoonful name. Since he did, it feels to a lot of people like the drummer was trying to pull a fast one on record buyers — though, to be fair, milking every last drop out of the name sounds more like the calling card of Kama Sutra and Koppelman-Rubin, not Joe Butler. The benefit it would have had for Joe (and all of us, frankly) is to check one more album off the seven-album deal and get us closer to recouping our advance.

But the fact that Joe got to make the album was a good sign, because it meant Koppelman-Rubin and Kama Sutra weren't just interested in John Sebastian, as we'd previously suspected. Also in 1968, they'd release Zally's uneven and half-serious solo album, *Alive and Well in Argentina*, which was produced by none other than his Lovin' Spoonful replacement, Jerry Yester. It might seem obvious now that, as a proven singer and songwriter, John was the most obviously marketable solo act in our group, but remember that in 1968, before The Beatles broke up, there wasn't a whole lot of precedent for singers breaking off from popular rock groups and becoming solo stars. This was also a time in the record business when companies were willing to develop artists and didn't think solely in terms of whether every record you released would sell millions.

It was in this environment that I walked into the offices of Koppelman-Rubin with my 12-string guitar, and my brother Skip's bandmate Steve Soles and his guitar, to try to convince them to let me make a record. I'd written a song called "If I Stare," a big country shuffle that I felt really good about. Steve Soles, a great player and singer from the Hamptons who would go on to work with Bob Dylan, T-Bone Burnett and Elvis Costello, among others, was there to help me present the song. Steve played guitar and sang the lead vocal; I played the 12-string and helped with the harmonies.

When we finished, Charley Koppelman was effusive. "That's a fuckin' hit!" Charley said. "If your other songs are as good as that one, we'll let you make a record, sure."

I told Charley and Don that, yes, I was working on some other things I was just as excited about. I may have also taken the opportunity to remind them of my writing credits on some of our hits. (I probably did not bring up my vocal on "Priscilla Millionaira" in this meeting.) I managed to convince them, and they booked me studio time.

For part of my backing band, I'd be using members of Skip's group, including Steve Soles, and a guy named Guy Phillips from The Oxpetals. Before summer's end, three old Hamptons summer friends of mine named Jock McLean, Arma Andon and Billy Beattie had brought these guys from a group named The Oxpetals out to the Hamptons to meet me. Jock and Arma, who had worked for The Beatles as part of Nemperor Artists (the American partner to Brian Epstein's NEMS) were trying to talk me into producing the group, which they'd begun managing. (Jock and Arma also brought me an acetate of "Hey Jude," which I listened to, loved and, much to my financial detriment, tossed in the trash!) I didn't have much interest — I was still on vacation — but they seemed like cool hippie kind of dudes. I particularly connected with Guy, who asked me to call him "Yug" ("Guy" spelled backwards). OK, dude. The Oxpetals were mostly pass-the-hat folkies who had come from Virginia Beach, Roanoke and Northern Virginia as part of the same small music scene that produced Emmylou Harris and later Juice Newton. In fact, three members of The Oxpetals were crashing with Harris, who was still working part-time as a waitress in New York when I met the group.

Once I got my record deal, I called up Yug to see if he wanted to work the sessions, which were to take place at Olmstead Studios on 40th Street in midtown Manhattan. I told all the musicians involved that I'd pay them union scale plus any overtime they worked, which was icing on the cake. The studio owner, Gene Radice, had just come off producing a record for The Left Banke and was a veteran engineer whose credits would come to include Hendrix and The Velvet Underground. My brother Skip would be assisting with the production.

Things were going well early on, or at least I thought so. We had good versions of "If I Stare" and another one I liked called "Mississippi Belle" in the can, but in retrospect I took too many liberties and the atmosphere in the studio was too freewheeling. I knew how to produce and arrange the music, but I wasn't a task-master like Erik Jacobsen, and at this time in my career was not one to foster a disciplined, controlled environment in the studio. Sessions would go all night long, and since I was abiding by union rules all the musicians went from making full scale to full scale with overtime. Quickly, and unbeknownst to me, the costs got out of control, which apparently set off alarm bells with Koppelman-Rubin, as did the fact that — no shock here — I couldn't really sing. I'd been getting drunk and gutting my way through the vocals, but they were not anyone's idea of quality singing. Skip tried to impart some of the same tips John and Jerry had on "Priscilla Millionaira," with similar results. Anyway, I showed up at the studio one day and was told by Radice that the plug had been pulled on the project. I was furious and felt like I'd been set up to fail by Koppelman and Rubin, who'd never relayed to me any kind of budget parameters or timeline for delivery. If they needed an album in the can in four days, wouldn't it have made sense to get me a veteran producer to keep things on task?

It was incredibly discouraging, and was for all intents and purposes the last time I'd deal directly with Charley Koppelman and Don Rubin. Which was sort of a silver lining. When people ask me about the direction The Lovin' Spoonful might have gone if John and Zally had stayed in the band and we'd recorded into the '70s, I tell them the sounds we were pursuing on my never-completed solo album offer a possible indication. Thinking about how "If I Stare" was pure country, and how Zally was a Floyd Cramer disciple who ended up playing behind Kris Kristofferson, plus the country tinges that were already part of our sound, I think you might have seen us go in a similar country-rock direction to The Byrds — combined with some of the folkie touches of John's solo work from that period. We certainly weren't going to become a psychedelic or jam band, but I do think we could have delivered the goods with a more Bakersfield-style country-rock type of sound. Too bad we'll never know.

With my solo project dead, I was free to produce The Oxpetals. The story of their one and only album, which was finally released by Mercury Records in 1970, is worthy of its own dramatic film release. I'm still not sure whether you'd file that movie under comedy or horror, however. Here's your cast of characters:

Benjamin Herndon (bass, group spokesperson, lead songwriter): Lead songwriter who was great at writing interesting album material, hits not so much. Marginal bass player at best but good guy who stayed with Patti and me frequently at our new apartment on West 79th Street, only after I recommended he stay at the Albert Hotel and he got his guitar stolen on the second day there.

Steve Pague (rhythm guitar, songwriter): Most spiritual member of the band, also into meditation and yoga. Had played in a Lovin' Spoonful tribute band in Virginia called Full Measure. Arrival in New York was delayed while he served a four-month prison term for dodging the draft. Wrote songs that were almost Krishna-themed, none of which sounded like single material either.

Guy "Yug" Phillips (lead guitar, songwriter): The sensible and level-headed one in the group. Experience in rock bands and playing behind folk artists. Highly skeptical of "fucking cosmic shit" being proselytized by almost everyone around him, in particular Steve Pague.

Bobby Webber (keyboards): Best natural musician in the band, could play anything and covered for Benjamin's inadequacies on bass via organ pedals. A difficult personality to manage.

Dan "Ace" Allison (drums): Biggest drug user in the group, most notably acid. As drug use increased, he preferred garbage can lids to a conventional drum kit.

Gene Kieffer (manager and initial financial backer): Successful owner of a four-color separation printing company called National Colorgraphics that had just moved to New York; had also run the successful 1966 re-election campaign for Harold Hughes, Democratic governor of Iowa. Natural PR guy and consummate bullshitter who'd had a midnight conversion to spirituality and the teachings of Edgar "the Sleeping Prophet" Cayce, which is how he got hooked up with fellow Cayce acolytes The Oxpetals. Also tried hard to convert The Oxpetals to Eastern-style philosophy. No experience in the music business, but loved The Moody Blues album *In Search of the Lost Chord* and was focused on matching its success via The Oxpetals.

Edgar Cayce ("The Sleeping Prophet"): Deceased since 1945. American psychic, prophet, reputed healer and philosopher who gave psychic readings while under hypnosis. Had some thought-provoking teachings that I still subscribe to today, focused on natural healing, organic health and quality sustainable living for a small planet. Some other teachings, including his belief in the lost island of Atlantis, I think less of. Probably would have been surprised to have his teachings be the focus of rock 'n' roll songs performed by five long-haired men.

In Search of the Lost Chord (Moody Blues album, 1968): Fine, spiritually focused second album by a band from Birmingham, England, that had been a professional group since 1964 and knew what they were doing both as a live act and in a studio setting.

Moosepac: Communal house and lakefront property in north-west New Jersey, rented to The Oxpetals and their associates by Dr. Harold Reilly, a physiotherapist and disciple of Edgar Cayce who ran Cayce's foundation in Virginia Beach. House at Moosepac was legendary for being the only place where The Oxpetals sounded good. I constantly tried to convince the group to do "out" gigs to help their sound come together, to little avail.

Simon Hayes (vice president, Mercury Records): Tall, skinny, red-haired Englishman who dressed in Carnaby Street fashions. Heard The Oxpetals demo and immediately wanted to sign the group.

Irv Green (president and founder, Mercury Records): Legendary music business pioneer who traveled to Moosepac at the behest of Simon Hayes to hear the band play. After four or five songs performed in the Moosepac living room, jumped up and said to Simon Hayes, "Let's go ahead," also signing off on a budget for equipment so the band could go on the road to promote the record. Became concerned when recording exceeded the planned budget and scheduled delivery date, and also at the lack of an obvious Top 40 hit on the record.

Muhammad Ali (boxer): On a visit to Mercury Records' offices on West 57th Street, I shared an elevator ride with him. He was very gracious and friendly, and said he even knew who The Lovin' Spoonful were. Quite a thrill. One of the best parts of The Oxpetals saga for me personally, and it lasted 35 seconds.

Steve and Patti Boone: Helped form Purple Planet Productions. Married November 23, 1968. Patti and I were together constantly right from the beginning — we were the ultimate cosmic lovebirds — and there was little doubt that marriage was in our future. Just as we were starting to make those plans, Patti became pregnant. Not wanting to do the hippie thing and have a baby out of wedlock, we decided in a kind of fevered rush to get married. There was a whole brouhaha over Patti's not being Catholic and my wanting to get married in the Immaculate Conception Church in Westhampton Beach (if for no other reason than the irony of its name), but in the end we gave the church some money and all was forgotten. Everyone under 40 was higher than the church bells that beautiful day in November, and my folks threw a great reception at their house. True to his everlasting nature, my dad managed to freak out Patti's mom with a very mild (for him) comment on the Jewish population of Westhampton Beach, resulting in Maxine refusing to come downstairs for the cake cutting. All in all, it was a very nice ceremony and reception, and what looked like the warming of the nest for the newest member of the Boone family. But shortly after, Patti tragically lost the baby in February, under the influence of a minor hallucinogenic we'd both taken. The good people at St. Luke's Hospital, who thought we were two hippies trying to get a free abortion in this pre–*Roe v. Wade* era, nearly let her bleed to death before they treated her. We lived part-time at Moosepac during this era.

Purple Planet Productions: A consortium including Steve and Patti Boone and Skip and Donna Boone, financed by Gene Kieffer and Mercury Records to produce The Oxpetals.

Warren Dewey (engineer): Fragile but talented engineer who quit midway through recording due to the incessant demands of the band, which already believed it was famous before it had sold its first record.

Magic PA system: Collection of speakers I flew to Indianapolis with Benjamin Herndon to hear, as Gene Kieffer had been told they could heal various illnesses. Sounded no better than the Voice of the Theater or contemporary speaker systems to me, but we had them built and they arrived at Moosepac three days before the band's important industry showcase. When they arrived they were enormous and four times louder than what we'd heard out in Indy, making the live sound difficult to mix and manage. Healed no illnesses that I know of. Also won the band no extra fans.

The Oxpetals (album, 1970): The country-rock-flavored record we somehow got made while meditating, eating vegetarian and saying no to fascism and imperialism, amongst other, more hedonistic pursuits. Album cover was an expensive four-color gatefold sleeve, done with help from Gene Kieffer's Colorgraphics company. After a lukewarm showcase for the press in 1969 before 500 people (including reporters from *Rolling Stone* and *Crawdaddy!*, as well as Zal Yanovsky), followed by a handful of even less successful gigs opening for Joe Cocker, Van Morrison and Traffic, Mercury quickly stopped promoting the record, which sank without a trace, and The Oxpetals were never heard from again, though I'd cross paths professionally with multiple members of the group over the years.

In spite of what we were up against, and some of the sarcasm above, I take full responsibility for the weakness of the record, and for The Oxpetals' failure to launch. I'd get better at it, but I was still new to producing and had a lot of trouble managing all the moving parts of the operation, especially amid all the extracurricular activities surrounding the band during that time. Right around the time of the press showcase at Moosepac, I quit out of complete exhaustion. The band was pissed and I'm sure Kieffer and Mercury were too, but I had no confidence I could get that band to where the members thought they belonged. They considered themselves artists, not performers, and I could never convince them that the key to success was developing their sound in a live setting.

Curiously, at some point in 1969 between the delivery and release of the Oxpetals album, I was called into a meeting with one of the band's initial champions, Nat Weiss, who knew I'd quit the project though I don't think he knew how harrowing it had gotten. Nat was a great guy who I knew through Jock and Arma, and he was trying to give me a pep talk to convince me to start on a new project of his.

He slid a record across the table to me.

"James Taylor," I said. "Yeah, I've heard this record. This guy's good. What does this have to do with me?"

"You want to produce his next record?" Nat said.

Nat had done The Beatles' merchandising deals in the U.S., and had expanded from that to go into business with Brian Epstein in 1966 in a company called Nemperor Artists, Inc. The purpose of the company was to be the American management arm for Epstein's artists. Epstein died in 1967, but when Apple Records was founded a year later, Nat and Nemperor became the U.S. management reps for everyone signed to Apple.

James Taylor had recorded his (mildly successful) first album in London for Apple in 1968, which meant he was managed by Nat through Nemperor. Taylor's producer on that first Apple album had been Peter Asher from Peter and Gordon, but Asher had recently gone to work for MGM Records in New York, meaning he was not free to work with Taylor, who was still under contract to record albums for Apple until 1970. Taylor was back stateside and plotting his next move.

Which is where I could have stepped into the picture, apparently. I'm not sure today how many people Nat was talking to or how it might have progressed once I met with James, but it sure seemed like I was being offered a production deal for James Taylor. Except that I didn't want it, not after the Oxpetals debacle.

"Sorry, Nat," I said. "I know this guy's talented, but I just don't think I'm cut out to be a producer."

Nat Weiss looked me straight in the eyes and said, "Steve, I like you. You're a great idea man. But you don't know how to finish up."

He was right, and I took his words to heart, even while rejecting his offer. And it all worked out for James Taylor, of course.

As it happened, Peter Asher got fired from MGM as part of the same corporate maneuvering that saw John Sebastian temporarily and unhappily signed to MGM Records, thus freeing Asher up to work with James Taylor again. With Apple in dire financial shape, Paul McCartney made a personal appeal to the other Beatles, probably at Asher's behest, to release Taylor from his Apple contract. By the end of 1969, Taylor was recording the album (*Sweet Baby James*) that would make him a megastar as part of the Warner Brothers stable. Would all this have played out the same way had I taken Nat's offer and at least met with James Taylor? Who knows. I'd like to think I wouldn't have ruined his career. Maybe he would have helped mine.

But the point was, after the demise of The Spoonful, the aborted sessions for my own album and the failure of The Oxpetals, I felt like I'd just taken my third strike in the music business.

I'd be my own umpire in this case — I was out.

Chapter 10
NEVER GOING BACK

There was never any official confirmation that I was no longer a rock star. It's not like the army — they don't give you papers that say you've been honorably discharged from tearing up hotel rooms without consequence, being recognized on the street and having random sex with strangers who think they know you.

But by the middle of 1970, I knew I was no longer a rock star because my bank account told me so. It had been three years since I'd gotten that sizable chunk of change as part of the seven-album deal, and that was gone. It had been two years since The Lovin' Spoonful had played its last show, not that I ever made more than scraps from touring — concerts were not monetized to favor the artist like they are today. The last real money I'd gotten had been when I signed the production deal with The Oxpetals, but a lot of that had gone into band-related expenses. Some had been nickel-and-dimed on drugs, but I also had a wife to support and our day-to-day living expenses were climbing and hardly anything new was coming in.

Publishing and record royalties, such as they were in 1970, when no one was buying our records in great quantities, were tied up thanks to mergers and acquisitions involving Koppelman-Rubin, our

206

record company (Kama Sutra) and its distributor (MGM Records). The owners of Kama Sutra had formed a new label called Buddah Records, which had started distributing our records when the MGM distribution deal expired in 1969, although at the same time MGM (erroneously) thought it had the rights to John's solo work via the terms of our old Lovin' Spoonful contract. John and Bob Cavallo thought differently, signing with Warner Brothers/Reprise, but the album got delayed a year while MGM and Warners (who concurrently released the same album with different covers) fought over John in court. In the midst of this, John was hanging out on Long Island with David Crosby, my old New York neighbor Stephen Stills and Graham Nash, who were talking about putting together a "supergroup." John had a chance to join but declined. John and Lorey broke up soon afterward, when John discovered she'd been having an affair with Graham Nash, who wrote the song "Lady of the Island" about her. John moved to California.

Meanwhile, in 1968 Koppelman-Rubin had sold the publishing arm of their business, including my songs, to a group called Commonwealth United, for the sum of $5 million. After pocketing that money, Charley and Don were retained to run Commonwealth United, but soon afterward the company went bankrupt, and somehow our publishing ended up back in the hands of Charley, Bob Cavallo and Erik Jacobsen, and our masters ended up in the hands of Buddah.

All this made my head hurt, and I didn't bother following the money, because I'd been told we never earned back our advance from the seven-album deal. Supposedly, any royalties that were coming in were just paying down the debt from that advance and my other pocket-change payouts over the years.

So I was broke, not that the IRS thought so. Sometime in early 1970 the government came to me with an enormous tax bill I had no prayer of paying. They were taxing me on my earnings from the past four years, which of course were mostly on paper. I had nothing saved in the bank to pay taxes with. Bob Cavallo had warned me this day would come, but I naïvely figured that since I'd been generating a good income since the middle of 1965, I could always work my way out of debt. But now there was no work, at least none that I wanted to do or that could make a significant dent in what the IRS said I owed them. I couldn't even sell my Ferrari, which was gone. I was underwater.

As soon as all this became apparent, I began getting more serious about my escape.

Getting away had been on my mind ever since the bust happened, frankly. I never adjusted to the lack of privacy of a rock 'n' roll life and was already growing weary of the non-musical obligations of a rock star. As early as January 1968, when I took the trip to the Bahamas with Denise, Peter and Sandy, I'd begun thinking seriously about sailing again. It had been in my blood since I was a kid, and the passion never left. On the way back from the Bahamas, we stopped in Miami, where I fell in love with a 40-foot schooner I saw docked on the Miami River. It was a yacht that had been converted from a small island freighter. It needed some work but had a price tag I thought was reasonable.

Back when I'd first started making money in The Lovin' Spoonful, I made a gentlemen's agreement with Peter, who'd traveled around Europe with me on a motorcycle a lifetime ago, that I would pay his bills and general living expenses until his inheritance came due; as soon as that happened, he would return the favor and buy me a live-aboard sailboat. But Peter hadn't gotten his inheritance yet, and I couldn't make the financials line up to buy this yacht, even though I went as far as putting down a deposit.

The seed was planted, though. By 1970, I wanted to sail and be at sea more than anything in the world, and had no work obligations that said I couldn't. In April 1970, Patti and I scrounged together some money and went to the U.S. Virgin Islands on what was our first official vacation. I had received listings on three sailboats that I wanted to look at, including one that sounded a lot like a vessel I'd been taken with when I'd seen a spread about the Virgin Islands in *National Geographic* back in February 1968. I looked at the first two boats, but they were not quite what I had in mind. I was told the third one I was scheduled to see, which was called *Cygnus*, had been booked at the last second for a chartered cruise to other islands. It looked like I'd struck out in my yacht quest, but as Patti and I were sitting on the beach at Trunk Bay in St. John, I looked out to see a boat anchored maybe 50 yards off the beach.

"I think that's *Cygnus*," I said. I was drawn to this boat, so much so that I spontaneously dived into the water and just started swimming out to it. Sure enough it was *Cygnus*. The owner, Bruce, was sitting in the cockpit, entertaining a couple who were also looking to buy the boat. He was surprised I'd swum up and I think was impressed with my enthusiasm, but asked me to come back in 30 minutes and said he'd show it to me then.

"That's fine," I said. "I'll be back with my wife." I swam back to shore and a half-hour later Patti swam back with me. Within five minutes I knew I'd found the boat I would buy. It not only looked like the one I'd seen in *National Geographic* — it was the exact same boat. Bruce told me he'd allowed *Nat Geo* to photograph *Cygnus* with the thought that the publicity might help drum up some business for his charter company. And it was absolutely perfect for living aboard. It had two private staterooms, a large galley, a large dining saloon and all the mechanical gear necessary to support an independent life on a sailboat. In my mind, I was already living on it.

The only problem was the price tag. It was priced to move because Bruce was anxious to move back to California, but he was asking $22,500. In 1970 you could buy a nice home for that amount. And, as mentioned, I was already looking at a serious IRS bill I couldn't pay, so how was I going to come up with 22 grand? But the only reason I'd been looking at all was because of the promise Peter had made to me. That evening back at our hotel, Patti and I talked it over. We both thought the boat was big enough to live on, and from the initial appearance it seemed to be in fantastic condition. We decided that whatever it took, we were going to buy the *Cygnus*.

As soon as we got back to New York I sold my one remaining asset, putting an ad in the Sunday *New York Times* to sell my Land Rover. I scraped together enough cash to put down a $10,000 deposit, then started working on Peter. I had to convince him to sign a letter of intent promising to pay off the balance, and since he hadn't fully inherited his money yet, it took a whole lot of him convincing his financial advisors to agree to give me the letter, followed by a whole lot more talking to Bruce and his wife to convince them I would come through when I said I would. But ultimately I made a deal on both ends and *Cygnus* was mine.

I guess I could have just as easily asked Peter to help pay off my IRS bill, but that hadn't been our deal, and it doesn't sound very rock 'n' roll, does it?

Patti and I had a yard sale, getting rid of everything we couldn't fit into a four-by-four-by-four packing crate. My belongings aboard *Cygnus* would consist of my Guild 12-string; some hippie books, including the *Whole Earth Catalog* and *The Urantia Book*; some how-to manuals on sailboat care and the cruising lifestyle; basic cooking utensils; a tool kit; a camera and lenses; and last but not least, my beloved harmonium, which I found a spot for in the main cabin. We stocked the boat with a 100-pound bag of brown rice for cooking, and by early fall of '70, we were living on *Cygnus*, which was docked in St. Thomas at the Yacht Haven marina. We'd brought along our German shepherd, Blitz, and tabby cat, Spider. I was in heaven, as far away from the music business as possible and loving every minute of it.

I hadn't lost interest in music, though. In fact, I was becoming more interested in the new sounds I was hearing in the Islands, and it was rekindling a spirit that had been trampled by the rancor in The Lovin' Spoonful.

One of my neighbors at Yacht Haven was this young surfer dude named Scotty, who turned me on to reggae over frequent rounds of banana daiquiris on his boat. He played The Wailers and Jimmy Cliff and Toots and the Maytals a good two years before anyone in the U.S. had heard of these people. I was captivated by these sounds, which had the most infectious beat.

One night after I first got to Yacht Haven and had gone to bed relatively early, I was awoken out of a deep sleep by the sound of loud music coming across the harbor. As I sat listening in the darkness, this music became so compelling that I put on a pair of shorts, a T-shirt and some flip-flops, and walked over to the lounge that was part of the marina complex. The only words I could make out coming from the singer's mouth were "drunk and disorderly," which was a phrase I could relate to. When I walked in, what I saw onstage was the oddest combination of two or three different steel drums, a small standard drum kit, electric bass and electric guitar and a couple of brass horns. The singer also doubled as a percussionist. I had just been introduced to Mighty Sparrow (real name: Slinger Francisco), and a style of music called soca. The last time I'd been this impressed by music had been when I'd sat in the Night Owl watching Fred Neil sing.

Soca wasn't anything like the reggae sounds Scotty had passed along. The beat was faster and the horns had a Latin-style influence. It was a lot like calypso, only with rock and Latin beats. The occasion of this show was carnival week, which in the Caribbean is a week of celebration and music. All the islands do it at different times of the year, and as I was just finding out, this was St. Thomas' week to celebrate.

I stayed at the bar until closing that night, and then returned to go to sleep with the sounds of "Drunk and Disorderly" firmly etched in my mind. The next day, I headed to the nearest record store in downtown St. Thomas to find Mighty Sparrow's album, or anything else that might contain the same style of music. I found that the record store was full of artists like Mighty Sparrow and Lord Kitchener, and I bought a handful of records, took them back to the boat and spent the next several days listening to as much of it as I could. I was hooked.

Other than that event, the early days when *Cygnus* was docked at the marina were worry-free. It was when we actually took the sailboat out to do what it had been designed to do — sail — that things got hairy.

Up until 1970 my personal experience with handling boats under power or sail had been limited to a 24-foot sailboat, an 18-foot speedboat and one week on a 30-foot Pearson Triton bareboat charter in the Bahamas. *Cygnus* was 72 feet from tip to tip. Taking a boat that size out of an interior position in the marina slip, backing it down between the row of piers and then heading out for open water, surrounded by other anchored boats with swirling 15-knot trade winds cascading down from the hills overlooking Charlotte Amalie, can be nerve-wracking for even the most seasoned sailor, which I was not. During my time at Yacht Haven I took advantage of every opportunity I could to watch other skippers having to deal with similar circumstances, though you really only learn by doing.

For our first trip we loaded up with some provisions to sail from St. Thomas over to St. John and then on to the British Virgin Islands for about a week-long voyage with my crew, which consisted of Patti, my surfer friend Scotty, his wife Cheryl and my friend Bob Davis, who'd been acting as part-time caretaker of *Cygnus* when I was going back and forth to New York to finish up my final business there. As I started to back out of the slip, the wind was blowing across the harbor, perpendicular to the way I wanted to go. The mast and rigging of a sailboat, even without the sails up, act like a wind catcher, and any breeze more than a ripple crosswise to your intended direction of travel had better be compensated for, or you're going the way the wind blows whether you like it or not. I didn't fully understand this yet. The wind blew me completely down into the closed end of the slipway without enough room to extricate myself. I'd floated practically right up against the bar stools at Fearless Freddie's, where the entire bar was watching and snickering as I died of embarrassment.

Fearless Freddie's was like the cantina scene in *Star Wars*. In 1970, it was a melting pot at a main crossroads of the cruising sailor's highways. People from every country, speaking every language, following every custom and sailing every type of vessel would eventually end up at Yacht Haven in St. Thomas and specifically at Fearless Freddie's. From the day I moved onto *Cygnus* with my dog, cat, hippie chick wife, long hair, totally skinny tall frame and rumors of some connection to the rock star world, I was viewed with suspicion by many, derision by some and just a hint of friendliness by a few. This episode — trying to back my big old sailboat out of the slip without the advance preparation that a proper skipper would've given to it — only seemed to confirm their dismissal of me.

The only way to get *Cygnus* free of that situation was to pass lines to onlookers, and a friendly fellow sailor in a small dinghy then pulled my stern off into the direction it needed to go so I could continue on my way with the only final damage being the red face of humiliation.

So we were off, sailing down the south coast of St. Thomas with my full set of sails up at the urging of my spirited surfer friends. *Cygnus* was flying. It was a beautiful Caribbean day and she was sailing along like the true thoroughbred I believed her to be. That is, until Bob popped his head up from below. His voice was anguished.

"The floorboards are all floating about the cabin, and the boat is filling up with water," he said.

When you buy a sailboat, especially a used one, it's pretty much standard operating procedure to get done what's called a survey. This is just as it implies, where a marine surveyor goes over the entire boat and its gear and writes up a written inspection report for the prospective buyer. Normally this would be done with the boat hauled out of the water so the surveyor can inspect its entire interior and exterior. To save money, and because I was so sure that this boat came into my life on a cosmic collision, I had the survey done while the boat was in the water and I wasn't even there. Big mistake, as I was finding out.

I went down below and noted that the bilge pump was unable to keep up with the leak — it was only designed to keep up with the very small amount of water that collects daily from rain and other moisture that drips in along the prop shaft. We had turned off the engine once the sails were up, and since I knew there was a one-and-a-half-inch emergency pump that would drain any bilge water at a very fast rate and was driven by the diesel engine, I decided to start the engine and drain the bilge with the emergency pump. But when I hit the start switch for the engine, nothing happened. I switched to the other battery, hit the switch again, and still nothing. Now I was worried.

The next step was to sail with the wind to the closest land at Buck Island, a little island in St. Thomas just outside the main harbor of Charlotte Amalie, leaving just enough of the sails up to keep us moving. Once the sails were down, the leaking slowed dramatically, so much so that the electric bilge pump was able to start making progress on the leak.

Putting two and two together, it became obvious that the leak was caused by the pressure of the mast on the keel when it was compressed by the wind in the main sail and club jib (the second biggest sail). The diesel engine couldn't be started because we had the boat so far heeled over that seawater had been siphoned back in through the exhaust pipe and had filled up the inside of the diesel, preventing the starter motor from turning and in essence locking the engine.

With the worst of the crisis averted, we managed to sail under limited power (but no engine) to the clear water of Francis Bay on St. John and drop anchor for the night, and the next day we got *Cygnus* back to Yacht Haven. A great mechanic, a Frenchman named Jean Archie who was also the dive master at Yacht Haven, came aboard and quickly discovered that the source of the leak that had drowned the engine and flooded the floorboards was the garboard plank, which is the first plank up from the keel on a carvel-planked boat (with planks fastened end to end, rather than overlapping). It turns out that the compression from the main mast on the keel, when the main sail was up, was pushing down and separating the keel from the garboard and letting in ungodly amounts of water. After talking to some marine surveyors and other experienced sailors, the conclusion was that if I could refasten the garboard plank to the frames of the boat she might be able to sail again under all sails up. Within an hour, Jean got my diesel running like a brand new engine. He told me to change the oil three times in a row and run the engine every day, and that after that, it should be good to go. And welcome to the world of living on a cruising sailboat. Jean would become a good friend of mine and would be a very valuable source of information to this young, skinny kid who didn't know much of anything other than actually sailing the boat.

My first sailing expedition with *Cygnus* had begun with humiliation at Fearless Freddie's and ended with one thought: What have I done? That would not be the last time I'd ask that question.

Though the engine had been fixed, getting the plank fixed was the only way to prevent the leak from returning and to get *Cygnus* fully seaworthy again. The place with the best reputation for that type of repair was 35 miles away by ocean sail in St. Croix, but given what we'd encountered, I'd have to wait until the winds were gentle enough to attempt it. On a beautiful day, I set out with Patti, Peter, Sandy and Bob for a picturesque sail into the harbor of Christiansted, St. Croix. There were two separate channels by which you could enter the harbor. One channel took a longer route along a major sandbar, and the other was a more direct route, but the water was very shallow and it took careful navigation to get through the shorter channel and avoid hitting the sandbar. Guess which route I picked.

As I approached and passed Buck Island on St. Croix at a slow speed of six knots (about seven miles per hour), the channel appeared to be deep and dark blue in color. After the six-hour sail in the sun, my vision was pretty good and I felt really confident I'd found the proper channel into the harbor. All of a sudden, kaboom! The boat pounded into the sand bottom and ground to a halt. Panic ensued. We had run aground. Taking the sails down and putting the boat into reverse did absolutely nothing. Every wave that washed under the boat would lift it up and crash it again onto the sandbar with a sound that suggested the boat was about to break in two. We put an anchor down and tried to pull ourselves backward off the reef, but *Cygnus* was a 30,000-pound boat, and even with its 100-horsepower diesel engine, 18-inch prop and mighty cranks on the winch, the boat did not move an inch. Every 30 seconds, another wave would come under the boat and lift it up and pound it down. After about 15 minutes of this, someone approached in a 25-foot launch and asked us to toss him a line so he could try to tow us backwards off the reef. It was a generous offer — it wasn't going to be long before the pounding of the seas was going to start taking a nastier toll on the boat's hull. The skipper of the launch revved his engine mightily, and we revved *Cygnus'* engine with equal effort in reverse for a good 10 minutes . . . with no progress at all. We then got an idea to take one of the main mast halyards, attach a long line to it and run a small anchor off to the leeward side to try to heel the boat over so that the keel would be less deep into the water. With the diesel engine launch straining at max revs and *Cygnus'* engine churning the prop for all it was worth, and a couple of us winching the mast over to get the boat to heel as far as it could, slowly the boat backed itself off the sandbar and slipped into deep enough water for the keel not to be hitting bottom. Relief.

After some very careful re-charting of the course, I managed to get the boat up to the main dock at St. Croix Marine Railway, and began to make an inspection for any damage. Miraculously, it seemed that all that pounding had not taken a toll on the boat's hull. The bilge was not too full and the water level in the bilge was not rising. The skipper who'd helped us get off the sandbar came over and said he would send me a bill, which I was thrilled to pay. As *Cygnus* was lifted completely out of the water via the marine railway in advance of its repair, I finally saw the half of the boat which had been hidden from view when it was sitting at the dock. It was a very impressive sight in more ways than one. It reminded me of how big a task it was going to be to own and maintain a sailboat of this size. The bill for repairs drove that point home.

The surveyor took me down into the bilge and pointed out something that hadn't occurred to me, which would have turned up had I done a proper survey before buying the boat. *Cygnus* had been converted in the 1950s from a racing schooner into a cruising ketch by legendary naval architect John G. Alden, which necessitated steel reinforcement of the heavier, newly added main mast. It was now over 15 years since the conversion, and the relatively lightweight steel, along with the iron fasteners that held the planks to the steel floors, had become corroded after being in contact with salt water for all that time. The recommendation was to completely redo the steel floors and refasten the affected planks with new, proper fasteners and hardware. The estimate for these repairs was nearly $13,000 — more than half what I'd paid for the boat itself. I just laughed right in the guy's face, though I'm sure I wanted to cry.

And of course I'd cut myself off from all sources of income to indulge in my sailing fantasy. The IRS had placed a levy on any on-the-books income, so we were essentially living on money from friends and relatives and what little savings I had left in the bank. I had made a deal with Peter so the boat was going to be paid for, but to keep it ship-shape and safe as a place that was my new home, it was obvious I had a whole lot of learning to do. I had a pretty good background in carpentry and basic mechanics, so I wasn't too intimidated by all the work that would need to be done, but as I was finding out, anything that had "nautical" or "marine" associated with its name could automatically be counted on to cost a lot more than a similar product that was not designed for marine use. Things like paint for the bottom of the boat, bronze and stainless fasteners and fittings, and other pieces of gear for the operation and upkeep of the boat also had to be serviced or replaced regularly. This was going to be the beginning of a three-year learning experience that at times seemed like it was all too much, but in the end would be one of the best learning experiences I ever had.

Anyway, since I didn't have that kind of money but didn't want to give up on my dream of living on the sailboat, I asked the mechanic just to sink some new fasteners into the old steel floors and re-caulk the seams, and I would learn to live with the boat and not push it too hard depending on the wind and sea conditions. It was a major disappointment, since I'd been a racing sailor and had gotten a glimpse of what *Cygnus* could do when she went fast, but the boat was now over 30 years old and had never been designed to last this long. I had to learn a whole new set of rules to prevent my home at sea from sinking out from under me. We headed back to St. Thomas, down but not out.

Patti and I soon got used to living on board. Before too long we had become friends with more of the local cruisers and charter boat skippers. Once back in St. Thomas at the marina, the boat looked terrific all freshly painted, and we were comfortable at Yacht Haven, which had 110V AC shore power and a continual supply of fresh water, as well as nice hot showers in the marina office building and of course Fearless Freddie's. The crowd there was becoming a little friendlier toward the hippies with the long hair. And after my initial embarrassing effort, I began to learn to maneuver *Cygnus* within the tight spaces of the marina. I'd always been a pretty good driver of anything mechanical, and once I learned how to anticipate the unanticipated on a big sailboat and didn't try to do anything too quickly, progress to becoming a capable skipper was slow but sure. Patti was a city girl when she arrived on *Cygnus*, but had adjusted to life within the confines of a floating home that was just 14 feet at its maximum beam. She'd by now become a great navigator when we were out at sea, and had learned to work the galley kitchen like it was all she'd ever known. Patti was a great cook, learning how to make amazing meals with just a combination of organic brown rice, the fresh vegetables we could buy right on the dock and the occasional fresh fish or goat for protein.

After a good home-cooked meal one beautiful night, Patti and I, along with Bob Davis and a girl he was friends with, were sitting in the cockpit of *Cygnus*, which was tied up to a slip at Yacht Haven. It was such a nice evening, so we all took some LSD and were sitting and talking in the moonlight. The subject had turned to dealing with unexpected calamities when living aboard a sailboat. Hurricanes and fires were all animatedly considered, and as the LSD reached its peak intensity, the talk turned to how best to deal with the tsunami created by a major earthquake. It was about 10:30 and there were not too many people still up, but what began as a banging sound, like a hammer hitting concrete, built in volume and ferocity, which, combined with the already heightened state of awareness from the LSD, began to frighten us nearly back to sobriety. It was an earthquake — what else could it be? Had we called it into being by summoning the gods of nature? We all stared at each other, too frightened to do anything. At first I thought it was a group hallucination, but then the hatch on the boat next to us slid open and out popped the head of its skipper Bill, a seasoned veteran charter skipper who joined in with "What the fuck is going on out here?" Now I knew we had to spring into action. "Where is my axe?" I thought, making ready to chop away the dock lines when the tsunami hit. But then, just as suddenly as it had started, the banging began to subside, and in a minute it was all over. I found out the next day there had been a major earthquake somewhere near Puerto Rico, but apparently no land damage was done. It took me days to believe we had not created the earthquake simply by talking about it.

My past life felt light years away. I knew John had released his debut album, *John B. Sebastian*, and had done an impromptu set at Woodstock, stoned out of his mind. He'd also played the Isle of Wight Festival, where he welcomed to the stage a special guest — Zal Yanovsky, who was by then in Kris Kristofferson's touring band. John and Zally even played "Darling Be Home Soon" together at the Isle of Wight, which was hilarious to me. I also knew Joe had been performing to rave reviews in a theatrical production of *Hair*, and that Jerry was back in California working on music with his wife, Judy Henske, and also doing some production. But I couldn't have told you what was in the Billboard charts, nor did I care. I was living the life I wanted to live, with no boss to answer to and no clock to punch. My brother Mike, who was 10 years younger than me and about to start his senior year in high school, flew down to Martinique, where we were trying to get some repairs done for our one and only down-island sail, which included stops at all the Leeward and Windward Islands. Mike ended up living with us for the whole summer of 1971, and we had an absolute ball.

Amid the postcard-beautiful skies and sparkling blue water, little could I have sensed the darkness that was around the corner.

In the late fall of '71, Patti and I scheduled a trip back to the States to take care of some business, including a meeting with the IRS to see where I stood with my tax bill and to check in on the members of The Oxpetals, toward whom I still felt some responsibility even after I'd left and they'd broken up. While I was there, I'd also agreed to go into the city and pick up Peter's right-hand-drive Rolls-Royce, which was scheduled for some repairs out on Long Island. By this time, Peter and Sandy had rented a beautiful house with a great deck up in the hills overlooking Magen's Bay, one of the nicest locations in St. Thomas. I was glad for this development as Peter had been dealing with an increasingly worrisome drug problem.

From the very beginning of our friendship, Peter and I had smoked pot and taken pills. But while I was on the treadmill with The Spoonful (and still smoking pot and taking pills), Peter had fallen in with a crowd of artists that were into heavier drugs — opiates and powder heroin. Sandy came from this same fast-lane crowd and was a user too throughout the time that I knew her. I was not into hard drugs — I'd gotten temporarily hooked on morphine after my accident in 1960 and saw the hell that went with that — and tried to be the one to say, "Pete, let's go, I want to get out of here." But I wasn't always around, and Peter had fallen deeper and deeper under the spell of the really bad stuff. He'd gone through periods of being clean over the years, but it was a constant battle, as all addiction is.

One of the rationales for him coming to St. Thomas was that he could get away from New York and the easy access to dope there.

That effort seemed to be working. Peter told us we could use his house in Springs, near East Hampton, while we were back in the States.

A few days into our trip, I left Patti at Peter's house and took the train into the city to hook up with Ace and Yug from The Oxpetals. I was going to be in the city a couple of days while I got my business taken care of, staying in the uptown apartment of Rich Chiaro, my road manager from the Spoonful days, who was by now working with singer-songwriter Laura Nyro. We were driving up First Avenue when Ace — who was not the world's most articulate human being — turned to me and said, "I think there is something you need to know, Steve."

"Really, Ace?" I said. "What's up?"

"Well . . . Webber and Patti are together right now at Peter's house."

I had no idea what he was getting at. Ace's wife's name happened to be Patty, so I figured he was saying his wife and Bobby Webber, the keyboard player from The Oxpetals, had gone out to the Island to party with Patti.

"And?" I said.

He just stammered, "It's not good . . . Patti and Webber are together and it's not good."

Slowly, my brain computed what he was saying, and that he was talking about my Patti, not his Patty. Ace was right. It was not good.

It was obvious to me when I'd first met him that Webber was just one of those guys women found irresistible. He was charismatic and good looking and an unbelievable player to boot, which made him the archetypal babe magnet. But I had never noticed anything unusual when he was around Patti, because Patti was smoking hot and every man I knew looked at her the same way. I'd never suspected anything between them, or between her and anyone other than me. I was floored.

"Stop the car here, Ace."

I went into a small bar on 30th Street, downed a shot to keep my hands from shaking and called Peter's house. When Patti answered,

I asked a few pointed questions and she just started babbling incoherently and being evasive. It was all I needed to know. I never made it to Rich's house that night. I walked to Penn Station, but the last train for the Montauk line had already left, so I just sat and waited for the first one the next morning. When I got off at the Amagansett stop, she was there waiting for me. We both just sat there and cried. It was over.

The next month was a blackout. I had not seen this coming. I thought we had settled into a great life on *Cygnus*, but I guess Patti did not see it that way. I think she saw me getting further and further away from the music business and the life that made sense to her. She looked around Fearless Freddie's and saw those old boat bums, and must have gotten a glimpse of a future she wanted no part of. Patti immediately moved in with Webber. I went back to St. Thomas a week later, alone and in a daze.

By Christmas I was still battling the heartbreak and humiliation, but was determined to move on. I headed up to Long Island for Christmas to reconnect with my family, and to try to find a real party amid the pity party I was throwing for myself. It seemed to be working. I helped my brother Charlie move into this little house my mom had found for him, and there was rum and lots of great pot every night. As New Year's came and went, I was starting to get antsy to get out of the cold and back down to the Islands, back with Peter and my friends and the life on *Cygnus* that I was more insistent than ever on making work.

Then I got a call, and for the second time in three months got knocked clean off my feet. Peter Davey was dead.

The story I got was that he'd relapsed and overdosed. Apparently he'd found out about a supplier in Charlotte Amalie while hanging out in St. Thomas with an Italian-American scumbag we both knew from East Hampton whom we'll call Fabio, who I'd also heard was screwing Sandy. My suspicion is that Fabio found the dealer in town and brought the drug around, and because Peter was an experienced user I'm guessing it was something pure and potent like China White. But Peter was trying to get clean, and that could have affected his tolerance for the drug. He and Fabio and Sandy went down in the middle of the day and boarded *Cygnus*, got high, and Peter at some point lay down to try to sleep it off. At some point, possibly because Peter was not coming to, Fabio injected Peter with a saline shot that was supposed to counteract the effects of the narcotic. But in this case it was administered wrong, or at the wrong time, and caused him to go into cardiac arrest. Sandy was there for the whole event but was also very stoned, and since I was not there, I can only guess what she was doing besides panicking. There were people in our circle of friends who swore Fabio killed Peter to get to Sandy.

I never found out the full story. By the time I got to St. Thomas, Peter was gone, his body quickly taken back to the States by his family, who didn't want a real investigation, didn't want a scandal to spread, and who I'd later learn blamed me for his death. They didn't have to make me feel guilty, because I already did. I was in the States, and I'm sure his family never knew I'd been trying to help him for years, but regardless, you always second-guess yourself and wonder what more you could have done.

He died right there on my boat, the one he'd bought for me to fulfill a pledge between two friends.

Peter was 29 when he died, but to me he'll always be that 21-year-old kid on the 500cc twin Triumph motorcycle, climbing those highways of the Swiss Alps with nothing in front of him but an open sky and a limitless future. He was my best friend, and he always will be.

It was sometime in early 1972 that Yug, to whom I'd grown closer and who knew I was hurting, came down to live with me on the boat, along with his wife, Lisa. Yug's presence kept me from what I would have been doing otherwise — wallowing alone — and he was determined to get me "out of the house." I was 29 and single, and as long as my newly grown, full-length beard didn't scare anybody off, there was no reason I shouldn't be out socializing.

We'd heard about this band that was playing at a club in Charlotte

Amalie, an American-style cover band with a kickass girl drummer. Now this I had to see. Women playing the drums was still quite the novelty in 1972 — the only ones I knew of were Moe Tucker from The Velvet Underground and the drummer from the all-girl Goldie and the Gingerbreads. We found the club and settled in to watch a group from Washington, D.C., that called itself Sun Country. The band was great, and sure enough, this drummer got your attention right away. She was beating the shit out of the drums, and it turned out she was a really good singer too. When she stood up from the drum riser I expected to see a big girl, but she was this cute little thing of maybe five-foot-two with short blonde hair. She wasn't much taller than the ride cymbals. We stayed for two sets and went back to the boat, but I could not stop thinking about how hard she was hitting the drums, and decided to do a little digging.

I knew the owner of the club, this guy Danny Davis who also owned the club right outside the entrance to Yacht Haven. When I saw one of Davis' employees one day at Fearless Freddie's, I pressed him for details on Sun Country and this amazing drummer.

He said, "Oh, yeah, the band with the girl drummer. Her name is Trudy Morgal. She and her girlfriends run the place for Danny, and they are all a bunch of dykes." I could tell he wasn't using the word to be insulting, he was saying this was not only a girl drummer but a gay girl drummer! For some reason I was even more intrigued.

The next night we took Lisa with us and listened for about three sets, and again they were incredible. I was dying to meet Trudy. Someone in the club, I don't remember who, approached her and told her I would like to meet her.

She came over and we made awkward small talk, but she seemed preoccupied, like she was looking for somebody. I asked her who she was looking for.

"I heard a guy from a famous band was in the bar," she said. I just laughed.

She said their booking was up in a week but she and her friends were planning on staying for a while longer. We talked a little about going out for a sail, and I said I would see her again before their booking was over.

After we left Lisa said to me, "Steve, you know she's a lesbian, right? Why are you interested in getting to know her?"

"She didn't say she was a lesbian, did she? . . . And you know, Lisa, I don't have to be romantically interested in her to want to get to know her, do I?"

By this point Yug was laughing his ass off and said, "Boone, you just want to get your dick wet again. I guess screwing a lesbian drummer is the only way to get a bass player off."

The truth was that while I did think Trudy was cute, I was also thinking of starting a new band and liked the idea of forming a rhythm section — the musical kind — with her. Drums and bass are joined at the hip in a good rock band, and yeah, the idea of having sex with a gal who kicks the shit out of the drum kit did turn me on. From that point on I became obsessed with getting to know this Trudy girl. We did go for a sail to St. John, and she brought several of her friends along. They were mostly from Baltimore or Washington, D.C., and they liked to party. Trudy was as wild socially as she was behind the kit.

"You know, you sure do pick some wild chicks to chase around," Yug said, and when I thought about it, he was right. Denise Mourges, Patsy Smith, Christine Biddle . . . all wild, unconventional girls, as was Trudy. She would not be the last girl in my life to fit that description.

It was through Trudy that I was introduced to the strange and wonderful world of sopers. This girl she knew named Ruthie and her husband, Pete, were both full-time St. Thomas residents who had a connection in San Juan for these little yellow pills. I took one and recognized right away that they were a form of quaaludes. For a while in the '60s they were sold over the counter as a sleep aid. While they worked well for sleeping, they worked even better for sex, removing any inhibition one might have. It was like being drunk without the aggressive behavior booze could cause — you loved everybody and everybody loved you. Also, they were cheap. You could fly over to San Juan on the airboat, buy two bottles of 100 pills each for about $50, use what you needed and sell the rest at a tidy profit. Things got mighty strange once sopers entered my orbit.

For one, Trudy and I did become romantically involved, despite the fact that she had a ubiquitous girlfriend named Zac (short for her last name, Zacharski). She hung around with a crew of definite lesbians but never gave me vibes of "stay away," so finally, one night when Trudy and I happened to be alone aboard *Cygnus*, I made my move and was not rebuffed. It was obvious she had been with a man before, and she confirmed as much after the deed was done.

So I began dating a bisexual with a girlfriend. Things got weirder.

After the rest of Sun Country had gone back to the States, Trudy invited this group of great players from Baltimore with whom she'd worked previously — Walt Bailey on guitar, Jeff Lutzi on bass and Rick Peters on drums and vocals — to play a couple of weeks at Danny's club. When the two weeks concluded and the guys went back, we started talking about putting together a pickup band. Back on St. Thomas during one of our regular frozen banana daiquiri parties, Scotty mentioned that there was a small grass shack on the road from Charlotte Amalie to Red Hook that could be used as a club. We had Trudy on drums and vocals, me on bass and Guy on guitar, but we needed another player who could sing and play keyboards. As it happened, I knew a guy who could do just that — Bobby Webber.

I don't know if it was the sopers or the fact that I'd moved on to Trudy, or both, but I found myself calling the guy who had stolen my wife and asking him to come down to St. Thomas to be in a band with me. What's even crazier is that he agreed. Before you know it, I was picking Webber and Patti up from the airport and heading out to Red Hook, where *Cygnus* was anchored. It had to be surreal for Patti to be back on *Cygnus*, but I didn't notice at the time (sopers).

Anyway the band, which I gave the good-time party name Wang Dang Doodle and Yug (again, sopers) was a blast but short-lived.

Our repertoire was mostly rock standards, and in short order we managed to round up some amps and a sound system that were better than what The Spoonful had used on tour. The first night at the new club — which Scotty and his partner Don Edwards appropriately called the Grass Shack — kicked ass, considering we had a week's practice and limited song repertoire. The second night it seemed like half of St. Thomas turned out, but they didn't come to hear us — they came so they didn't have to hear us. Apparently because the club was located down at the bottom of a ravine, the sound from the music was traveling up the mountainside and blasting into houses of folks who preferred the sound of the trade winds in their living rooms. We agreed to turn it down at first, but the sound got louder and eventually the cops showed up. So we turned it down permanently, but the crowds got smaller by the end of the week and apparently we were still too loud for some of the local residents. Yug was standing onstage near the end of our short run at the Grass Shack and some big guy got in his face about the noise, so Yug wheeled and took a full swing at this guy with a 20-pound mic-stand base. It hit him square in the midsection, but the guy didn't even flinch. Bystanders got in the middle before any blood was shed, but that was the last call for the Grass Shack. The folks with the real influence in St. Thomas had the law on their side and, citing a noise ordinance that I doubt had even existed on our first night there, they told us no more live entertainment with amplifiers and drums was allowed. It was fun while it lasted, and it lasted less than a month in total.

The episode was also a sign that perhaps my time in the Islands was drawing to a close.

By January 1973, even with the sopers flowing and a new, albeit strange relationship with Trudy, I'd had enough of living on the boat. Peter's death and the breakup of my marriage had definitely damaged my overall mindset when it came to Island living, but the bigger thing was that I was back into playing music — I believed in Trudy's talent and wanted to help her pursue the stardom I believed she could attain. She'd had enough of the Islands and had moved back to Baltimore around Christmastime, but not before asking me to join her.

I thought long and hard about buttoning up *Cygnus* and leaving Brad on board as caretaker — he'd been de facto captain when I'd gone back to the States a couple of times — but that was beyond my means financially, with maintenance expenses and upkeep. Ideally I would have sailed *Cygnus* back to the States, where I could keep an eye on her, but she wasn't in good enough shape to do that and the costs associated with keeping her there would have been even higher. I'd put some for-sale listings in various publications, but almost all the prospective buyers were little more than "keel kickers" looking for free boat rides. Just as I started to get pretty discouraged, I was approached by two guys who flew down from Baltimore, one of whom was Brownie, the brother of Trudy's ex-bandmate (and ex-boyfriend, I'd recently found out) Rick Peters. They'd found out about *Cygnus* and me through Rick, and inquired about buying a half-interest in the boat. They didn't tell me what they were up to, but I knew immediately. In those days, anyone with a big enough boat, myself included, was being approached to make some "easy" money by hauling bales of pot back from South America. At that time, the Coast Guard had no clue what was going on, and the risk — at least from a getting-arrested standpoint — was minimal. I'd been asked to make runs but didn't really have any interest, as I'd become laser-focused on Trudy and getting back into music. But, although I didn't press for any details, I knew these guys from Baltimore had been convinced to make such a trip.

Although I needed the money, and selling half-interest made sense on paper, I was worried. These guys had done some sailing around the Virgin Islands and weren't novices, but sailing the open ocean en route to South America was a totally different ball game. The Atlantic Ocean enters the Caribbean through three different passages. Waves can start all the way in Africa, unimpeded by land masses along the way, and the winds that come down from Canada can cause waves to go from five to 20 feet in minutes. I told them about the major leak we'd had in the garboard plank the first time we'd taken the boat out back in 1970, and that before any big ocean voyage was even considered, they had to get the significant repair done that had been recommended to me back then. They swore up and down they would make and pay for the necessary repairs, and I believed them. One of the members of their crew was going to be Brad, who was a veteran sailor and understood the dangers of not making the repairs. Or so I thought.

I took their $5,000 for a half-interest in the boat and I left for Baltimore in February 1973.

A couple of months later, I got a call from the Coast Guard, asking me if I knew the whereabouts of *Cygnus*, which was a documented yacht officially protected by the U.S. government. She'd disappeared without a trace, and they were looking for the five-person crew at the behest of a worried-sick father whose daughter had apparently been aboard. My heart dropped into my stomach. I hadn't heard from my co-owners, I told them, but would help however I could.

Apparently they'd gotten a crew together and left from St. John, and got as far as St. Croix, where they had a leak and some other problems that were fixed with assistance from a U.S. Navy submarine. They were subsequently spotted somewhere near the ABC Islands (Aruba, Bonaire, Curaçao) and were never heard from again, nor was *Cygnus*. The Coast Guard did a four-day search, which turned up nothing, followed by an investigation at their offices in St. Thomas, where they grilled me very hard for information. Other than my suspicions and my acknowledgment that the boat was in need of a major repair when I'd left, I knew nothing. For the sake of those families, I wish I did know more.

In the years that followed, I heard all kinds of rumors. That there had been a distress call — which seems unlikely to me, because the boat was not equipped with a single sideband radio, and a distress call would not have been heard beyond a 12-mile radius. That some Colombians had convinced them to come down to Santa Marta to load the boat with pot, and that they'd either been lost at sea on that trip (the most likely scenario, given what I knew about *Cygnus*) or been killed in Colombia when the deal went bad. I've also had people swear they saw *Cygnus* out in California, or that they saw one of the crew members in New Orleans, which I really hoped was true but had to be total bullshit. I did find out later that Brownie and his friend had federal warrants out for their arrest, but the rest of that crew were not really criminals; they were amateurs who had no reason to want to disappear. The families have accepted that they're gone, and so have I, though it still makes me sad and angry every time I think about it. Those guys didn't listen to me — there's no evidence they ever made the necessary repairs — and they and three other people paid with their lives.

What a terrible waste.

Between Peter's death and the fate of *Cygnus* and her crew, the rock 'n' roll life I'd been running from suddenly felt like leisure. The irony was not lost on me that I'd gone to the Islands to escape the stress of the music business, and had ended up burdened with as heavy an ordeal as I could ever imagine. Suddenly, all I wanted to do was make music again, and I was rediscovering that joy almost daily during my first few months in Baltimore.

When I arrived there in 1973, I knew virtually nothing about Baltimore other than Fort McHenry and the Orioles, and the fact that Trudy had come from there. We'd played a couple of gigs there with The Lovin' Spoonful, including one with The Supremes and another one where I'd met a cute young teenybopper I decided to bring with me on the rest of the tour until I was reminded by Rich, our road manager, that doing so would be a violation of the Mann Act and I'd go to jail. Five years later, I was back there with Trudy, who was cutting a demo at a studio in the suburbs of Baltimore with Walt Bailey, Rick Peters and Bob Grimm, the band she'd played with briefly in the Islands. I had no feelings for Baltimore one way or another, though it seemed like an unusual place for a recording studio.

I walked into ITI Studios — which was actually outside the city in an industrial park in Hunt Valley, Baltimore County — expecting to see something like the old Sun Studios with two rooms and an old microphone hanging from the ceiling. Wow, I could not have been more wrong.

This was one of the nicest studios I'd ever been in, with a huge live room and a recording console unlike anything I'd ever seen. The board was equipped with something called parametric equalization, which allowed producers and engineers to retain precise control over the sound of recorded instruments. Is this what recording studios had become in the three years I'd been away? No — ITI was special.

The studio had begun life as Recordings Incorporated at 1130 West Cold Spring Lane in North Baltimore in the early '60s, and was the area's only fully functioning music studio at that time. Because it was in an obscure off-market, the studio did a little bit of everything to pay the bills, including commercial recording, mastering and even pressing. From the time he was 15 years old, one of the mainstay employees at Recordings Incorporated was a local kid named George Massenburg, a music obsessive but also an inventor and electronics whiz who'd gotten a job through a next-door neighbor who worked there. In short, Massenburg was a genius who, while studying electrical engineering at Johns Hopkins, experimented at Recordings Incorporated with parametric equalization. He wanted to make the things he was recording sound better, so he started by building a new kind of board.

But soon after Massenburg left Hopkins, Recordings Incorporated was sold to a local telecommunications magnate and shady Spiro Agnew associate named Jack Best, who was hated by the studio's employees — including Massenburg — due to his reputation as a racist, a sociopath and generally just a terrible studio owner. Jack Best changed the name of Recordings Incorporated to ITI (International Telecom Incorporated), and by the time I walked through the door, George Massenburg had moved to Paris with his actress wife, and Best had pretty much run the business into the ground before moving to Hawaii with earnings he'd received from a patent on the world's first portable color-cam.

I'd been in Baltimore a few months working with Trudy when I was approached in late 1973 by Vance, the manager at ITI, about picking up the lease payments. I guess ITI figured that since I'd been in a successful band, I had a lot of discretionary income to play with. I made no bones about how much I loved the facility, but I had to stifle a laugh when they asked me about taking over the studio payments. I'd been living solely off the $5,000 I'd made selling the half-interest in *Cygnus*. Basically to avoid embarrassing them and myself, I said I'd consider the kind offer and get back to them.

As I started thinking about it though, the notion of running the studio appealed to me. I was really growing to enjoy Baltimore, which I found to be full of cool people, a high percentage of gorgeous women and more great local music than I ever would have guessed. What cemented my affection for the city and increased my desire to live there was probably the Fells Point Festival of '73, an outdoor gathering where I experienced all of the above. I reached out to some of the contacts I still had in the music business, to see what they thought about my making the studio venture my new job. One of the calls I made was to Bob Cavallo.

I told him about the fertile music scene in Baltimore, and the size of the facility, and the parametric EQ board designed by George Massenburg, and . . . he stopped me.

"Oh, Lowell George loves George Massenburg."

"Who's Lowell George?" I said.

"Lowell George . . . from Little Feat," Bob said. "I've been managing them."

I'd never heard of Little Feat, but then neither had most of the world — they'd made three albums for Warner Brothers, but none of them had cracked the Top 200. When I asked Bob what kind of music they played, he couldn't really tell me. They were a multiracial group from L.A., fronted by Lowell, who was this heavy (as in weight) Frank Zappa disciple, and their style was a fusion of rock, country, blues and some New Orleans influences. The commercial performance of their first three albums had Little Feat on the verge of breaking up, but Warners at that time was known as the most nurturing, artist-friendly label out there, and they still believed in them and were willing to invest in the group. Bob Cavallo had become their manager after he moved to California with John at the end of the '60s, and had never left.

As dumb luck would have it, Lowell had heard of this studio in the Baltimore suburbs because he'd worked with Massenburg when they'd both participated in sessions by Dobro player Mike Auldridge and his band The Seldom Scene, as well as a track on Linda Ronstadt's breakthrough *Heart Like a Wheel* album, in early 1973. So Cavallo called me back and said, "Little Feat might be interested, if George Massenburg is going to be there. If he is, Warners will bankroll the sessions."

"Great," I told Bob. "Consider it done."

With the money from Warner Brothers, I would have enough to make the lease payments and take over ITI. There was only one problem — George Massenburg was in Paris and didn't know me from Adam.

Somehow I tracked him down and explained the situation. Massenburg loved Lowell George and Little Feat, but was newly relocated to Paris and didn't sound greatly enthusiastic about leaving his wife behind to work the sessions. He'd also been burned at the end of his time at ITI, which he'd almost single-handedly built into a state-of-the-art facility only to see Jack Best run it into the ground. He was familiar with The Lovin' Spoonful but didn't know me personally, and I don't think he was too keen on being under a new studio owner's thumb.

"George, you built this place, I'm not going to mess with anything you want to do in the studio," I said. "If you want complete autonomy, you got it." He said he'd think it over. I updated Bob Cavallo, who in turn had Warner Brothers vice president Clyde Bakkemo make a call to George for another recruiting pitch.

The next day, Massenburg called me to say he was in, and I called the management at ITI and told them I accepted their offer. "Oh and one more thing," I said. "The new name of the studio is Blue Seas Recording Studios." I'd had the name in my head for years. A guy I'd encountered on Hassel Island in the Caribbean, a sailmaker named Manfred, had salvaged a freighter and asked me to spec out putting a recording studio in it. That project had ultimately been aborted — the ship was all steel and the acoustics could never be worked out — but I loved the concept. The freighter was called *The Blue Seas*.

The first few months at this version of Blue Seas were a whirlwind. When I took over the facility at Hunt Valley, I had no experience managing a staff or planning a strategy to run a business, but as the boss I had to appear to have a grip on all of this. I had very limited resources to hire staff, so I wore as many hats as I could and hired contract employees who would get paid based on the earnings of the studio. I lured in Yug to be the de facto manager of the studio on a salary of zero dollars and a job description that included being on call 24/7. Who could say no to *that* lucrative offer? I'd met this young guy named Mark Ritter at the Latin Casino, where Trudy was playing a gig, who'd basically been selling popcorn at the club. He asked me for a job, and while I was trying him out I was so impressed with his ability to learn the recording console and studio machinery that I made him the chief engineer — like Yug, no salary, no specified work schedule. Trudy went on the road with a band from D.C. and when they got back, their keyboardist, Scott Johnson, came and toured the studio and asked if he could be in charge of in-house production. I agreed. His salary would be 50 percent of whatever business he could stir up for the studio. This young man named Butch Roach came out to the studio with a local act that had booked some time there. He hung around after the group left and was quickly made assistant engineer. Looking back on the audacity of all this stuns me. These people were in the right place at the right time, but they were also very good and highly committed to our growth.

We had networked out to other bands who came in to record demos that helped keep us in business, and Scott Johnson got work for the studio by making contracts for one-off holiday albums, jingles for local TV and radio, and "soundalike albums," which were the hits of the day played in note-for-note copies and subsequently sold on the cheap at bargain stores like Kmart. It was not exactly the kind of work going on at Columbia or EMI Studios, but this is what you did for survival at a studio in the Baltimore suburbs. Our band for these endeavors would consist of me, Guy, Scott, Trudy and her bandmates Walt Bailey and Rick Peters, a local ace named Victor Giordano, and Jim Lawler and Lee Diamond, hired guns from a band named Bull. Leo McLaughlin and Jim would eventually become production assistants at Blue Seas.

We all worked our asses off and learned so much in those first couple of months at Blue Seas, because really, there was no alternative.

But the highlight was undoubtedly getting a chance to watch Little Feat up close and personal.

Lowell George had come out from L.A. with his wife, Elizabeth, who already had two small children and another one on the way. They rented a house in Cockeysville, just a short drive from the studio. The other guys stayed in a hotel in nearby Hunt Valley and made themselves at home rather quickly. The band's great piano player, Bill Payne, met his future wife, Fran Tate, when she arrived at Blue Seas along with her friend Emmylou Harris to provide backing vocals for a session. (Bonnie Raitt also worked a Little Feat session at Blue Seas.) Little Feat guitarist Paul Barrere met his future wife, a girl from Towson named Debbie, during the sessions. It was a really good time in the personal lives of these guys, and it carried over professionally.

You could tell they were thrilled with the studio and loved working with George Massenburg. They were monsters, just unbelievable players, with Lowell the leader of the pack. He'd go in the studio and just listen to drum machines for hours before he got the rhythm he wanted, then he'd plug his guitar directly into the board and start working on the grooves. None of this was unusual to the rest of the band, who had learned to adapt to Lowell's idiosyncratic approach and to give him what he wanted. During those first few days they cut his "Rock and Roll Doctor," and Bill Payne's "Oh, Atlanta," and Paul Barrere's "Skin It Back." This was the sound of a band at the height of its powers. It was just stunning to me that they had almost broken up and hadn't yet broken through with a successful album.

But that would change. The album they recorded at Blue Seas, *Feats Don't Fail Me Now*, ended up being their first to hit the Top 200, going all the way to No. 36 and rewarding Warners' faith in them. Adding to the happy memory of the time is the fact that Lowell and Elizabeth had a baby girl, Inara, while in Baltimore on July 4, 1974. Lowell's friend, the songwriter Van Dyke Parks, was there at the hospital. (I still have a vivid memory of Lowell and Van Dyke trying to make off with my Mighty Sparrow and Lord Kitchener albums from Blue Seas. Van Dyke had recently produced an album for Sparrow, but I wasn't letting him get away with taking my records!) Inara George would eventually make up one half of the highly respected indie duo The Bird and the Bee.

And Little Feat didn't stop working when *Feats Don't Fail Me Now* was in the can either. English singer and eventual '80s superstar Robert Palmer, who was recording his second album for Chris Blackwell and Island Records, had also booked time at Blue Seas. Lowell had worked on Palmer's first album along with The Meters down in New Orleans, but Palmer wanted to use all of Little Feat for this album. Fine, Lowell said, but you'll have to come to Baltimore. So that's what Palmer did, showing up with a talented American producer named Steve Smith who had cut his teeth at Muscle Shoals Sound Studios, as well as a fabulous engineer named Phill Brown. My crew at Blue Seas really benefited from getting to watch guys like Massenburg, Smith and Brown work on the technical side of the recording. Those guys were major league. They cut great funk tunes for the album that would become Palmer's *Pressure Drop*, including "Fine Time" and "Work to Make It Work" and a version of the Toots and the Maytals title track that was about as good as a group of (mostly) white guys was going to do.

While I knew these were great artists, I never would have believed how long these two albums that were made over a period of maybe a month in the early summer of 1974 would endure upon their release. *Feats Don't Fail Me Now* was in a list of the Top 100 albums of all time put together by the *Times* of London, and Elvis Costello listed it on his "500 albums you need" list a few years back. More recently, *Pressure Drop* was named one of the best 50 albums in the history of Island Records by *MOJO* magazine, alongside records by Bob Marley, U2 and many others.

It was a special time for me and probably the most fertile period in the history of the Baltimore recording scene. Blue Seas was off to a blazing start, but as great an experience as I had with Little Feat overall, there was an incident near the end of the sessions that would sour me on working with the band.

Everyone in Little Feat but Lowell, who was back in Cockeysville with his family, was drinking and partying with me at this bar called Mother Lode's Wild Cherry on Greenmount Avenue. I'd been hanging out with these guys for weeks and had a good rapport with them.

To my surprise, somebody in the band — I think it might have been Bill Payne — said, "Hey Steve, what was the deal with that bust in San Francisco?"

Now, the bust had never been far from my mind in the eight years since it happened, but I wasn't sure how many people remembered or even knew about it. I hadn't talked to anyone about it much, if at all, since Zally was fired in early 1967. But I had a lot of respect for the guys in Little Feat and it seemed like the respect was mutual, so instead of brushing off the question I was honest.

I laid out all the gory details, that the cops improperly searched us, that Zally was being threatened with immediate deportation, that our management team and label hadn't been through something like this and didn't really present us with a lot of options, and that ultimately Zally and I made a decision out of fear that we'd regretted almost instantly. The guys took in the story and seemed to get it. The party continued; as usual with Little Feat, it was a raucous time.

The next day, I was in the studio with the band, and Bob Cavallo was coming to visit them for the first time. I was looking forward to seeing Bob, with whom I'd always had a good relationship. Even after The Spoonful broke up, I'd been friendly with him. My mom had rented him a house in the Hamptons in the summer of '68 right near mine, and I'd taken Bob's son, Rob, out waterskiing and had other friendly interactions with the Cavallo family. And of course Bob had played a major role in delivering Little Feat to Blue Seas and allowing me even to take over this studio in the first place. I was thankful, and wanted to tell Bob so in person.

But when he walked in that day, before I could even greet him, Paul Barrere got the first word in. "Hey Bob," Barrere said, "how come you made Steve fink out the band?"

Cavallo's face turned ashen. I was furious and felt like I could have killed Barrere right there in the studio. It was such a low blow. What I told them wasn't at all translatable to "Bob made us fink out the band." I guess Barrere was trying to be funny, and I suppose he didn't know how sensitive the bust was in the lore of the band, but frankly he should have guessed. I tried to smooth things over with Bob, but things were noticeably awkward between us after that incident. I'm sure part of him always wondered whether I blamed it all on him when I talked about the bust, which was crazy.

My personal dealings with Little Feat after that day were few and far between. I personally told Paul Barrere to stay out of my airspace if he knew what was good for him. Even after *Feats Don't Fail Me Now* had become a success, I wasn't about to actively court Little Feat to come back to Blue Seas to record a follow-up, and they never returned as a band, though Lowell visited frequently to record by himself and sketch out ideas, and I was always happy to have him.

Would Little Feat have returned to Blue Seas had it not been for one stupid comment that set me off? I don't really know, but I sure wish it hadn't been said, because the business would suffer for it.

It wasn't long after Little Feat and Robert Palmer left that a different sort of problem emerged with the studio.

I was at my house in Pikesville when I got a phone call from Yug who said Blue Seas was being visited by a sheriff's captain, along with some man named McCormick and a bank officer from Maryland National Bank. They were there to evict us from the premises. I raced to Hunt Valley to see what the hubbub was about.

I knew it was serious when I heard the name McCormick. The McCormicks — as in the venerable Baltimore family behind McCormick spices — owned an industrial park and pretty much all of Hunt Valley. When I got there, this McCormick guy — I still don't remember which McCormick it was — gave me the lowdown. An enormous sum was owed to the McCormicks, dating from the time when Jack Best owned the facility, and I had to pay up. Now, of course, this supposed bill had never come up when the lease had been transferred to my name, or in any of the first few months I was running the studio, so I quickly figured out that it wasn't really about money. The problem was the long-haired hippies doing business and keeping crazy hours at this otherwise buttoned-down corporate center. Other tenants had been complaining about parties and drug use and sex going on inside the studio, and I can't say all of those complaints were unfounded. The mattresses on the floor of the studio were a tell-tale sign, though those were less about sex and more about the fact that my round-the-clock, unpaid studio employees were mostly poor and starving and had nowhere else to sleep.

Anyway, I put up a fight. Who knows what these guys thought of the lanky hippie with the beard down to his chest, but I read them the riot act for their dirty-dealing eviction caper. I pointed my finger at McCormick and said, "You people don't know what you're doing, you're going to throw rock 'n' roll out of Baltimore County. Baltimore will regret this day." To his credit, McCormick just stood there and took it. But it sure looked like we were finished. Since I had no chance of paying this trumped-up bill that went back years, the McCormicks started eviction proceedings, including an auction to sell the studio, which was to take place in January 1975.

There were to be two separate auctions, one for the entire studio and all of the equipment it housed, and the second an itemized auction for just the equipment. The higher total of the two auctions would determine whether the studio was sold as a lot, or piece by piece. I thought we might at least be able to rescue some of the equipment, so I went to the auction. A guy I knew named Tom Anderson — an entrepreneur from New York and a pothead like me who had become sort of a silent financial partner in Blue Seas — had agreed to come with me and see if we could salvage a piece or two of the business. But when the auction started, Tom was nowhere to be found. Apparently he was doing a deal somewhere in New Jersey and had gotten stuck on a train in a snowstorm, along with Yug. So I was on my own, though George Massenburg had shown up too to see what would become of the parametric EQ console he designed.

It was clear right away that the potential bidders, who had come from around the world to attend the auction, were more interested in the high-end equipment than in owning a studio in Hunt Valley, Maryland. This included the console, a 16-track recorder, some state-of-the-art Neumann microphones and various other trinkets that the bidders had their eyes on.

They started the auction for the studio, and very little bidding was going on. Even though buying the studio would have given you all the equipment that came with it, apparently no one wanted all that stuff, or to deal with managing the next steps for the studio operation itself. The bidding got up to $17,000. I looked around for Tom Anderson, but he was nowhere to be found. The auctioneer said, "Any other bids?" And I just blurted it out — "$18,000!" I of course didn't have 18 cents on me, but as they prepared to start the piece-by-piece auction, I held the high bid. Not that it mattered. That 16-track recorder alone was going to command 18 grand, and my measly bid for the studio was about to get swept away.

But then a funny thing happened. The McCormick guy pulled

the auctioneer over to the side. They conferred for a couple of minutes, and the auctioneer banged his gavel on the podium and said, "Ladies and gentlemen, the auction is over — Steve Boone, you've bought the entire studio complex."

I heard people gasp, and I'm sure one of those gasps was mine. I was stunned. Of course, there was the little problem that I didn't have $18,000. The auctioneer told me I had an hour to come up with at least 10 percent of the $18,000 price tag, and 24 hours to pay off the remaining 90 percent. The only way to do that was to conduct my own auction, selling off some of the pieces of the studio to the disappointed buyers who were getting ready to leave. George Massenburg helped me. We sold an eight-track recorder, two vintage EMI echo chamber plates and a couple of other items that wouldn't really be missed, and paid off the debt to the auctioneer and the McCormicks.

What I heard later was that McCormick had been so impressed with my impassioned speech when I read him the riot act that he conferred with Maryland National Bank and changed the nature of the auction to favor my bid. Maybe he was a secret music fan, who knows. But word got back to me that since the McCormicks had done us a favor and let us keep the studio, they were expecting one in return. They wanted us out of Hunt Valley. Message received.

Ever since the experience with the freighter on Hassel Island, I'd been thinking about the concept of housing a studio on a boat. With Blue Seas in limbo, there was no time like the present to try to execute that idea. With Tom Anderson's financial support, I began studying the logistics of relocating the studio to Baltimore's Inner Harbor. One of the primary challenges would be moving all of the high-tech recording equipment. The other one would be getting that equipment to yield quality productions. Even if you found a boat that could accommodate the proper acoustics, there was the noise of the water and of the city to think about. It seemed like everyone to whom I mentioned the idea thought I was crazy, but they also said, man, if you can figure it out, that would be a hell of a cool studio. I liked the challenge and pressed forward.

Pretty quickly, I found a beautiful modern houseboat that had been converted from an old slag barge by a local lawyer named John Armor. I thought it could be perfect. Tom Anderson fronted me the money to lease the barge, and we were off and running.

The most important piece of the studio was George Massenburg's parametric board, which we were going to need to relocate if we'd ever have a prayer of getting big-time acts to come record there. The problem, as Massenburg was quick to point out when I was pitching him the idea, was that the 400–500 wires to the board were housed in a conduit that was encased in cement underneath the floor of the studio. We were going to need to snip all the wires (which weren't color-coded) and totally rewire the board to get it functioning on the harbor. I know George thought I was crazy, but he stuck around and helped me get it operational. As for the noise, we devised a shock-absorbing system that would live just off the pier and would cut down on unwanted sounds dramatically. My team and I worked for six months, night and day, to transform the barge from a house-boat into a professional recording studio, and damn if we didn't defy all the skeptics and get it done.

The business community in Baltimore City was much more supportive than their counterparts in Hunt Valley. Part of the reason was probably that city folk understood these long-haired hippie artists better than they did in the suburbs, and part was that the Baltimore Inner Harbor in 1975 was in almost total decay due to "white flight," which had started back in 1968 in reaction to the inner city riots following the Martin Luther King assassination. When we told the city fathers we were planning on docking a floating recording studio at Pier 4 right in front of the old, unused Power Plant building, we were met with a collective "OK, sounds pretty good." Baltimore was looking for new revenue streams, and the fact that we'd already had two national artists on our roster must have given them some confidence we could succeed. William Donald Schaefer, the mayor who would later play a pivotal role in revitalizing the decrepit harbor into a tourist destination, practically threw the key to the city to us.

Our first year on the barge was wonderful. Lowell George came by a couple of times to do some recording. Bob Cavallo must not have been too mad at me, because he turned Earth, Wind & Fire's bass player Verdine White on to the facility, and Verdine came through town and produced demos for various acts. Blues legend Sonny Terry came in and recorded an album, which Yug in particular was over the moon about. We were also tapping into the small but promising rock scene right there in the city. Really the only two clubs that featured live rock music at that time were the Marble Bar and No Fish Today (the more famous Hammerjacks didn't open until 1982). We'd open the studio at 3 a.m., and the bands that had been playing at those bars would lug their gear over and record. The Marble Bar was run by a part-time blues singer named Scott Cunningham, who recorded with his band at Blue Seas and would become a personal friend of mine. There was a great communal spirit around music in Baltimore, and Blue Seas was at the center of it, at least until it all went bad.

Tom Anderson had been sinking money into Blue Seas but wasn't too crazy about the return he was getting on his investment. We were not making a lot of money, and he thought I should be doing more to change that. Noting that I was the "name" guy who had come from a popular group, he wanted me up in L.A. and New York, trying to recruit top acts to Baltimore to record. But even though our prices were dirt cheap and we'd recorded some popular albums at Blue Seas, it was a tough sell for the record companies in particular to send groups to record on a boat in Baltimore. I'd even put out some feelers to the other guys in The Lovin' Spoonful about coming to record either solo or as a group. The timing wasn't right, though Joe Butler did come to Baltimore and help me record some commercials and jingles for a short period. Joe had also visited me on *Cygnus*, and it was good to bury the hatchet (well, most of it) with him. Anyway, I grew weary of being a salesman. I was a musician, and by this time I was involved in various other projects outside of the studio, including my band, Blanche Ltd., which was playing clubs three to four nights a week and had recorded songs for a demo.

By the time late 1977 rolled around, it was clear Tom wasn't going to invest any more money in Blue Seas, which put the whole enterprise in jeopardy. While I was figuring out the next steps, the unthinkable happened.

I was on Long Island visiting my family on Christmas Day 1977 when I got a phone call at my parents' house. It was Guy Phillips.

"The barge is sinking," Yug said. "You'd better get back here fast."

I raced back the four hours to Baltimore and discovered quite a sight. The studio was almost completely submerged. I got there to find trucks from the Baltimore City Fire Department trying to pump the water out while members of my studio staff tried to salvage whatever equipment they could from the bone-chillingly cold water of the Inner Harbor. Yug literally fished my Martin D-28 guitar out of the water with a hook. But while some of the equipment was salvaged, a number of important items were not recoverable. The tape library was on a shelf that was just sitting against a wall — it was not screwed to the wall — and when the studio listed because of the weight of the water, the whole library tipped over. Hundreds of two-inch tapes and stereo mixes went into the salt water and could not be salvaged, including a lot of Lowell's solo demos, some eight-track Lovin' Spoonful outtakes and almost all of our in-house production. It was a crushing blow.

What happened? For starters, both of the bilge pumps had failed at some point in the previous 24 hours, which aroused great suspicion when the boat's sinking was investigated by the authorities. The state thought that since the boat was housing a struggling business, it had been scuttled for the insurance money, and that myth persists among many in Baltimore who remember the event. But it's a myth. There was no insurance money. The insurance had lapsed six months earlier.

There were also rumors that the sinking of Blue Seas had been revenge by a competitor, or someone who'd been burned in a drug deal involving a high-level employee at Blue Seas. At some point, somebody in a bar either in Fells Point or up on Eutaw Street had been heard boasting about sinking the barge as an act of vengeance. That person got tracked down and the police investigated the lead aggressively, but the ultimate conclusion was that it was just a drunk trying to be tough and talking shit.

What I'll always believe is that Blue Seas sunk because of its design. It had a wooden hull, and so it had gigantic seams between the planks that constituted that hull, and the whole boat was only caulked to about a foot above the waterline. Even though we had two bilge systems, we were in trouble if one malfunctioned. It would be up to that second one to account for all the water that came in, and at only a foot above the waterline, anytime the sea became choppy due to passing boats or weather or whatever, you could take in a foot of water pretty quickly. Once that happened, the bilge pump was outmatched, and water would come in as though a hole had been punched in the boat.

No matter the cause, the studio was officially finished, another endeavor begun with a lot of optimism and promise that ultimately ended with disappointment.

I certainly didn't want to see it end like that, but I didn't have time for mourning — I already had my eye on a different sort of business.

Chapter 11

RESPOKEN

In May 1975, about two and a half years before Blue Seas sank, I was invited to a party along with Scott Johnson at a bar called O'Henry's on East Centre Street in Baltimore. When I arrived, Scott was already there. He told me to meet him in the john, where he produced a very small packet of cocaine, which we both proceeded to sniff from a spoon. I didn't do coke often, but in 1975, in the crowds I and many people in their twenties or early thirties ran with, if someone offered you coke at a party you didn't turn it down. Unbeknownst to us, there was a guy in the bathroom at the same time who was an off-duty officer and had witnessed our indulgence. He forced the owner of the bar to call the cops, and Scott and I were arrested on a misdemeanor charge of cocaine possession.

The charges were penny ante shit — they never even found the coke; I think Scott tossed it away — but it ruined what could have been a great party. Anyway, as I was being debriefed by a detective, he asked me if I'd ever been arrested. Since Zally and I had made a deal in San Francisco to have our arrest records expunged in exchange for our cooperation, according to the law I was supposed to have a clean arrest record.

"No sir, I've never been arrested," I said.

"Really? What's this then?" he said, throwing a packet of papers on the table.

And there it was. My arrest sheet from San Francisco.

"How about we slap you with a perjury count in addition to the possession charge?"

I was stunned and speechless. That bust had helped take down one of the biggest bands of the '60s and had negatively impacted my career to this day, and the authorities hadn't even held up their end of the bargain? I shouldn't have been surprised, but I was.

The coke charges were later dropped due to a lack of evidence, but I'd made an important discovery. In the eyes of the law, I'd been a criminal since 1966. If they were going to label me a lawbreaker, I might as well be a damn good one.

I remembered back to the jobs I'd turned down in the Virgin Islands, and the activity that had been swirling all around me in those years.

The week I'd arrived in the Islands, my friend Scotty told me about how he and his pals had been sailing over to Jamaica with empty scuba tanks and filling them up with weed for easy import and sale in St. Thomas. There were no serious custom checks for sailors at that time, and no hassles to speak of. All around me during those years, young guys like myself were taking their boats down to Jamaica and Colombia and loading them up with quality ganja and offloading it in the States or the Islands and making a pile of dough.

My friend Gilly, the captain of the schooner that was anchored right next to us in Yacht Haven, had gone down to Colombia on a dive charter and brought back a bag of genuine Colombian Gold pot, the first of its kind I'd ever seen. Gilly was a newbie at dealing in pot and asked for my advice on whether this "gold-colored weed" that he had a bag of was worth anything. I told him to keep it under his hat, but yes, it was worth twice as much as regular good pot. He was getting the good stuff without even trying.

Those memories remained in my mind until sometime in 1977,

when Jody Porter, my old friend from the New York days, came back into my life. Jody was visiting his parents down on the Eastern Shore and asked if I wanted to grab a beer. Sure thing.

Jody and I made some small talk and then he came out with it.

"How would you like to make some easy money?"

"Doing what?"

"Well, if you're keeping up with your sailing skills, I know a guy that needs somebody with local knowledge to pilot a sailboat up the Chesapeake to Talbot County."

"Is this what I think it is, Jody?"

"Yes," he said. "You want to meet my partner?"

At this point we were in a public place and I was afraid to talk openly. I wrote him a note and slid it across the bar. The note said I might be interested but needed to know more. He must have understood my concerns because when we left the bar and took a ride, he showed me he had no wire, no camera. I agreed to move forward and talk to his partner to find out more.

The next day, I met the person Jody was answering to, a preppy but athletic-looking guy, my age, named James Dwight. He asked me to call him Bubba. Basically the deal was that if I could go down to Riohacha, Colombia, as part of a three-man crew, help pilot the boat during the trip up the Chesapeake and also find a house in Talbot County to make a drop, I'd share in the earnings as soon as we made the drop.

At this point, Blue Seas was still a going concern and I needed the money badly. Tom Anderson had withdrawn his financial commitment, and we weren't going to be able to get a loan from the bank. The IRS was still seizing anything that was coming in off Lovin' Spoonful royalties. I'd also recently scrounged together $13,000 for an unbelievable 11-room rowhouse at 800–802 South Bond Street in the Fells Point section of Baltimore, thanks to a $10,000 loan from Patti and her business partner Marge. I was attempting to renovate it and I needed to repay Patti, which brought with it a need for cash flow.

With the money I stood to make off this deal with Bubba, I'd be able to keep the studio going, keep my renovations moving forward and have leftover money to spare. Jimmy Carter had just taken office, and the risk of arrest at this time seemed really low. I knew dozens of people who were making similar runs, and no one had reported as much as a close call with the authorities. Still, I don't think I would have done it had I not found out from the Baltimore arrest that I was a branded man. Knowing I'd been fucked over in San Francisco was the final justification I needed to drop any pretense of being John Q. Citizen. My attitude was, fuck the authorities. It was time to make their lives as difficult as they'd made mine.

The first drop did not quite go off without a hitch. Strangely, the other two members of the crew on this 45-foot Coronado sloop called the *Carolina Garnet* seemed to be well-off, straight-laced guys. The captain claimed to have been a skipper for Jimmy Buffett, when Buffett had his first 35-foot sailboat. (He told me Buffett was scared of the ocean.) We left from the West Palm Beach city marina, made a fuel stop in Grand Turk in the Turks and Caicos Islands, got down to Colombia and waited off shore for two nights for the call to come from the loaders. The captain and first mate wanted to turn back, but I wasn't having it. Even though I was the low man on the mast, I practically had to mutiny to get them to stay one more night. I was right, because the loaders called the next night. The rest of the run, including my skipper's turn piloting the boat through foggy conditions up the Chesapeake and offloading it at the house I'd found on Harris Creek in Talbot County went relatively smoothly, although I was a little nervous when we got passed by the U.S. Navy trying out their experimental hovercraft in the middle of Chesapeake. I got paid for my services in product, which amounted to one 135-pound bale of the 6,500-pound load, and once back in Baltimore I sold the product and converted it into a pile of cash thanks to a couple of local sources. The studio survived, then died under the most bizarre circumstances, which had nothing to do with money problems. But even with Blue Seas gone, I was hooked.

Being a pirate gave me everything I wanted. An opportunity to sail, all the free weed I could smoke and more money than I'd ever seen in my life. Again, I did not have any more of a moral hang-up about smuggling pot than I did about smoking it. I did not consider myself much different from a bootlegger during Prohibition, supplying the thirsty masses with the product they desired against the wrong-headed objections of a bunch of tightasses who didn't even understand the substance they were banning. Later, I'd grow to understand that any type of business that isn't regulated and monitored has the potential for exploitation and violence somewhere down the chain, but then as now I felt like an equal amount of blood was on the hands of the authorities who had incorrectly criminalized the practice in the first place. The only thing "bad" about pot, in my mind, was its prohibition.

My series of expeditions as the captain of a pot-smuggling enterprise could probably fill their own volume, though not telling those tales at all would be conspicuous in a story about my life. In the interests of space, I'll concentrate mostly on the basics of what was a complicated three-year story with a number of twists and turns, not the least of which was the reunion of the band that made me famous, smack-dab in the middle of all this madness.

Knowing that Blue Seas was gone and that I had no forthcoming commitments, Bubba asked me to make another run on the *Carolina Garnet* in May 1978. This time would be different, he said, because I would be the captain and could put together my own crew. This was significant, as I'd vowed during my near-mutiny the last time out not to commit to a situation where I couldn't be in control and working with people whom I could trust and who were of the same mind. My crew for this expedition would consist of my brother Mike and his friend Fred, who'd been one of his classmates at Westhampton Beach High School.

The trip was not without its share of tension and nerve-wracking moments, but I knew the terrain and felt much more comfortable than I had last time around. We left from Charleston, South Carolina, where the *Carolina Garnet* had been docked, and our trip down to Dibulla on the northern coast of Colombia was particularly pleasurable. We again stopped in Grand Turk for refueling, and then onto the southern tip of Haiti, where we were able to swap a box of T-shirts for freshly caught lobster tails.

My skills as a sailor prior to my first Colombia trip had been line-of-sight point-to-point navigating. Using the onboard electrical aids to navigation were new to me, and little use once we got 30 or so miles from shore. As a result I had to rely on plotting my course carefully on a chart and following that planned route using a type of navigation called "dead reckoning" — not a good choice of words, I agree. I was therefore very pleased to spot a landfall noted on the chart of Colombia that placed me right where I needed to be.

Once in Dibulla, the *Carolina Garnet* was loaded with 7,300 pounds of pot, a slightly bigger load than the last time, with considerably more money at stake for the captain. The paranoia was high on the return sail, as we followed the same route back through the Windward Passage. Every boat you see has to be viewed with suspicion. I was sure we were under surveillance several times, but never knew for sure. Soon we saw the familiar sight of the Chesapeake Bay sea buoy, and continued to the Severn River. Our drop point was at a safe house in Crownsville, Maryland, which had been found by Patti, who'd been working as a pot broker for a Vietnam vet named Tom whom we'd met in the Virgin Islands. Arriving was a great relief, as the trip had taken a heavy emotional toll. I had nothing left in the tank when the bales of pot were being brought up the dock into storage in Crownsville, so I pulled rank and let the crew handle hauling the load up what seemed like 100 steps from the pier to the house.

At the end of the day, I'd made more money off this pot run — $125,000 — than I'd ever received at any one time in my life. It was even more than I'd gotten from the seven-album deal with The Lovin' Spoonful. Now, of course, any good heist movie will tell you it's always a good idea to lie low when you make that kind of a score, but all that money was burning a hole in my pocket. So I loaded stacks of cash into a borrowed Samsonite briefcase and headed down to the bank for a cashier's check that would land me the car I had my eye on — a BMW 733i stick shift that was the only one of its kind in Maryland. The bank transaction would have been very cinematic had I been able to get the goddamn briefcase open once I got there, but I didn't know that after flipping the tumblers, I had to turn the briefcase over to get it to open. Had I known that, I wouldn't have gotten out my buck knife to cut it open, ultimately resulting in $100 bills flying through the air of the bank branch. Once that happened, they couldn't give me my cashier's check fast enough. I then went to the dealership and handed the incredulous staff a check for $23,000, which was a hell of a lot for a car in 1978. They must have known what I was up to — they begged me to finance that car, which would have been the smart thing to do. But I was feeling bulletproof.

By this point, the *Carolina Garnet* was considered slightly radioactive after two successful runs to South America. We didn't know if anyone had seen us out there, but it was best not to push our luck.

So when the funds and supply were running low and it was time to get another load, a new vessel — the *Do Deska Din* — a well-built, 68-foot steel motorsailer stored in English Harbor, Antigua, was secured. This run, which was to net 19,000 pounds of pot — nearly three times what we'd brought back last time — had to be carefully orchestrated. Instead of bringing this load into Crownsville, we arranged to have two 40-foot trawler yachts meet us off the coast of Ocean City, Maryland, to offload the shipment. I sent my crew, including my brother Mike, Fred and their friend Chuck Burke, to Antigua two weeks in advance to get the boat ready. They called and said they'd need some supplies before we could make the trip, including some electronics and a four-man lifeboat. I was planning on flying to Antigua to meet the boat, and the only way to bring the supplies was to take an American Airlines DC-10 out of BWI and check the items into excess baggage. To add to my already elevated stress level, this was just weeks after Flight 191, an American DC-10, had crashed just after takeoff in Chicago, killing all 271 people aboard.

But I arrived in Antigua without incident, and the crew and I began our sail down to the agreed-upon load point in Santa Marta, Colombia. As we were leaving town, we happened to see the cutter *Diligence*, known as the U.S. Coast Guard's top pot-busting boat. As it happened, a film crew was aboard, making a movie about drug smuggling. How ironic, and slightly unsettling.

Our nerves would become even more frayed once we got to our rendezvous at Needle Point, between Santa Marta and Riohacha. It was a rough and stormy night on the Caribbean side of the Colombian coast, which because of the trade winds was always rough sailing to begin with. We called out to our contact with the agreed-upon code name and awaited confirmation. Nothing. After three hours of waiting, we decided to come back again the next night. We laid low and dropped anchor just off shore, trying to remain as inconspicuous as possible. The next evening I moved the *Do Deska Din* back to Needle Point and tried again. Nothing, just fisherman talking in Spanish. After another night of choppy seas and not much sleep, I huddled my crew and told them if we didn't make contact the next night, we would have to consider turning back. You can't stay out of sight forever, and the chances of an unfamiliar ship being photographed go up exponentially with each passing day. On the third night, at the three-hour mark, with things looking desperate, Fred came back to the helm and said, "Do you think they could be using 'Screamin' Chicken' as the call sign?" While that was not our agreed-upon code name, it did happen to be my nickname, and my CB handle known to our South American liaison for this run. We had contact.

We arranged where to transfer the load, and my contact gave me a meeting place that happened to be right in the middle of the Santa Marta harbor. Why this very active harbor was agreed upon as the transfer point remains unknown to me, but I did have visions of what the inside of a Colombian jail must look like. It was now midnight, and we needed to get in and out of there as quickly as possible to avoid detection. We had five hours until dawn, during which time at least 200 bales, weighing 80 to 100 pounds each, needed to be loaded carefully and quietly through the narrow passageways of the cabin, and stacked floor-to-ceiling below deck so no room on the boat was wasted. That gave us about 100 seconds for transport per bale. Storing the cargo in hidden compartments was a non-starter — you could never make the trip profitable enough that way. We also had a language barrier to deal with, given the presence of the Colombian crew, none of whom we had met before. For all we knew, we were going to load the boat only to have them blow our heads off, throw us overboard and sail it away to God knows where. If you think this was an easy way to make a buck, think again.

But as the first light of dawn was creeping across the harbor, we said farewell and headed north for the Windward Passage and home. The sail northward was about 90 percent boredom and 10 percent sheer terror, with the presence of the Coast Guard and the eventual 15-to-20-foot waves accounting for the latter.

Once out of the Windward Passage we started sailing through the Bahamas and into a 36-hour thunder and lightning storm that made everyone wary of standing watch holding the steering wheel on the all-steel boat. There was another headache as we got near the Maryland coast, when it was discovered that the offload spot where the two trawler yachts were coming to get the pot was in a highly trafficked commercial fishing hole. Using coded language, I managed to change the drop point, but it was something of an ordeal, as the clock was ticking and it would be broad daylight by the time the second trawler yacht found us. As bales were being tossed onto the second yacht, I heard the sound of a jet engine. I looked up to see a single-engine jet fighter, probably from Naval Air Station Oceana, circling overhead. Without much of a choice, we just kept on tossing. When the pot was gone, we cleaned the boat with a fine-tooth comb, ate a big dinner and waited for instructions from the safe house.

After the jet fighter saw us, for all we knew our photo had made its way to the bridge of every Coast Guard cutter in the area. I reported this to the house. Just after coffee the next day, out of the morning haze, making not a sound, came the prettiest Coast Guard cutter I had ever seen. I will never forget the boat passing by us about 50 yards away, with about eight uniformed officers on the bridge with binoculars, looking us over from stem to stern. The name came into view: it was the USCGC *Dallas*. It just idled by, but now we were definitely damaged goods. Soon after I reported being sighted by the *Dallas*, the call came in to disconnect the electronics and sink the boat. One of the trawlers came back to rescue us, and we watched the *Do Deska Din* slip into its watery grave.

Despite the scuttling of a fine Motorsailer, this was viewed as a successful trip, and it pocketed me $180,000. I would not be required to work for a while.

Lying low in the fall of 1979, I received a surprise call from John Sebastian. I hadn't talked to John much in the past couple of years, but I knew he had experienced some peaks and valleys throughout the '70s. His solo career had started with a lot of promise with his appearance at Woodstock and the *John B. Sebastian* album, but he hadn't been as prolific a writer as he was in the Spoonful days, and critics found his albums uneven. He'd had a surprise No. 1 hit in May 1976 with "Welcome Back," the theme song from the TV show *Welcome Back, Kotter*, but hadn't been able to do much to capitalize on the success.

Anyway, John wanted to know if I'd be interested in getting The Lovin' Spoonful back together for a theatrical film starring and written by Paul Simon, called *One-Trick Pony*. John explained they were looking for some '60s bands to play a concert sequence that would be part of the movie, and that The Lovin' Spoonful had been asked to re-form and take part.

I was intrigued but nervous about this proposition. For one, music had not been on the front burner for me (see above), and in particular I had not played or thought about those old Lovin'

Spoonful songs in years. Also, I had a growing drug problem and wasn't sure whether I could make it through the production without the necessary supply. But I knew this was a great opportunity and ultimately could not say no. John had even gotten Zally to commit, and if John and Zally were both willing to play in The Lovin' Spoonful at the same time, there was a chance this reunion could go beyond the film. So I gave John my commitment and began working on a supplier I could count on to get me through the filming.

It had been more than a decade since I'd been in a room with John, Joe and Zally, so when I walked into John's house in Woodstock to begin rehearsals, it was more than a little surreal. For the most part, it was a happy reunion. Joe grumbled a bit about not being able to sing any leads on the film (the producers only wanted our biggest hits), but given that he was driving a cab by this time, he wasn't really in a position to make any demands. When Zally finally showed up, bearded and late, to our weeklong rehearsals, he seemed to be in pretty good spirits and decent form. He'd been out of show business for the last couple of years and had just opened a restaurant in Kingston, Ontario, called Chez Piggy with his second wife, Rose Richardson, that would go on to be wonderfully successful.

For obvious reasons, I couldn't talk about my recent endeavors. I wonder if anyone (or everyone) could tell I was using.

Given the time that had passed and the quick turnaround time, we clicked extremely well. I think the time away had given us enough perspective to understand what we'd lost when the group broke up, and there was legitimate excitement about our possible future. I was more than happy to forgo my sailing adventures and the riches that came with them if we could recapture some of that old spirit again.

Our parts of the film were shot at the Concord Hotel near John's house in the Catskills, in front of a live audience that included fans, extras and industry types who were there for a fake "Salute to the '60s" concert. Also playing the faux show were Sam & Dave and Tiny Tim. I don't know how much we understood this until we saw the film, but it sure seems like we're being demeaned. The character

Paul plays clearly thinks the type of nostalgia package show like the fictional one we're playing is beneath him. Was the real Paul getting back at us over those arguments about show billing from 1967? I don't know, but whatever his motivations, we played a fabulous concert. It was about 10 of our best-known hits played over 35 to 40 minutes although only one — "Do You Believe in Magic" — made it into the final cut. We were told that it was the only song that was tracked, though I'd love to know if footage of our complete show exists in a film vault somewhere. If so, my memory says it would be as worthy of release as any performance the classic lineup of The Lovin' Spoonful ever did. I also had a line in the movie, which got cut. I don't remember what it was, but I do know I was so much taller than Paul he had to stand on a box so we could both fit in the shot!

When the Spoonful were done with the film, we retreated to our respective camps, expecting to see one another soon. The show had gone down so well that both the group and Bob Cavallo thought we'd get some offers to reunite on a more permanent basis via an album or tour, but if those offers came they never made their way to me. It didn't help that when *One-Trick Pony* was released in October 1980, it was trounced by critics and sank like a stone at the box office. But I think the bigger issue when it came to our potential re-formation was that we were just a little bit ahead of the curve when it came to the demand for '60s groups reuniting. Within five years, many of our contemporaries were getting back together. If *One-Trick Pony* had been made in 1985, I think something could have come of it.

As it was, it would be another 22 years before the four of us would be in the same room again.

And so I returned to my life as a pirate, taking the *Carolina Garnet* out of storage and preparing for another run. I would captain two more expeditions in my career as a smuggler. Both would offer suspense and excitement. Neither would end with the success of my previous missions.

In April 1980, after the *Carolina Garnet* had been outfitted with a new mast and rigging that turned her into a hot-rod sailboat, I was sent with my usual crew down to the ABC Islands, where Bubba had told us to go and wait for a load to develop in Colombia. The new-look *Carolina Garnet* handled rough weather well, and with plenty of room below for a crew of three, it was not hard spending time on it. And spending time on it was what we did on this trip. There was never a clear plan for where we were going to load the boat, or when or even where we were going to bring it back after it was loaded. I didn't like not having a clear timetable, and I knew my crew would not like it either.

We stopped in Grand Turk to refill the jerry jugs and fuel tanks and get some last-minute fresh veggies and fruit, after which I decided we would beat to windward for a few days and then turn south and go through the Mona Passage between Puerto Rico and Hispaniola. We were making terrific time and by nightfall had covered a lot of territory, so we settled in for night watches and I went below around midnight to get some sleep. About 3 a.m. I heard Fred call the code name he used for me.

"Stanley, I think you better come up and see this." I rubbed my eyes and stumbled to the cockpit. "What do you make of this?" he asked.

All I could see for 360 degrees around the boat was large military ships, traveling much faster than we were and heading in the same direction. The closest ones were less than a mile away, going 20 or so knots. My first thought was it was U.S. Navy ships from Roosevelt Roads Naval Station in Puerto Rico, but why so many? Was this an aircraft carrier battle group on maneuvers? If so, we were in trouble in more ways than one.

We'd all heard tales of ocean-going ships coming into port to discover the rigging or remains of a small sailboat entangled in their anchor gear. A ship that big going that fast at night would not even hear the impact of a collision. And even if they did see us, can you imagine a 1,000-foot, 100,000-ton aircraft carrier, traveling at over 20 knots, finding a tiny little 45-foot sailboat in its path with no lights on, and having to do an emergency turn to avoid collision? Think the military would just brush off that kind of incident?

All I could do was turn on our tiny running lights with a thought that maybe they'd be seen in these 10-foot seas, get out the spotlight and shine it on the main sail, and hope for the best. I decided I'd rather be spotted and potentially disciplined by the Navy than run down by a ship that never saw us.

We must have had good karma or something on our side. Soon the dawn was upon us and in full daylight we could see there was not a ship in sight; the entire fleet had somehow passed us by. Bullet dodged.

The good karma would not continue. We hung out in Curaçao for a couple of days and waited for a call that never came. The next day, Bubba showed up at the dock and told us to go hang out in Bonaire, where visibility was lower. By 1980 the feds were starting to catch on to the small sailboat as a means of smuggling loads of pot, and Curaçao was rumored to be one of the islands they were monitoring. One week in Bonaire turned into two, then a call. We couldn't get a load done because the quality of the marijuana was too low. We were too late in their harvest to get quality stuff. We were told to take the boat to Jamaica and wait there for word. This was getting annoying — we'd now been in the boat over a month. But we blasted up to the Windward Passage and then flew down the coast to Montego Bay, where by virtue of the fact that we'd docked there, we earned guest privileges at the Montego Bay Yacht Club.

Jamaica in June 1980 was in political turmoil, with the leftist reform movement at violent odds with the interests of the business community. Rumors of a communist takeover were all about. The crew and I had all gotten short jarhead-type haircuts before this run, thinking it would reduce suspicion, but we stood out like a sore thumb at the club. That evening I was confronted by one of the members, and we were very loudly denounced as CIA operatives. We kind of laughed it off, but the next day another sailboat pulled in and docked right down the pier from us. We watched the immigration agents and police board this sailboat and were shocked to see the crew being taken off in handcuffs. During this same trip I was offered a pound-for-pound match of quality ganja for as many fresh onions as I could bring in — the political turmoil meant the import of fresh vegetables had been all but cut off by authorities. Too bad I had no idea where to get that many onions.

This was all very interesting, but not the reason we'd come. Over a week after we landed in Jamaica, Bubba finally showed up, and he and I drove up to a resort in Negril to try to negotiate an agreeable conclusion about loading the boat. We could not — Bubba got in an argument with the guy brokering the deal — and as we were leaving at about 3 a.m., you could hear a giant twin-radial engine plane taking off from the Negril airport, no doubt loaded to the ceiling with Jamaican weed.

We hung out for a couple more days, hoping something would materialize, but it didn't, and we took the *Carolina Garnet* back to the Bahamas to be stored. It was a long and wasted trip, and my first real setback in a business I thought I was getting pretty good at. More disappointment was around the corner.

Sometime after *One-Trick Pony* had been released and promptly dropped out of sight in October 1980, I got a call from Bubba, who asked if I wanted to finish what we started earlier that year.

I was pretty well out of money by this time (money goes fast when you're just spending it) and agreed, but Mike didn't want to go, so I asked my old friend and Trudy's ex-bandmate Rick Peters to be part of a crew with Fred and me. We sailed from Green Turtle Cay in the Bahamas to Grand Cayman, where to avoid potential suspicion we changed the name of the boat to *Miss Sun* (the name of a then-popular Boz Scaggs song).

Bubba and I flew from Grand Cayman to Montego Bay to sort out the deal, which went much better this time: we arranged for a place and time to pick up the load in Ocho Rios, Jamaica. Bubba and I parted company, and he went down to set up the drop while I went back to the airport to fetch the *Miss Sun* in Grand Cayman. All I had in my possession for this one-night trip were the clothes on my back (cut-off jeans, T-shirt, flip-flops), my shaving kit and the Cayman-issued temporary driver's license that functioned as my

ID. My flight back from Montego Bay to Grand Cayman had a stop-over in Kingston on the other end of Jamaica, which I thought was no big deal until I tried to board the flight from Kingston to Grand Cayman. I was told that because this was an international flight, I would need to show proof of U.S. citizenship, which was sitting on my sailboat in Grand Cayman. I tried to explain, but they wouldn't budge. Time was ticking — I had a tight window to get back to the *Miss Sun*, get her over to Ocho Rios and pick up the load. So I decided to board the plane anyway . . . and was promptly escorted off by two soldiers with machine guns. I wasn't arrested, but I was stuck. A ticket agent explained that the only way I could get back to Grand Cayman with my ID was to fly from Kingston back to Miami, then Miami to Grand Cayman. This was getting ridiculous, but I did it. I had to go through immigration in Miami, fly back to Grand Cayman and go through immigration again.

By now it was sundown. I took a cab to the beach but the boat was not where I'd left it — it was anchored offshore, and I had no way of signaling to Fred and Rick to come get me. So I swam out to *Miss Sun*, took the dinghy back to the beach to pick up my shaving kit, and finally prepared to make the trek to Ocho Rios. Tick, tick, tick.

As if all this wasn't stressful enough, I was supposed to be back in Baltimore on Sunday, December 7, to perform in the wedding of two good friends of mine, Bob Hieronymous and Zoh Meyerhoff, who had frequented the studio when I ran Blue Seas. I couldn't tell them what I was up to, but I assured them I'd be there. I was determined not to let them down, but it was now December 3 and I was going to be cutting it close.

By the afternoon of the 4th we had reached Ocho Rios, contacted our people and eventually found the load zone. The coast of Jamaica is very rocky with few beaches, so the bales of pot, totaling 6,500 pounds, had to be loaded onto small boats at the shore, motored out and thrown over the gunwale before being stashed below. By the time the last bale was on and the anchor and boat secured, it was well after midnight on Friday morning. There's an old sailor's superstition that says you're not supposed to leave for a long journey on a Friday. Were we tempting fate? Time would tell.

The seas were rough leaving the north coast of Jamaica and heading into the Windward Passage, and the fact that the boat was loaded down with more cargo than it was designed to carry wasn't helping. As Friday turned to Saturday, we were making progress, but not as much as I had hoped. We were about halfway through the Windward Passage when I grew concerned because the wind and current had moved us too close to the Cuban shoreline, perhaps even into their territorial waters. I had heard stories of smugglers boarded by Cuban gunboats; the crews were never heard from again, or got locked up in terrible Cuban jails. The U.S. Navy base at Guantanamo was also off to our port side, and we didn't need to be making contact with them either. So as I got ready to lie down for some rest, I had Rick change course to put us a little more toward the east. This would get us out of Cuban waters, but because it brought the wind closer to the bow, it would also make us pound harder into the head seas and put more stress on the boat's rigging.

I had just drifted off to sleep when I heard a loud crack and the sound of lines whipping against the hull of the boat. I put on my slicker and crawled up to the cockpit. The boat was pounding up and down and the seas were whipping over the deck, so it was hard to see on this pitch-black night. But with the sheet line for the jib flopping around like it was, I made my way up to the bow to see what had happened. The news was all bad. The forestay, or main wire that holds up the mast from the bow, had broken at the deck fitting and was just hanging out loose over the water. The only thing keeping the mast from falling down was the jib's luff wire, acting as a stay. We could not take the jib down or the mast would fall, and as I examined further, I found that one of the jib sheets had become wrapped around the rudder and we had very limited steering.

We started drifting closer to the Cuban shore. We tried various fixes over the next few hours to mitigate this major issue, but by the first light of dawn I could see the very dim outline of the Cuban coast in the distance. I tried to activate the emergency tiller to get us some steering, but the entire rudder and stock sheared its retainer pin and fell off the boat in thousands of feet of water. We were now literally rudderless, and by now I estimated we were already inside the 12-mile territorial limit of Cuban waters. I did not want to spend the rest of my life in a Cuban jail. Who knew what would happen should a patrol boat come by and board us?

I made the only decision I thought was reasonable: I decided to burn and sink the boat and call in a mayday. If we just called for help, we were either going to go to jail in Cuba or the U.S., and with this load of pot on board, neither outcome was going to be good. We could try throwing the bales overboard and then call for help, but that would leave a trail right to us. If we sank the boat without a trace, the theory was that we'd be losing the load and a boat I'd been planning to keep, but no one would be going to jail. Whoever owned the load we were carrying was not going to be happy, but if we got caught with it still on board they would lose it anyway, combined with the pressure of the crew getting busted, a legal defense and maybe the trail reaching back to them. Around 9 or 10 in the morning of December 7, we got out the emergency life raft, packed our passports and some cash and set about scuttling the *Miss Sun*.

It is not easy to sink a 45-foot sailboat with three and a half tons of pot aboard. We wanted it to sink as it burned so that the load would go down without a trace. We soaked all the bales in diesel fuel, then busted out the thru-hull fittings to let the seawater start to fill the boat. When all of that was done and the life raft was launched and ready to cut loose, I called in a mayday. We got an answer back from a freighter coming down the straits and heading for the passage. I gave them my position and said we'd had an uncontrollable engine room fire. They acknowledged our position, gave me an ETA and we thanked them. Rick and I got in the life raft. Fred's job was to use the last of our gasoline to soak the nearest bales to the companionway, then get in the cockpit and throw a match down into the cabin to start the blaze. Rick and I were watching as he lit the match. When he threw it into the cabin, the fire started with such force that it blew Fred right out of the cockpit and into the ocean. We pulled him into the life raft, and from the end of our 30-foot painter, we watched the boat go up in flames like a bonfire. She burned beautifully.

It was only a matter of minutes before we were hauled up onto the freighter and offered a hot shower and some coffee and food. I watched as the sailboat slipped under the waves, at which time I spied the unmistakable orange stripe of a U.S. Coast Guard cutter coming toward the freighter. The cutter stopped right where the *Miss Sun* had sunk, and seemed to go nowhere for about 20 minutes before resuming its course for the freighter. It pulled up alongside and sent over a longboat. The captain of the freighter came in and said that since he was going south, the Coast Guard would take us to a port closer to the U.S. We thanked him for the great hospitality and rescue and got aboard the longboat. We expected to be taken by the Coast Guard to a nearby port where we could arrange transportation home. But on the trip back to the cutter, the officer in charge of the longboat radioed the ship and I heard him say, "We've got the prisoners on board."

We were busted.

When we made it to the ship — a new and already legendary medium-endurance cutter called the USCGC *Decisive*, a sister ship of the *Diligence* — we were taken to the aft deck, where mattresses were brought out and we were chained to the deck with an armed guard watching over us. The three of us were able to have a private conversation, and I reminded everyone to keep the story between us straight, that we were delivering the boat from Jamaica to Florida and that was all. All of a sudden two seamen appeared carrying a dripping wet bale of marijuana, and dropped it on the deck just out of our reach. I could tell by the wrappings it was one of ours. We were allowed to lie there and look at this bale for about an hour and then one by one we were taken into an inner cabin and questioned by the second officer. You could tell these guys were newly assigned to this duty and did not know anything about marijuana smuggling on small sailboats. They were actually very polite and businesslike, and after they had interviewed all three of us, it was just about dark and we were fed and taken to the head and then we talked ourselves to sleep.

As I drifted in and out of sleep, I ran through the possible scenarios in my head, much as I had after being busted 14 years earlier with Zally in San Francisco. I did not see any way they could make charges stick. The bale was found floating on the ocean. We were miles away on a freighter, and the sailboat was at the bottom of the Windward Passage; they certainly couldn't present it as evidence. The crew of the freighter saw nothing illegal, and as a foreign crew they would probably not make cooperative or credible witnesses. As dawn broke, I was pretty sure we weren't headed for Puerto Rico, where they'd be sending us if we were going to be arrested. It looked like we had just done a big circle during the night and were probably right back in the Windward Passage. After we were up and getting our breakfast, the same officer who had debriefed us came onto our deck and told us the federal attorneys in Miami had decided they couldn't proceed with charges against us and that we would be taken to Great Inagua in the Bahamas and released. Phew.

An interesting thing happened then. After the handcuffs and chains were taken off, I asked to use the head. I had to be escorted, and as we went into the sailors' quarters where the bathroom was, the off-watch crew was all sitting around on their bunks. Almost in unison, they all gave a cheer of "freedom" to me. I gave them a raised fist back. No one had great affection for these anti-pot laws in 1980, yet here we are 34 years later and they're still locking people up for smoking weed. History won't be kind to these draconian laws. I also asked the officer if I could get a tour of the bridge, and he looked and me, paused a minute, smiled and said, "No — you have your secrets, and we have ours."

By mid-afternoon on Monday, the three of us were on a plane headed from Nassau to Baltimore. I'd missed my friends' wedding, which I felt awful about. If only they knew what I'd gone through to try to make it. On our way through the Nassau airport, I'd stopped in the duty-free store and bought a liter bottle of Mount Gay rum, which Fred and Rick and I proceeded to knock off on the flight home. As we were walking through the airport, I saw a pile of the latest newspapers on the floor. The headlines said John Lennon had been shot dead in New York.

One of the most horrific days in music history was memorable to me for another reason altogether — I was out of the pot smuggling business for good.

I took that audience with the Coast Guard as a sign that maybe it was time to move on to a new line of work, though it wasn't the only such sign. The game was changing. This rasta guy I had met through a St. Thomas connection tried to get me to smuggle guns into the country — he would get them and put them on the boat. I just had to sail them down from Texas. The money involved was huge, even relative to what I was making smuggling pot, but I turned it down. Pot was one thing, but guns were a much more dangerous and risky enterprise, plus I did not think I could look at the reflection of an international arms smuggler in the mirror. Ronald Reagan was about to become president in early 1981, and I knew the wrong guys were going to be in office for me to carry on with this lifestyle. Also, I was about to get married for the second time.

I hadn't been in a serious relationship since Trudy and I had "broken up" back in 1974. Trudy was technically bisexual but it became clear that if she was ever going to commit herself to one person, it wasn't going to be a guy. We'd remained very close friends, to the extent that she lived in my house on Bond Street and most people in our circle during the Baltimore years still considered me her boyfriend. But there was no romance between us, and I'd casually dated a bunch of women since that time.

Between pot runs, I'd been doing general handyman work for a little bit of extra money and because I liked doing it, when I was referred to a woman who needed some plumbing and electrical work done in her rowhouse on Compton Street in Federal Hill. Her name was JoNell Ryan, and she was known to Trudy through her friend Mary, who'd referred me to JoNell.

So I knocked on the door and it was answered by this beautiful five-foot-four woman who was totally in charge of the situation and what she wanted. JoNell took me up to show me the repairs she needed done, and as we walked through her third-floor bedroom past her bed, there was a big bowl of cocaine sitting there on the night table.

"Want a line?" she said. And that's where it began.

As I got to know her, it turned out JoNell was quite the interesting person. She was an upper-middle-class girl whose family owned a Chevy dealership out in Laurel, but she had willfully taken her life in another direction. She was a dealer at the time I met her, and had also done some side work as a hooker. She'd go up to New York on the train on weekends and come back with wads of cash stuck inside her boots. Sounded like my kind of girl.

When I told Trudy about JoNell, she flipped out. "You don't want to mess with that girl," she said. "She's a hustler."

And I married that hustler. Soon after that meeting, I moved in with JoNell and we decided we would clean up from drugs, get health insurance and plan to have a child. Jo agreed to give up her lifestyle and with the obvious changes in mine coming down the pike, I had little choice. Jo, on the other hand, was doing very well by herself, and her independence would now be at stake. On October 30, 1982, we were married by my good friend Dr. Bob Hieronimus, whose wedding to Zoh I had failed to show up for two years earlier. Our wedding was attended by the largest gathering of two Irish Catholic families I had ever seen. Held outdoors at JoNell's family home in Laurel, it had all the trappings of an upper-middle-class wedding. An outsider never would have guessed the lives we had recently left behind.

What attracted me to Jo as much as anything was that she was totally in charge, smart, independent and completely disciplined when it came to both money and drugs. I'd always been terrible with money, but she made sure the bills got paid on time and debts were not put off until tomorrow. It was while married to Jo that I would clear up my tax problems — she forced me to sit down with the IRS, negotiating a settlement by which they forgave the rest of my debt. Because of JoNell I was making money off publishing royalties for the first time in 15 years.

Being settled down again also appealed to me because the shit was hitting the fan with the smuggling operation, thanks in large part to wife number one.

Patti had been in the pot business in Baltimore for years, making good money as a broker and high-level dealer in the same operation I'd been a part of. She'd had a daughter, Rania, with Webber (I'm her godfather), but not long after that Patti got it into her head that, like me, she wanted to be a loader, putting crews together and heading down to the Islands and South America, where the even bigger money was. I thought that this was a horrible idea and Patti was going to be in way over her head. But she pressed forward, finding a 41-foot Morgan sailboat called the *Green Sea* and putting a crew together to go down to Jamaica on a run.

Of course, Patti was using at the time, and her whole crew was comprised of junkies. They were due to bring a load in through the Ocean City inlet when they ran aground on a sandbar in the middle of the night. Instead of trying to get the *Green Sea* off the sandbar, they just left it there and took the dinghy back to shore — to do what, God only knows. A fisherman discovered the abandoned sailboat and notified the Coast Guard, who, when they boarded the *Green Sea*, found bales of pot everywhere, identification for everyone on the boat, and an address book that had names, numbers and addresses for all of Patti's associates in the pot business. My worries had been well founded, it seemed.

The feds began a high-level investigation using the information they'd picked up from the *Green Sea*. I warned Patti to clean up before they started pressing her for information, but she didn't listen to me. Members of my crew were openly talking about killing my ex-wife before she could talk, discussions that I was luckily able to shut down.

But sure enough, the investigators got her in that room and started making threats about what would happen if she didn't talk. They told her she'd lose Rania if she didn't cooperate. She believed them, and she sang. Patti knew a lot. She told them everything and gave up everyone, including me, my brother Mike and his friend Fred, my friend Rick and the whole rest of my crew. By that point we knew it was over and just waited for the call to come.

I was arrested in October 1981 and charged with 64 counts of importing a Schedule 1 narcotic. I pleaded it down in 1983 to a single charge of felony conspiracy, for which I was sentenced to 30 days of confinement and another four years and 11 months on probation. I also needed permission to leave the state while on probation. All things considered, it was a pretty good deal. The confinement, which was at a halfway house on Boston Street just a stone's throw from my house on Bond Street, was kind of a joke. It was work release, and so from 8 to 5 every day I'd go to my job, which was helping to renovate a bar JoNell's mom owned down in Laurel, Maryland. After work every day, the Mount Gay rum would come out, and I'd stumble back to Boston Street not feeling much like a prisoner. Sure, I was locked in at night, but since I could look out my window at the Inner Harbor, it wasn't much different than being in my backyard in Fells Point. The only difference was that the state paid for my meals.

Still, when the 30 days were up, I was committed to walking the straight and narrow, or at least trying to, knowing that if I slipped up during my nearly five years on probation, I could be looking at real time in a real prison. I started by selling the house on Bond Street, which I'd bought seven years ago for $13,000 and now unloaded for $135,000, to pay off my fines and put some cash in my pocket (today that property is worth well over a million dollars). I sold another house I'd bought with pot money on Lancaster Avenue in Fells Point. There were always people trying to pull me back into my old life — I was even asked to make a significant sum of cash bombardiering bales from an airplane soon after I was released from the halfway house — but I thought better of it.

What I really wanted to do was get back into playing music, and I did, almost immediately. My friend Scott Cunningham had been the owner of the Marble Bar on 306 West Franklin Street in Baltimore when artists ranging from Muddy Waters to The Talking Heads to Phil Collins' jazz fusion project Brand X played there. Scott also happened to be a great singer in a band called The Scott Cunningham Blues Band. They'd even recorded an album (at Blue Seas) called *Blues Take You Over*, which featured other Blue Seas players, including Yug Phillips and Bob Wyatt. After my conviction, Scott would invite me frequently to play with his band, which featured some of the best players I had ever played alongside and ever will, including a monster drummer named Dennis Chambers, who played with many of the big-time funk acts. Other major league players who would sit in with Scott included Ralph Tucker, Ralph Fisher, Dave Carrero, Tommy McCormack and David Smith, and others from Baltimore's seemingly endless pool of top-shelf players. You had to be on your game to hang with those guys, and I was developing an appreciation for the blues that hadn't been fully formed when I was a member of The Spoonful.

Also during this time, John Sebastian extended me a musical lifeline. A friend of mine named Billy ran a pool and tennis club down in Sugarloaf Key, just northeast of Key West, and I'd go there pretty frequently to get some sun and hang out at Billy's bar, which was part of the facility. On one trip down there, I sat at the bar with Hunter S. Thompson, just him and me, getting drunk and bullshitting well into the night. I wish I had that conversation on tape. Anyway, Billy had booked John as entertainment at the club and had asked him whether he'd be amenable to my sitting in with him as a duo. John said he'd love that, and we were billed as "The Lovin' Spoonful with John Sebastian and Steve Boone." It was a low-key gig on an outdoor stage, but it went really well and reminded me how much I enjoyed working with John. We might have played more gigs there if John's idiot substitute road manager, some mobster's kid named Vinnie, hadn't trashed the Sugarloaf Lodge in a cocaine frenzy.

The next year, John called me to do a higher-profile duo gig in San Francisco for Bill Graham and the 20th anniversary of the legendary Fillmore club. John had been playing with NRBQ as his backing band but wanted to do an acoustic set with just him and me before NRBQ came on to join him. I had to really stretch to learn the chords again, but I sat with John and learned them all. It would have been a great gig, were it not for the fact that Howard Hesseman — at that time starring as Johnny Fever on *WKRP in Cincinnati* — got in my face with a look that told me he would always consider me a fink. That was nice. Also in the mid-'80s, Joe and I were called up for mini-sets with John at shows held at Johns Hopkins University and the 9:30 Club in D.C., but those did not go down so well. A lot of the old resentments between John and Joe were right there at the surface, and it was clear the arrangement was not going to last. But all these gigs were great evidence I could bring to my hard-ass probation officer, Ed Watts, to show him I was out working and staying out of trouble.

Unfortunately, while I played a lot of music during the rest of my time in Baltimore, which lasted until 1987, I also did a lot of drugs.

I had of course been a pot smoker for as long as I could remember, and other recreational substances like acid, PCP, coke and various pills had found their way into my bloodstream over the years. I'd always been able to manage my usage and keep my life relatively under control — until China White heroin entered my world.

I'd been introduced to it back in 1979 by Rick Peters after we'd scuttled the *Do Deska Din*. Until that time I'd stayed away from opiate use. I remembered what the withdrawal had been like after my accident; Peter had OD'd on the stuff; and things like heroin were not in everyday circulation in the crowd I ran with. Plus, you never knew whether the source was authentic or whether it was cut with bad substances that could kill you. But one day Rick came by with some powder that he said was completely uncut and straight from Thailand. He caught me at the right time, I guess. I snorted a line, and my entire world changed. This high was a quantum leap from any memory I had of opiates. And while with badly cut powder drugs you could always count on waking up the next day with hangover symptoms — stopped-up nasal passages, terrible-tasting drip in your throat, upset stomach — with the pure China White I woke up the next day feeling good. The dam had burst. Within weeks I had what was then called a "chippy," or mild addiction, where stopping was becoming fairly uncomfortable. By the end of the summer of 1979, I was going through cash far too quickly and snorting too much China White, which seemed to be in endless supply in good quality. After wrecking my BMW on Long Island earlier that summer — mostly because of being too high — right after I'd been stopped by the police with an open bottle of Mount Gay on my seat, I knew I had to try to clean up.

I got this crazy idea to get sober by going on a cross-country trip in my repaired BMW with Trudy and my Chesapeake Bay Retriever, Gruff, doing some business along the way and bringing along a car full of camping gear and a then-new VHS camcorder. The idea was to drive across the center of the country, first to Nashville for some music business and then on to San Francisco to rent an apartment for a month and get clean from the China White. Why I picked San Francisco, which still held so many painful memories for me, I couldn't tell you. Of course, I brought the rest of my stash of China White with me on the trip.

It was quite the adventure — while we were out in San Francisco we met up with Webber (now divorced from Patti), who had just passed his Single Engine Land certification as a pilot. This was a guy who, despite being a brilliant musician, was so scatterbrained as a person that it was nearly impossible to imagine him not only passing the written test for a pilot but passing the much harder check ride with a licensed instructor. I was so high on the dope that my sense of impending doom was very diminished, and we agreed to go up with him for a flight over San Francisco. Trudy was not getting high and she did not at all like the idea of letting him pilot us around the skies, but despite her trepidation she and Gruff went along for the ride. It all went well until the landing approach. I was in the front right-hand seat, and Webber turned to me and said, "Here, you land it." I had been taking private flying lessons on and off since 1967 and had accumulated enough dual hours to qualify for my licensing (all of which is a story unto itself). But at this point I was high out of my mind, and although I managed to wrestle the plane to the ground without crashing, I don't think Trudy ever forgave me or Webber for that thrill ride.

By the time October rolled around, the last of my stash of China White was going up my nose, and I didn't really have any choice but to go cold turkey. I found a very nice apartment to rent on Telegraph Hill, but my first attempt at cleaning up didn't take. I spent a big chunk of my remaining cash to fly back to Baltimore for more China White, then flew back to San Francisco. When that was gone, I entered withdrawal hell. The first two or three days off heroin were just as bad as any movie or account I had ever read. Gut-wrenching nausea and cramps, sweating buckets, and chills and fever continuously. I had no appetite for food and did not eat for at least three days. At the end of my rope on day three, I put on some clothes and had Trudy drive me to a hospital. I jumped out of the car and pushed through the entrance just as two attendants and the gurney were coming out. They took one look at me and knew exactly what I was doing there. The emergency room doctor sent me packing with a message of "get straight on your own time." It was a low point. I did manage to get through the withdrawal, though I wasn't totally through with drugs on this West Coast sojourn.

Trudy and I went down to L.A. to visit a young friend of hers from Baltimore named Gina Schock, a rock drummer who had been inspired by Trudy's playing. Gina had just replaced the original drummer in an all-girl band called The Go-Go's. We went to a rehearsal, and when the band cranked for the first song, my dental fillings began to vibrate — they were loud, and sounded great, though on this day in 1979 I couldn't have predicted how famous they'd become. I'm not sure how much they appreciated my sense of humor (I referred to lead guitarist Charlotte Caffey as "snarl-face," which didn't go over so well), but by coincidence their rhythm guitarist Jane Wiedlin and I had a mutual acquaintance — John's wife, Catherine Sebastian — who happened to be in Hollywood visiting at the same time I was there. The day after the rehearsal, Jane and I picked up some cocaine and went and partied with Catherine until it was gone. (Coke was nothing like China White — for whatever reason, I could still do it recreationally without any worry about becoming addicted.)

So the trip ended on a good note, and while I'd eventually kicked the China White habit, the addiction was at the back of my brain, still gnawing through my conviction, through my marriage to JoNell, and through my attempts at getting back into music. Once your body tastes opiates, you develop a craving that can overpower the strongest of wills.

After getting together with JoNell, I'd developed a taste for her drug of choice: Dilaudid, a medical-grade form of morphine that can be taken in pill form or injected. (I mostly did the former.) I managed my Dilaudid usage at first, but inevitably the habit got stronger, and whatever little money I had was going to getting more of the drug. Eventually, the addiction got bad enough that I started "busting scripts": using forged prescriptions so I could get more of the drug. I consider busting scripts to be the worst thing I ever did related to drugs, which is saying something for a guy who smuggled pot from South America and was addicted to China White.

It was extremely stressful. You couldn't hit the same pharmacy too much or they'd catch on to you pretty quick, so I must have known every pharmacy within an hour's radius of Baltimore. You had to play it cool so the pharmacists wouldn't think you were a junkie and scrutinize the script. If I'd gotten caught while on probation, I would have landed myself in prison. My habit required three pills a day, so I'd submit a prescription for 10 Dilaudid, keep enough for two days, and turn around and sell three at a cost of $20 or $30 per pill to finance the next transaction. Jo also knew a pharmacist who would sell us a bottle of 100 Dilaudid for $1000, and we'd keep what we needed and move the rest. It never got to the level of street dealing — most of our sales were to musicians and artists we knew, including some semi-famous ones — but if I hadn't cleaned up, it might have come to that. It didn't, but it did ruin my second marriage.

Drug addiction makes it easy for the addict to rationalize behavior and to overlook common sense. By 1987 I was using Dilaudid to the point that I could not stop cold turkey. Jo had cleaned up, but I tried to a couple of times and the withdrawal was just too severe. I was finally getting publishing royalty checks in increasing amounts, but I would blow through them quickly. The addiction and my inability to stay at a maintenance level of use was causing financial issues and driving a wedge between us. In 1987, she announced that she was leaving for — where else? — the Virgin Islands. Her mother had an unoccupied condo down near Fort Lauderdale on Hallandale Beach, and Jo proposed that I go there to try to get myself cleaned up so we could take some time off and see whether the marriage could be repaired.

I wish I could say that event was the start of my sobriety, but it wasn't. I went down to Florida, but not right away.

I was about two months out from the end of my probation when I got a call from the lead agent in charge of the feds that had busted me, a guy named Dennis Bass, asking if we could meet. I'd been getting high throughout my probation, so I was always paranoid that I was going to be found out and sent to prison. But Bass had a painfully familiar proposition for me. Without mentioning any awareness of my continued use on the street or low-level drug trafficking, he said he needed me to live at a house on the Eastern Shore of Maryland with two agents who were investigating drug smuggling in that area. I was to be their front person renting the house, and my task would be to hang out with the agents, go out to nightclubs and basically keep an ear to the ground for possible illegal activities. I had a bad case of déjà vu. I was convinced that if I did not go along with this, they would have charged me with violating my probation. Unlike what had happened in San Francisco two decades before, I was completely on my own here, and the potential penalty for my lack of cooperation would have been real prison time, not just the end of a band. Either way, I was trapped again, and this time the indecent proposal had been all my doing. I told the agent I would do it under one condition — that I would not have to have anything to do with buying or selling drugs. Dennis agreed, saying my only role there would be as someone with local knowledge of the area. They were also going to pay me a salary and lease me a car, which was significant since I had just wrecked my Ranchero and was broke. In the throes of a Dilaudid addiction and not seeing much of an alternative, I agreed to be a paid criminal informant for the feds.

To the Eastern Shore I went. The house was a pretty large estate on a creek off the Chesapeake Bay, oddly enough not far from where I had brought in my first load of pot back in 1977. They also had a 50-foot sportfish boat that had been seized from other smugglers and that I'd get to take out a couple of times with the two agents. I remember thinking after I met them that they were pretty nice guys but were going to stick out like a sore thumb. If there were other smuggling operations going on in this area, they weren't going to friend up with these guys. Of course, I was still using, so I had to go back and forth to Baltimore every couple of days to supply up. All I ended up doing was driving around the Eastern Shore in the daytime and going out to nightclubs on the weekend nights. I was using an alias, as I had friends on the shore and sure didn't want my name used in association with these guys. One night we went into one of the swankier places in St. Michaels, Maryland, and there was a singer I knew from Baltimore, with her band. I told the agents we'd better get out of there because I was going to be recognized, but before we could, the singer spotted me. I basically said I was just there visiting with some fishing friends of mine, and quickly got the hell out of there.

That was about the most exciting event of the whole two months. Nothing ever came of it and no arrests were made, thank God. It was around that time that I got a letter saying my probation was over, and I was free to leave the state without permission. I exhaled and plotted my next move. Baltimore was becoming radioactive for me.

This was underscored when, as I was preparing to move down to my mother-in-law's place in Florida, a connection of mine called and said he had the best China White and would I be interested in getting some. Even knowing what I'd been through, I couldn't say no. I snorted some and nodded out. I might have overdosed had Trudy and Zac not called and woke me up, saying they were coming over — with some cocaine. I did some of that too . . . at least it woke me up. But it was clear I had to get the hell out of town.

I packed up Gruff and my remaining Dilaudid and hopped in the '67 Mustang I'd bought with my earnings from the informant gig and headed down to Florida for Jo's mother's condo. The place was fine, but I was as depressed and low as I'd ever been. I tried to get clean and figure out where the hell the last 10 years of my life had gone. My life consisted of watching MTV and VH1 while lying on the couch, and occasionally going out to the pool and baking in the sun. By New Year's I was essentially clean. Bruce Burrows, a friend of mine from Baltimore who was also a sailor and lived in South Florida part-time, would come by with some pot, or would take me out for a pasta dinner, or to a bar.

One night in mid-January 1988, Bruce borrowed a classic Chevy convertible that belonged to a friend of his, and took me and another friend out to a club. We had a pretty good time and when it came time to head back to Hallandale and my home, we piled into the car and were traveling through the only vehicle tunnel in the whole state of Florida, which goes under the New River on U.S. 1 in Fort Lauderdale. Bruce was driving with me in the front and our friend in the back. We were passing around a joint when we entered the tunnel, and the friend yelled out "There's a car in the roadway!" I turned back around just in time to see a car that had stalled in the tunnel, right in our path. Bruce had very poor eyesight in perfect daylight and after a few drinks and nighttime conditions, he did not see the car until it was too late. He slammed on the brakes but not enough to avoid a collision, and we hit the car going about 40 miles per hour. There was no one in the other car — it had apparently stalled and been abandoned — which was a good thing, because this old Chevy knocked the other car up onto its side. An ambulance came and took all three of us to Broward General Hospital, where Bruce had to go into immediate surgery to relieve a blood clot. He also had a concussion and was in the hospital for a couple of weeks. The rear passenger was not seriously injured. I'd hit my forehead on the windshield frame, not too hard, but they diagnosed me with a mild concussion and gave me a prescription for Percocet, a pain-killer. And the cycle began anew.

Between January and May 1988 I must have fallen on and off the wagon a half-dozen times. I was invited out to St. Thomas with Mark Ritter, my old engineer at Blue Seas, who had a proposition for me. If I could bring him up a couple of ounces of cocaine to Baltimore to sell, it would finance the trip and put some extra money in my pocket. I went down to the Keys, where I had a drug contact, and did as asked. And of course every time I went to Baltimore, I would look up my old connections and start getting high all over again. With opiates you can clean up for a month, not touching a pill, but if you get high one time, you are right back to square one.

We went from there to the Islands and I checked in on JoNell. It was cool to visit St. Thomas again, having not been there in almost 15 years, and I could see why Jo had decided to move there. She was working for a sailboat charter fleet and had gotten herself sober and now had a boyfriend. It was obvious the marriage was over — not that I was surprised.

In the early spring I made another run for Mark, except this time I decided to fly and not drive. Big mistake. My flight out of Fort Lauderdale got canceled at the last minute, so I booked a flight out of West Palm Beach, an airport about an hour's drive north. I was on a tight schedule to get this trip done, and having to get to West Palm Beach airport in a rush was stressing me out. I had a business suit on, and not wanting to carry the coke in my carry-on bag, I'd wrapped it tightly in two Ziploc bags and stuffed it into my underwear. I barely made the flight in West Palm and I had been doing coke all day, so I was totally wired and — with cocaine still shoved in my underwear — I tried to calm down by having a couple of drinks on the plane. All that did was make me more paranoid and nervous, and when I got to Atlanta to change planes for my flight to Baltimore, I found out that it had been canceled. I was sweating and stressed out — not what I would recommend when you're trying to smuggle two ounces of coke. In Atlanta, coke-addled, mad and unreasonable, I stormed off to find an Eastern Airlines ticket agent. As I walked up to the customer service counter, ready to erupt, the agent took one look at me and said, "You need an upgrade!" Well, yes, I did.

I looked in the mirror of the first-class bathroom at a guy I barely recognized. I was down to 145 pounds and in terrible shape. It was right there that I had a talk with myself. Boy, you'd better get a grip. (When I got to Baltimore to make the coke transaction, the coke was bad and I never even got paid.) Once I got back to Florida, I started taking my own advice. I didn't know exactly what I wanted to do next, but I wanted out of this life. I was more determined than ever to get clean.

A couple of months into my latest attempt at sobriety, Bruce — who had recovered from the accident — came by to take me out to eat. We went to a cool sushi place on 17th Street in Fort Lauderdale called Sagami. On the way into the restaurant I saw a Volvo station wagon parked in front with a little Casio electronic keyboard on the front seat. It caught my eye and I said to Bruce, "Let's see if we can guess who the driver of the Volvo with the keyboard is."

I saw a blonde woman sitting at the bar a few seats down from me — she kind of looked like an artist. "That's your Volvo driver," I said. Displaying unusual boldness for me, especially because I was looking pretty pathetic at this point in my recovery, I leaned over and asked the blonde if her car was a Volvo station wagon. Well it turned out that no, it wasn't, but we struck up a conversation anyway. I was not particularly attracted to her, but she looked just like the woman from the Rick Astley video they were running constantly on VH1. Because she was an artistic-looking hippie type, we soon found out we had some things in common, became friends and swapped phone numbers.

I had just met Susan Peterson, who would become my third wife. And I took my first deep breath in a long time.

Chapter 12

FOREVER

March 6, 2000, was a triumphant night for The Lovin' Spoonful. John, Zally, Joe and I stood onstage at the Waldorf Astoria in New York, accepted our Rock and Roll Hall of Fame statues and played the hits just like we had on so many nights in 1966.

John Mellencamp gave a really fine induction speech, talking about the summer of '66 and the joy of hearing "Summer in the City," "Nashville Cats" and the *Hums* album for the first time as a teenager in Indiana. John was a fan of ours, and the feeling was mutual. He said we should be honored to know that people will be "dancing and fucking to [our] music in the 21st century," which we were. He told the audience gathered there that we were the band that had inspired him to pick up a guitar and become a musician in the first place.

Zally got up and thanked his old whipping boy Bob Cavallo first, and I got a chance to thank my brother Skip for helping to start me on my journey in music. I managed to work in a shout-out for his band Autosalvage, which got a shout-out back from a table in the audience. John got choked up talking about Mama Cass and while thanking his wife Catherine and their boys. Joe said he always wanted to be "one of the music makers," and was thrilled to have been a part of it. Our gratitude was sincere. We should have left that ballroom floating above the rafters, feeling like we'd been accepted, like our position among our musical peers had been cemented.

And yet instead of basking in the triumph of a terrific honor, we had so many things go wrong leading up to it and during the actual performance that an adult-size dose of joy was sucked from the experience. And then there was the question asked by *Newsday*, my hometown paper on Long Island, which we might have expected to be among our greatest champions but instead asked in the next day's edition, "Now they're letting jug bands in the Rock and Roll Hall of Fame?"

Ultimately, the experience was bittersweet at best. But nothing in the career of the band, at least since May 1966, had been free of pain. Why should this be any different?

The truth was it had been a hell of a journey over the previous decade just to get those four people to agree to set foot on the same stage.

My own march to sobriety had been one of the major steps along that path.

Meeting Susan in 1988 had been an important mile marker for me. We shared some common interests, including the fact that she'd just bought a 30-foot sailboat that was docked behind her apartment on the New River in Fort Lauderdale. Also, significantly, she was not a drug user. She had a good job at the University of Miami, teaching English as a second language, and she was into a healthy lifestyle. Once I started exercising and eating better, I started to look and feel like a normal human being again. Susan had a connection at the International Swimming Hall of Fame in Fort Lauderdale and convinced me to become involved there. In addition to swimming at the Hall of Fame regularly, I became an official for U.S. Swimming and YMCA meets and also DJ'd big events at the pool, activities that I thoroughly enjoyed. Some of the young girls who swam in meets at the Hall of Fame started harping on me about my smoking, so I quit. That place and those kids meant a lot to me.

I also have a vivid memory during my DJ gig of playing AC/DC's "You Shook Me All Night Long" at the request of a swimmer named Seth Van Neerden at the U.S. Nationals just before a 200-meter breaststroke final. After he edged future U.S. Olympian and world record holder Mike Barrowman by 1/100th of a second to win the event, Seth sought me out to say that my blasting the song had helped him give the extra push he needed to win. Another lesson in never underestimating the power of music.

Not long after I met Susan, I knew it was time to move out of my ex-mother-in-law's house. Jo and I had made our divorce official with a simple and amicable swap of papers, and her mom was planning on using the condo in Hallandale on a more regular basis. Meanwhile, Susan was unhappy with her landlord and needed to move too. So almost as a matter of convenience, maybe a couple of weeks after we'd started casually dating, we took her sailboat up the north fork of the New River and moved in together at a cool little cottage we'd found there for rent. Not long after, Susan and I started working together, which was when I discovered her "mermaid" persona.

She fantasized she was a mermaid — at first I thought it was an act before I realized that she truly believed she was a mermaid — and that became the theme of her children's shows, in which she would put on a big flipper and swim, and also tell stories and play her guitar. She got me involved with it too. We found a frog costume somewhere down in Miami and I adopted the persona of "Mr. Frog." We'd play environmental showcases, and I had a little remote control speedboat I'd put in a pond or fountain while "the mermaid" would tell environmental awareness stories focused on water safety and respecting marine life. It was a long way from my past life, but it was fun and for a good cause. Another good cause I'd take up during my time in Fort Lauderdale was working as a New River tour guide for the Fort Lauderdale Historical Society, which I got into through curator Sue Gillis and associate Patsy West, the daughter of my next-door neighbor Cappy West — and that was also a blast. I branched off from this to write some articles about Fort Lauderdale's history for local publications, the first creative outlet I'd had in a while.

It was around that time that I started working for Alan Bliss. Alan was a friend of Bruce's, a legend in the Biscayne Bay sailing community, a great storyteller and native New Englander who'd been on active duty in World War II as a radar guy on Navy destroyers. Alan contracted me in 1988 to do some repairs around his house and on his sailboat, mostly handyman work, which got me out of the house and put some money in my pocket. One weekend he was going up to New England and asked me to look after his dog, Charlie Brown, which I was happy to do. I came and got the dog, but when I went back to his house later that weekend, I was shocked to see that Alan's house had burned not quite to the ground, but pretty much. He had a female roommate who had apparently spilled nail polish on the carpet, somehow ignited a fire and then just bailed. Alan came home to quite the scene. I asked him if there was anything I could do to help, and he asked me if I would help rebuild and renovate his house. He said he'd pay me time and materials, so I said sure. Alan was kind of a cheapskate with the material allocation, but I did spend all of 1989 rebuilding the inside of that gutted house, with a little bit of help from Bruce on the carpentry. It was a massive project, but perfect for someone in recovery who needed to stay focused on a task.

At what had become a good time in my life, I agreed to marry the mermaid. I say "agreed" because the pressure was coming all from her side. Susan had been a great friend at a time in my life when I really needed someone in my corner, and was (and is) a big reason why I'd been able to put my life back together. But I wasn't in love with her, and I'd seen a little bit of a crazy streak in her that concerned me. One night before I'd hooked up with Alan, she started harping on me about not having a job, in the midst of which she smashed six Corona bottles, one after the other, on the stone floor of our house. Still, my rationale at the time was that she deserved to be married because she was going on 50 years old and never had been. We went down to a public office in Fort Lauderdale that had a big heart on the wall, and made it official. It's a decision I would come to regret. We should have stayed friends.

Sadly, in the first year or two after I got to Florida, I played very little music. I had no bass, thanks to my old friend Mark Ritter, who turned out to be something of a con man. He'd convinced me to leave my valuable 1961 dual concentric Fender jazz bass and my gold records at his house when I was moving from Baltimore, but when I came back for them, Mark and my stuff were gone. I later got the gold records back from someone who contacted me through Zoh Hieronimus' Baltimore radio show, which I was doing a guest spot on — he'd bought them from a pawn shop right near Mark's house. But the bass had vanished without a trace, my Martin D-28 guitar was in bad shape and with limited funds at my disposal, I put most of my energy into getting better. Then late in early 1990 I discovered an authentic Irish pub on Andrews Avenue down in Fort Lauderdale called Maguires Hill 16. They had a great band there called The Irish Times, which featured one of the owners, Alan Craig, doing some singing, and a lead guitarist I would become great friends with named Dan O'Brien. Dan and I co-produced an album there called *Live at Maguires Hill 16* that I am very proud of, and we've continued to work together. It was working with The Irish Times that got me excited about playing music again.

Subsequently, I decided I was fed up with the fact that no one in The Lovin' Spoonful had received any record royalties since 1968. I'd been receiving publishing royalties for the songs I wrote thanks to the performing rights agency BMI, which has served me well for going on 50 years. But I hadn't received a dime from any of our records, including the innumerable compilations and gray-market repackages I'd seen in record stores over the previous two decades. John and Joe hadn't received a dime either. Zally hadn't, but wouldn't have anyway because he'd waived his right to future royalties when he got his settlement for leaving the band. By the time we started really pressing, through our new, determined lawyer Nick Gordon, the CD era was in full flower and all our fans (and some new ones) were buying new, digital-quality copies of our albums from which we still weren't making a cent.

Early on, the excuse had been that we hadn't earned back the advance on the seven-album deal. Once the IRS levy came in and none of that would-be money was going to make it into my pocket anyway, I stopped asking and was tied up with my various other pursuits. When we had lawyers try to look into the situation in the '80s, they threw up their hands in frustration. Charley Koppelman and Don Rubin had somehow "inherited" our record contract in the late '60s, and had sold our masters and the right to license them in the early '70s, to Buddah Records, which was run by a guy named Neil Bogart, who had worked his way up to running the label by age 24. Bogart left the label to run Casablanca, at which point the masters ended up in the hands of a company called Viewlex, which went bankrupt, after which they returned to ex–Kama Sutra owner Art Kass, who was running Buddah again by this time but was in debt to notorious rock 'n' roll gangster Morris Levy, whom he'd been forced to take on as a silent partner. When we started looking into this puzzle in the '80s, it was impossible to follow the money during the time Bogart (who died in 1982), Levy (died in 1990), Viewlex and Kass would have been in charge of our royalties. We were told Bogart and Levy and Kass had been shielding money through dead relatives during those years and that any chance of getting a proper accounting of our royalties, much less the actual money due to us, was virtually nil.

But we caught a break when the catalog ended up in the hands of a company called Essex Entertainment (later bought by Sony), which operated like a real business and hadn't been distributing our albums long enough to make it worth fighting us over money. They couldn't do anything about the royalties we'd earned before they took over, but Nick eventually got them to admit that they did owe us money from at least the past few years of sales. They proposed a settlement, which didn't inspire a trip to the Ferrari dealership but was a good start. The most significant thing, in my mind, was that they'd be paying us going forward and we should now be able to keep a handle on who exactly was licensing our back catalog.

But when it came time to split up the settlement and plan the future allocation of royalties, a problem emerged. A three-way split of royalties for me, John and Joe is what I'd expected, but one member of our group was proposing a four-way split — John Sebastian wanted Zal Yanovsky to be cut in on royalties.

It had been John who'd instigated Zally's firing in 1967. He'd never explicitly admitted it, but I know he was regretful. That's what things like their appearance together at the Isle of Wight had been about. John had become a huge cheerleader for Zally over the years, rightly lauding his innovative guitar work and positive impact on our band. Their friendship had been repaired, and that was commendable. I also loved Zally and wanted to see him get his due, but to include him in this settlement would be to ignore a business reality. Zally had accepted a lump-sum settlement in 1967 that took care of all royalties, past and future, at a time when no one else in the band had seen a penny. While the rest of us fought for years to get our own due, Zally already had his lump of money collecting interest in a bank. My understanding was that the money from the settlement had helped him and his second wife, Rose Richardson, start two famous restaurants — Chez Piggy and its bakery, Pan Chancho — in Kingston, Ontario.

Now, would Zally have taken that deal when he was 22 had he known he still could have been making money off Lovin' Spoonful royalties in his mid-40s and beyond? Probably not. Very few of our contemporaries could envision middle-aged people buying the same records they'd bought in their teens, only at three times the price tag. We certainly didn't see that coming. Did Zally contribute to those records, and play a major role in making them great? You bet your ass he did. But he'd taken that severance payout directly from Koppelman-Rubin in 1967 and he'd also been paid from the seven-album deal, which meant that by 1991, he'd made more money off The Lovin' Spoonful record sales than anyone else in the band. Sure, it would have been a wonderful gesture to loop Zally in. But it wasn't fair to the other three guys in the group, who had been working for years to try to get the royalties back, to just cut him a check when all indications were that he didn't really care anyway. And frankly, we were a little bugged that John was the one insisting on the four-way split. John made far more from publishing than me and certainly more than Joe, so dividing the pie four ways instead of three impacted him very little financially. It impacted us. The bottom line was that it felt like John was trying to clear his own conscience on Joe's dime and mine.

"This is the right thing to do," he said. "I also think we could get Zally to a rehearsal if we made this offer to him."

John was talking about a potential reformation of The Lovin' Spoonful, but I'd seen Zally the year before, when Susan and I had gone to Kingston to visit him, and I doubted this was so. He'd told me explicitly that he never wanted to play music for a living again.

"I think you're wrong about that, John," I said.

"Well, we'll never know if we don't cut him in on this . . . it's the right thing to do."

Joe spoke up. "I agree with Steve, John. Zally made the deal."

The three of us took a vote, just like we'd done 24 years before, sitting in John's living room in Greenwich Village, when we'd decided Zally's fate with the band. Again, the vote was two-to-one against Zally. This time, one of the majority votes was mine.

"You guys will regret this, wait and see," John said.

It was after the royalty situation was cleared up that serious discussions began about putting The Lovin' Spoonful back together for the first time since our *One-Trick Pony* one-off in 1979. It had been discussed previously, but it was hard to muster the support when we knew we'd be on the road promoting a catalog we still weren't getting paid for. But by 1991, the royalties were back in our control, and promoters were interested in having us tour. From my perspective and Joe's, the time felt right. We reached out to John and Zally and their answers, almost immediately, were no. That wasn't a huge surprise. Zally responded simply, and professionally, just saying he wouldn't close the door on doing something in the future but that he wasn't interested at this time. If he was angry at me and Joe over the royalty split, he certainly never made that apparent to me. John also deferred interest, though at first he didn't give any specifics on why he was saying no. We just figured he was more interested in his solo thing, and that was his right.

But Joe and I didn't feel that no John and Zally meant no Lovin' Spoonful, and neither did the promoters who were courting us. We were going to need a solution when it came to who was going to sing the hits — I certainly wasn't going to, and Joe couldn't carry the whole show vocally — but if we could replicate the sound credibly, we were told, it was doable. One of the first people we talked to, interestingly enough, was Mark Sebastian, John's brother. Mark had never been a member of The Spoonful but could sing and play guitar and knew our repertoire as well as, if not better than, anyone in the band. I'd always gotten along great with Mark, who was a little more down to earth and approachable than his more famous older brother. I got the sense that Mark really wanted to do it. He hemmed and hawed over it for a short period before ultimately saying no — he just didn't think it would sit well with John, which was more than understandable.

I'd originally thought Jerry Yester was a non-starter for the reformed Lovin' Spoonful. Jerry was living in Hawaii when we first started making plans, and logistically I didn't see how that would work. But as things were taking shape, I learned that Jerry had recently moved to Portland, Oregon, so we approached him, and indeed he was open to the idea. Jerry had a great voice, could play several instruments and could handle some of the songs John had sung lead on. Knowing we were going to need another singer and guitarist, Jerry floated the idea of inviting his brother Jim, who had played on all of The Association's biggest hits and was also available. We got together as a foursome in late 1991, and the chemistry and sound were very good. This looked like it was going to work.

Once we'd decided to move forward, we sent courtesy letters to John and Zally to notify them of our plans for using The Lovin' Spoonful name and to confirm their lack of interest. Our lawyer and my old friend Scott Johnson (who'd come a long way since our coke bust in the '70s) sent letters on our behalf, written on the stationery of his Baltimore firm, Ober, Kaler, Grimes and Shriver, and shipped them off. Apparently this attempted courtesy did not sit well with John. He fired back:

Dear Scott:

Thank you for your incredibly presumptuous letter. Yes, I know you represent Joe Butler and Steve Boone, and now, by default, Jerry Yester.

But do you represent or can you speak for The Lovin' Spoonful? — Believe me Scott this isn't the one that's gonna get your name on the letterhead. Let me fill you in on a little history.

The Lovin' Spoonful were four guys — me, Zal Yanovsky, and eventually the guys you represent. We earned our reputation by playing our own instruments in a day when studio substitutes were the norm for bands. I felt then as I do now, that anything less than that was foreign to the spirit of the band and dishonest to the public. Joe and Steve's 'many efforts over the years' consisted of trying to get me to do it without Zally — the guy who provided our on stage whammy! And during that time, Steve lost his bass, Joe didn't even own drums. I know because I fronted the money, found him a kit (which he hasn't paid me back for) and still had to listen to vague ideas of regained stardom and not once the simple, responsible idea of getting together to see how we might sound.

Are you surprised that I didn't think highly of this? So now they go back to Zally to try to get him to do it without me. He laughed in their faces. Now they got mad and when the opportunity came, they cut Zal out of a measily [*sic*] royalty statement that morally should be his. The irony here is that if they'd just not been so greedy and politically stupid, I could have had Zal at a rehearsal within a month.

During the course of The Lovin' Spoonful, we all had equal chances to create and contribute. When I left the band they had every opportunity to pick up the flag. Have you ever heard 'Revalation/Revolution' [*sic*]? Have you even seen the cover? The reason for your clients' obscurity was not lack of opportunity. The songs they will be trading on were mostly written by me.

So now these guys want to be in show business. And America's appetite for nostalgia is great and these guys are hungry. And when they tire of the unscrupulous promoters that will hire them, they can go back to contracting and carpentry and leave a spoiled reputation for a band that had The Beatles as fans. And do you know, Scott, who will be asked to explain this, before and after? The calls won't be coming to Scott Johnson, representative of Joe Butler and Steve Boone. Be glad.

Yours truly,
John Sebastian

Wow. Now this I hadn't expected. I couldn't help but think of the lyrics to our song "It's Not Time Now": "But we've taken sides in anger and we can't back down/ Now we're fightin' just to bring the other down." Right there in black and white, John was completely dismissing anyone's role in the band other than his and Zally's, forgetting the fact that I'd co-written some of our best-loved songs, including our biggest hit; using Joe's de facto solo album from 1968 as evidence that we had no individual talent; calling Joe a deadbeat and also apparently putting down carpenters and contractors everywhere. Yes, the calls always came to John when it came to The Spoonful, and he'd never thought twice about speaking for all of us then, so why should this be any different? He hadn't thought promoters' billing of NRBQ as The New Lovin' Spoonful in the '80s had been "foreign to the spirit" of the band, or at least not enough to object to that billing, but Joe, Jerry and I taking on the name of a group we'd been members of was? John obviously believed we were unworthy of our individual success, and even though my own musical history was arguably more diverse than his, he did not think we were up to the task of carrying on the band's name without him. The irony was that we would have had an even harder time carrying on its name *with* him, due to a gradual change in his vocal ability.

This fact was underscored by our performance at the Rock and Roll Hall of Fame induction in 2000, by which time we'd patched up our differences enough for the classic lineup to appear onstage and attempt a couple of songs. John's growing vocal problems had started to become apparent as early as the late '80s, when a sort of atonal growl became apparent in his voice. The changes in his voice have mostly remained shrouded in mystery even to his former bandmates, but he admitted on a New York radio show once that they were partially physical and partially psychological. By the time we went out on the road in '92 without him, the simple fact was that John was having trouble getting many of the Spoonful songs over during his own solo shows. Even when acknowledging the fact that no one's singing voice sounds at 50 like it did at 20 (not even Paul McCartney's or Mick Jagger's!), we would have had to reconcile this issue had he decided to come back to the group when we reformed. I felt bad for John over his throat problems — it had to be very difficult for him to go through that — but I thought it was a little disingenuous for him to send a letter effectively saying, "You're nothing without me" when he had to understand the reality of his own performing abilities.

And anyway, he was wrong. More than 20 years after The Lovin'
Spoonful became a live entity again, we're still a live entity. We've
done our classy, professional, well-produced show all over the world
to positive reaction, and have done nothing to diminish the standing
of The Lovin' Spoonful in the hearts and minds of music fans and
record buyers. The lineup has seen some shifts during that time, but
the '91 core of Boone, Butler and Jerry Yester remains.

Strangely enough, not long after John wrote the letter, we were
rehearsing the new lineup at a large house in upstate New York
when who walked in but John Sebastian. He'd driven down from
Woodstock, and though there was definite tension in the room, we
had a friendly chat, he wished us well, and that was that. I guess I
could try to psychoanalyze why this visit came so soon on the heels
of what was at the time a very hurtful letter, but I won't. Bands
have fights and end up not talking to each other for 20 years, which
benefits no one, so I was just glad he was there. I still don't think
he wanted the band to go on, but to his credit he knew there was
nothing constructive to be gained from holding a grudge. Maybe he
files away that letter, along with the circumstances of Zally's dismissal from the group in '67, as a moment he wishes he had handled
differently. I guess you'll have to wait for his book to know for sure.

There were some bumps along the road for the new lineup of The
Lovin' Spoonful. Jim Yester left after about a year — his personality
was not a match with the rest of the group — and we added a short-
lived keyboard player (David Jayco) and a guitarist (Randy Chance)
who didn't work out. Joe relinquished the drum stool so he could
come out front and sing, which meant we needed a new drummer.
We used this drummer nerd from Chicago named John Marrella for
a while, but booted his ass when it turned out he was shit-talking
the band behind our backs. In 1996 we added a terrific drummer
named Mike Arturi, who has been with us ever since. As a rhythm
section, Mike and I have developed the best chemistry I've had with
any drummer. A really wonderful second guitarist from Harrison,
Arkansas, Phil Smith, joined the group in 2000 after coming to us

through Jerry. Phil also owns a fabulous music store, GuitarSmiths, in Harrison.

But the most significant addition to the band for me, both personally and professionally, was Lena Yester. When Jim announced that he did not want to continue with the band, Jerry suggested his 17-year-old daughter Lena might be able to fill the sonic void. A musical prodigy, she had composed her first song at age two and was proficient on both keyboards and guitar in addition to being a great singer. I'd heard the songs she'd written and produced with her sister, Hannah (both Lena and Hannah are a product of Jerry's marriage to his second wife, Marlene), and I knew she was extremely talented. Of course, both Joe and I found the suggestion of her being in the band outrageous. The Lovin' Spoonful had always been an all-male lineup, and what would our fans think? We'd made our bones *singing* to teenage girls — they didn't come up onstage to play with us.

I was dubious, but we had a television show appearance booked in Holland, and with few other options, we gave Lena a try. She showed her professionalism and commitment level right away by learning all our songs, note for note. At the age of 17, playing in her dad's band with her first-ever gig a television show no less, Lena handled the entire experience with skill and grace. She sounded great — I thought she made us sound like Fleetwood Mac, a band I loved! She was also a songwriter, and I felt like her original songs could give us another dimension beyond being a "nostalgia band." Joe finally realized that Lena was a valuable asset too, and she became a full-time member. For the next few years the band got better and better. The new songs Lena brought to the band were extremely well received by fans, which was great to see. With the bookings continuing to increase, I actually saw the potential for a whole new Lovin' Spoonful.

Along those lines, as the late '90s approached, Joe and I talked about adding Jerry to The Lovin' Spoonful corporate structure. Jerry was our musical director and had really been such a big part of what The Lovin' Spoonful was, dating back to his work on our very first demos in 1965. Joe was not in love with this idea, but I finally convinced him it was a good move, so I laid the groundwork with our lawyers for Jerry to become a shareholder of Spoonful Concerts, Inc., stock, with an equal vote on corporate business. The greatest benefit of this, in addition to the fact that we'd have another trusted partner to share in decision-making, was that we'd have a tiebreaker in the group. Joe and I had been the only two votes on every decision since the group's reformation, and whenever we disagreed, one of us either had to relent or that piece of business just wouldn't move forward. This had led to some agendas not being advanced, in particular the fact that I wanted to pursue new music and Joe was content just playing the old hits. Unfortunately, at the last second Jerry decided he didn't want to get caught up in business matters and opted to continue concentrating on the music alone. I was crushed. Joe and I have carried on as equal partners with sometimes differing views on the way the business should be run. Luckily, we still enjoy playing together.

In the meantime something else was happening that I was finding hard to suppress, and had become a major distraction for me. By 1997 the band was playing a lot of dates, which meant I was on the road nearly as much as I was home. Jerry wasn't really one for hanging out after the show, and Joe and I have socialized together enough since our days in The Kingsmen that it's not strictly essential that we ever hang out again. We love each other, but I'm sure he feels the same way. So Mike Arturi and I got locked in as traveling buddies, and occasionally we'd see Lena in the bar after the show, once she came of age. Lena was a mature young woman, and the more I got to know her, the more I liked her and respected her talent. I also found myself developing feelings of attraction for this woman who was 32 years my junior, and who, by the way, was the daughter of my bandmate. We would flirt and I would compliment her, but I was married and of course there was always the very big, dark shadow of her dad standing not 15 feet away onstage. This was all very difficult to handle.

A couple of days before my birthday in September of '97, the band was in Buffalo for a gig at the Buffalo Bills practice facility and also got a chance to go to the game against the Colts. Lena was not much on going to football games, and I thought it odd that she stayed and sat right next to me for the whole time we were there. After the gig most of the guys wanted to go to Niagara Falls, but I stayed behind at the hotel bar to watch the Sunday night game and have a few drinks. Just as I was about to leave, who walked up but Lena, and I asked her if I could buy her a drink. She ordered a glass of wine and we talked, in the midst of which I confessed that I had dreamed of kissing her. She leaned over and gave me a kiss. Happy Birthday! We've been together ever since, though Lena left The Lovin' Spoonful in 2000. Other people might find our relationship strange, but for us, age is just a number.

To answer the million-dollar question, Jerry and Marlene were super cool about my relationship with their daughter. There were some initial cautions having to do with our age difference and my existing marriage, but as great parents, their primary concern is that their daughter is happy. Jerry has stayed in the band and has not to date attempted to strangle me with a guitar strap.

Susan was not quite as understanding, as you'd imagine. I handled everything totally wrong with her, copping to the fact that I was running off with Lena instead of just telling her I wanted out of the marriage for my own general happiness (which would not have been a lie). This admission led to years of legal wrangling over our divorce, with the result being that Susan, who at the time was dealing with ongoing problems related to a chemical reaction to pesticides, continues to receive a court-awarded alimony payment from me each month. I was going to fight the terms of this divorce in court, until it was explained to me by my lawyer that judges tend not to find in favor of adulterers who leave their disabled wives for women 32 years younger. Well when you put it like that . . . And yet somehow, through all of this, Susan and I have remained friends. She comes to my shows in South Florida and we still talk on the phone occasionally. As I've said, friends are what we probably should have remained.

In late 2000, I got the call that I'd wondered whether I would ever receive — it was Joe, saying The Lovin' Spoonful was being inducted into the 2000 class of the Rock and Roll Hall of Fame. We became eligible with the 1991 class, and watched nine straight classes of our contemporaries and select others get inducted while our phone never rang. I have my own thoughts on why this was so, and they start with Jann Wenner and the group of faceless "industry insiders" who control the induction process without a shred of transparency about their criteria or their process. There have been stories about last-minute switches of inductees due to concerns over the quality of the televised show, which, if true, is just appalling. We heard rumors that the bust had not put us high on the list of Wenner and his cronies, though I can't verify that. Maybe they just didn't think we were very good, though I'd wear it almost as a badge of honor that The Beatles liked us and Jann Wenner didn't.

But being mentioned alongside others we respected in the business and giving a thrill to our loyal fans was what the Hall of Fame was all about, so I was ecstatic when I got that call.

We'd expected that the four guys pictured on the "Do You Believe in Magic" single sleeve would be the four people honored as part of the induction process, but I pushed hard from the moment we got that call to have Jerry Yester honored as part of our group too. Jerry had been in The Lovin' Spoonful for just one of our four official albums, but he'd played on important singles like "Do You Believe in Magic" and "She's Still a Mystery to Me," had played *Ed Sullivan* and other key gigs with us, and did an incredible job in helping save the *Everything Playing* album when our producer bailed on us. It didn't seem like an outlandish request that he be honored, and certainly all four of us, including Jerry's friend Zally, thought his inclusion was appropriate and warranted. But the people at the Rock Hall said no way. They had no specific guideline or precedent they could quote as a reason to leave him out, mind you. If they had, perhaps they would have prevented The Grateful Dead from including 12 people as part of their official Hall of Fame entry, including a keyboardist who had left in 1970 and been with the band a total of 14 months, and another keyboardist who had joined the band four years before their 1994 Hall of Fame induction. I guess Jann Wenner really dug The Dead's keyboardists.

We could have opted to boycott the ceremony (which Jerry wouldn't have wanted us to do), but decided to go out of respect for our peers and our fans and so we could thank the people from inside our circle who'd helped make it happen. The four of us had also been getting along over the previous few years, which was a most welcome development.

I'd been in contact with John over business and other related matters, and had also seen Zally a few times — first when he came to Gulfstream Park in South Florida for the Breeders' Cup horse race, and again on a trip down to the Keys with two other friends for a week of drinking and partying. We didn't really talk about The Spoonful, except for me to tell him when he'd asked that we were having a good time touring as The Lovin' Spoonful.

Just like at the Concord Hotel 21 years before, once we picked up our instruments in the rehearsal room and started jamming in advance of our scheduled musical appearance on the show, things clicked. Paul Shaffer from the *Late Show with David Letterman* was the musical director for the induction ceremony, which also included inductees Eric Clapton, Earth Wind & Fire, Bonnie Raitt and James Taylor. Paul and his band were in the audience when we started jamming, and you could sense their appreciation for the sounds. Until John sang — then the quiet reverence seemed more like a pall. God love John, who knew what was expected of us during this show and only wanted to deliver. But he just couldn't hit the notes, and you could tell Shaffer and his people knew it. I wish Shaffer had stepped up and said, "Guys, this isn't going to do it," but he let us go on.

I pulled John aside. "Hey, why don't we do 'Night Owl Blues'? It was our signature piece, people would love it."

"They want the hits," he said. "It'll be fine."

But it wasn't. John got through "Did You Ever Have to Make Up Your Mind" passably thanks to Zally's harmony vocal, but "Do You Believe in Magic" sounded awful. Somebody told me Howard Stern played clips of the performance on his radio show the next day, talking about how The Lovin' Spoonful was one of his favorite bands and how let down he was by the performance.

Hindsight being 20/20, we should have been stronger in that situation and insisted on doing something that wouldn't have embarrassed us. We would have knocked them out with "Night Owl Blues." Whatever John's limitations in 2000 were as a singer, he was still an unbelievable blues harp player and rhythm guitarist, and people would have seen that even if he didn't sing. If they wanted to cut the performance from the TV edit of the show, then so be it, but we had earned the right to do that slot on our own terms. I wish we had. As soon as it was over I left the stage and went upstairs to join up with Lena, who was smarting over her dad not being allowed up there. Zally called my room and asked me to come down and party with him, but I was bummed and not in a party mood.

I knew this appearance was not going to help our legacy, and what has happened to the legacy of the The Lovin' Spoonful since the group last recorded in 1968 is a sore subject for me, I'll admit.

Back in '68 I wasn't focused on how we'd be judged 40-plus years on, because pop music wasn't really thought of in those terms. Pop music, the kind that kids listened to, was viewed as disposable. I'm sure The Beatles and Bob Dylan and those rightfully judged to be the most important rock acts of the '60s never dreamed that kids would still be buying their music when they themselves were at retirement age. But that's what has happened, and in addition to the music itself, an entire industry of commentators and critics and pundits has sprung up just to curate what's cool for the subsequent generations who weren't there to live it.

This phenomenon doesn't boggle my mind or anything. I really believe the '60s and '70s were a golden age of popular music, and will be judged that way long after we're gone. The evidence of the music's staying power is right there when you turn on your radio and hear 20-year-old guys playing recycled Led Zeppelin riffs, or see a teenager wearing a John Lennon T-shirt almost 35 years after he passed away.

What bothers me is the thought that The Lovin' Spoonful might be relegated to footnote status when the master class on the music of the era is taught.

I don't want this to sound like sour grapes, I really don't. The Spoonful were successful on a grand scale, and I wake up every day and consider myself lucky to have been a part of it, and to still be a part of it. Our records are still in print; people still come to our shows and can hear our songs on oldies or classic rock radio. Tens of thousands of acts, many of whom deserved a much wider audience than they ever achieved, would have surrendered their first-born for the degree of success The Lovin' Spoonful had. I get it. I'm grateful.

In spite of all this, I can't get over the fact that we're viewed as second-tier among some of the real aficionados, and what gives me that feeling more than anything is the way we're treated relative to some of our American peers.

Take The Beach Boys, with whom The Spoonful toured, and whom I've always loved. There was a point in the late '60s and early '70s when The Beach Boys were uncool to the point that *Rolling Stone* wouldn't even bother to review their albums. They're now held up right alongside The Beatles in terms of critical respect. Brian Wilson is a singular genius beyond any question, but let's remember that The Beach Boys didn't even play on their best-known records.

The Byrds, another of our American contemporaries and another group I think is terrific, didn't play on their early material either, nor write some of their most popular songs. Yet they seem to hold a place of great reverence among the rock establishment, and are considered one of the era's most important acts.

Even The Monkees have been shown some love. Though all four members of that act were musically talented, it seems to have been forgotten by some (though not Jann Wenner, who is rumored to be staunchly opposed to their induction into the Hall) that this was a boardroom creation — cynically created to capitalize on the success of The Beatles — made up of TV actors who didn't write or play instruments on any of their biggest hit songs. You wouldn't know this by looking at the state of their catalog, which now includes lavish box-set reissues of individual albums.

Again, I don't begrudge any of the above their period of critical re-evaluation and praise. They deserve it. I just feel strongly that The Lovin' Spoonful deserves it too, and I'm going on 20 years of wracking my brain over why it hasn't really happened.

I'm convinced it's not the music. You'll never hear me call myself an otherworldly bass player, but John Sebastian and Zal Yanovsky were incredible, gifted musicians by any objective measure. Go listen to some of Zally's guitar playing on those recordings — or better yet go ask his mega-fan Eric Clapton about it. We wrote and played on all our biggest hits, and it's not like they were cookie-cutter copies of the other songs on the radio, or of each other. Every single we released — and all of our hits were written by us — was specifically designed to improve and build on the last, which was not exactly business as usual in the pop recording industry of the '60s.

And though art and commerce don't always have an easy relationship when it comes to pop music, I think the popularity of our songs and their success during this period is indicative of the quality of the music. Seven straight Top 10 hits is a hard thing to fake. So our second-tier status isn't a result of us not being popular or successful enough, is it?

So what was it? Well, for starters, there's no doubt that the timing of our demise — just before the explosion of "the album era" and alongside the birth of *Rolling Stone* and formal, thoughtful rock criticism — was poor.

Today we're largely viewed as a singles act who never had one grand album statement, and that's a problem. Even though you could make a solid case that "album rock" was just a marketing construct the labels came up with to justify and help cover increasing production and studio costs, and that really every album is just the sum of its songs, album success is something close to a prerequisite in the arena of enduring critical respect. *Pet Sounds* is sort of retroactively cast in the role of the first important, cohesive rock album, but most serious rock fans know *Pet Sounds* was effectively a critical and commercial flop upon its release in 1966. *Sgt. Pepper's Lonely Hearts Club Band* was really the game-changer, and by the time *Sgt. Pepper* hit the racks near the end of 1967, The Spoonful were already fractured and incapable of attempting something on that scale. *Everything Playing* probably could have been viewed as "our statement" if our attention and commitment level was still at 100 percent, but that wasn't the case.

Even if we had been clicking as colleagues, I'm not convinced we had the label and management support to pull it off. If we did, they probably would have been pushing us in the right direction before we came off the rails, or at least during the making of *Everything Playing*, when their attention to the group was minimal. As mentioned, Koppelman-Rubin and Kama Sutra were great for us in the respect that they knew how to break hit singles. That's why we signed with them over Elektra and other suitors back in '65. The rub was that they and our management were behind the curve when it came to albums, both in terms of marketing and the type of environment that needs to be provided to accomplish something like *Sgt. Pepper*. The Beatles stopped touring in '65 and put all their efforts into creating albums. We made *Hums* and *Everything Playing* on the run amid tour dates and other obligations, because our management focused on us performing the hit singles, not creating masterpieces in a studio. Had we stuck together long enough, maybe we could have changed those attitudes, but it's a hard thing to know.

And though I'm not into conspiracies, you'll never convince me that the bust and its fallout didn't have a direct impact on the standing of The Lovin' Spoonful today. Remember that the American rock press — in particular *Rolling Stone* — grew out of the San Francisco counterculture, and during the period that followed the bust there was definitely an understanding and shorthand among those types that The Spoonful were finks. I think that feeling certainly subsided and softened in the years that followed. The bust remains out there as a part of our history for those who dig deep enough, but it doesn't get mentioned all that frequently, and what happened isn't even widely understood. The bigger problem is that the five- to 10-year period after our breakup when we weren't deemed worthy of mention was a pretty bad time to be invisible. When the Rock Lists were being devised during those years — when even dead artists like Morrison, Hendrix and Joplin were being anthologized and deified — we weren't on those lists and weren't part of the conversation. For the most part, that's the way it's stayed.

We've had some bones thrown our way, including the Hall of Fame, but even that felt like a hollow victory. The way some of our peers — The Beatles and Dylan, Phil Spector — continued to hold us in high esteem probably helped us get in, but we were more or less treated as an afterthought by the writers and rock establishment who judge such matters. Things like that hurt, and make it hard to feel like your work is being judged fairly.

I don't go around looking for credit, but I'll admit it bothers me, and I'm left to wonder why. If we'd concluded our career by making a bunch of bad music, I could understand, but we didn't. We were extremely successful, popular, well regarded, and the reasons we fell away had nothing to do with the quality of our music.

But wider respect eludes us. I hope not forever — that's not for me to decide, though, and unfortunately when that day comes Zal Yanovsky will not be there to see it.

The morning after the Hall of Fame induction, I saw him and his wife, Rose, off on their journey back to Kingston. It was the last time I would see Zally.

On December 13, 2002, the phone rang as I was getting ready to walk out the door for a week-long gig on a cruise ship The Spoonful was booked to play. It was John calling from Woodstock. Zally was gone of congestive heart failure just a week short of his 58th birthday. I was stunned but not shocked. He had made his deal with his lifestyle, and if ever a man is to be happy it is to follow his own charted course. While we all want to live forever, I really believe Zally went as he wanted. For me the shock was tempered by the image of a man who had overcome a terrible mindfuck and was still able to rise to the top and achieve his goals on his own terms. How I would love today to be able to go down to the Keys and sit dockside and eat and drink and laugh and remember. Remember what no one can take away from me, which is what we accomplished as that shooting star called The Lovin' Spoonful. Of all the friends who had come to my house and met my father, Zally was by far his favorite. A peacenik Jew and a gunny sergeant goy, the two of them would talk into the night long after everyone else had gone to sleep.

And, of course, The Death Duo — we fought for death to hypocrisy and pretension, yet that night in May 1966 we had to deal with our own hypocrisy and foibles. "The Dance of Pain and Pleasure" didn't survive beyond the womb, but in another universe perhaps there's a Yanovsky/Boone single high atop the Billboard charts. We remain The Death Duo, and though I hope it doesn't happen anytime soon, I'll be joining him on the other side one day.

John Sebastian and I have remained friends over the years, playing together live as a duo a few times and getting together a time or two a year at his house in Woodstock to jam. John has made some terrific, underrated music over the past decade, including his fine collaborations with David Grisman, and recently his problems with his voice have diminished somewhat. I'm not sure what will come of it, but we've worked on new songs together over the past couple of years that I believe have some potential. The 50th anniversary of The Lovin' Spoonful's first record is coming in 2015, and it would be nice to see John's contributions recognized alongside those of the rest of a group that was far more than the sum of its parts.

In light of some of the disagreements I've had with John over the years, many of which are chronicled in this book, I have always considered him a friend, and Joe too. No relationship or business partnership that occurs over the course of nearly 50 years is going to be without its share of dissension and conflict, and hopefully he and Joe and my other bandmates understand my desire to tell the truth about those disagreements rather than sanitizing them for public consumption. I'm certain that if this were John's story, or Joe's, the perspectives on the last half-century would be very different, and they would take issue with a number of my decisions, both personal and professional, along the road. And that's OK.

I've continued to work on music both inside and outside The Lovin' Spoonful. Lena is a fabulous artist and animator, and sometime after we got together we came up with an idea for a band that was also a cartoon, called Forq (pronounced "fork"). We had "Guido" (Mike Arturi) on drums, "Shoqura" (Lena) on guitar and vocals, "Alanna Down" (Lena's sister, Hannah) on vocals and percussion and "Flasher" (yours truly) on bass. We cut what I thought was a great album of mostly Lena and Hannah's songs, called *ForqChops*, although I contributed two including the long-lost "If I Stare," which I also sang. We made a cool video and played a gig before I approached Bob Cavallo, who at the time was running Hollywood Records, with the idea of this virtual band. He was interested enough to assign a producer to us, but I sent in some early mixes from the album and never heard from the label again. About a year later the cartoon band Gorillaz, devised by Blur singer Damon Albarn, took off with a very similar concept. Oh well. Forq was the greatest rock band nobody ever heard (except on iTunes, where you can still download the album!).

In addition to my work with The Irish Times, I played in another terrific Irish band called The Molly Malones in Wilmington, North Carolina, where Lena and I had moved from Fort Lauderdale. I moved onto an 11-acre farm near Wilmington with the idea of starting a new recording studio there, but when the economy tanked,

Lena and I put it on the market and are now living the good life in Flagler Beach, Florida, not far from where I lived as a boy.

In all, I'm in the best place in my life as of 2014, but it's been a hell of a long and turbulent journey to get there.

It's almost like a genie came to me in early 1965 and posed the scenario: You can be in one of the biggest groups in the world for three years and enjoy all the benefits of that life — fame, adulation, sex, cars, money, creative fulfillment and the respect of your peers. But once those three years are up, you can't ever go back to a conventional life, and you have to accept that your life will forever be judged primarily on what you did during three years that occurred in your early twenties.

Would you take that deal?

That's not to say I ever lost control of my destiny — my choices were my choices in 1965, and they're my choices now. And it's not to say that if I had gone to college as planned and become an auto engineer in 1965 instead of joining this new, nameless band, I wouldn't have made mistakes. I know I would have — maybe even some big ones.

But it's hard to imagine a path outside of rock 'n' roll that would have led me to four marriages, including one to a convicted drug felon who would turn me in to the federal authorities, one to a former hooker, one to a lady who thought she was a mermaid, and one happy one to a woman 32 years younger than me whose dad has been my workmate for going on 50 years. There are addicts in all walks of life, but it's a lot easier to draw a straight line from rock 'n' roll to China White and Dilaudid addiction than it is to make that connection from a career in the military or as an auto engineer. It's true that there are not a lot of professional musicians who go on to become high-seas pot smugglers — though Kenny G may be hiding something from us (just kidding, Kenny) — so I can't blame rock 'n' roll for that one, although there's no doubt that the ubiquitous presence of marijuana in the creative process of my band

and our contemporaries helped me to embrace a life with an illegal substance as its focus.

Rock 'n' roll opened a lot of doors for me, and continues to. I'm so grateful for getting the chance to experience things millions of people can only dream of. But everything in life's a trade-off, and my choice to take that genie's deal in 1965 has led to some pain and heartbreak that maybe I wouldn't have experienced otherwise. And naturally, I'd take that deal again because I've so enjoyed the music that I've been a part of both inside and outside of The Lovin' Spoonful. I've certainly directed my share of contempt at the music business over the years, but I've never stopped loving the music, and in the end the power of the music has helped me deal with all the other bullshit that comes with it. Deep down, I'm still that kid who got knocked out of his seat by "Peggy Sue" in the fall of 1957. The magic *is* in the music, and after all these years, the music is *still* in me.

And to answer the man's musical question, even after all these years, the answer is yes. I do believe in magic.

ACKNOWLEDGMENTS

It's impossible to mention everyone who played a role in making this book a reality, but there are some who deserve special recognition. My inspirations: John Sebastian, Zalman "Zally" Yanovsky, Joe Butler, Jerry Yester. The team: Bob Cavallo, Erik Jacobsen, Rich Chiaro, Dan Moriarty, Bobby Miller, Walter Gundy, John Forshay, William "Fudge" Whiting, Charlie "Curls" Boone, Skip Boone, Mike Boone, Joyce Boone, Guy Phillips, Trudy Morgal, Linda "Zac" Zacharski, Doctors Bob and Zoh Hieronimus, and Scott Johnson. Joe McMichael, Gary Belich, Henry Diltz, John Einarson, and Dennis Diken for their research and contributions to the archival history of The Lovin' Spoonful. Gordy Singer and Ron Lemen who put The Lovin' Spoonful back to work. Mike Arturi and Phil Smith for their talent and dedication to The Lovin' Spoonful's great live shows, and to Skyline Artists and Steve Peck for getting us those shows. To my exes — Patti, JoNell, and Susan — who have remained good friends, and my little pals Lily and Katya, who love me rain or shine.

I also want to express thanks to my co-author Tony Moss, our agent Uwe Stender, and our publisher Jack David of ECW Press. Tony, for taking the time out from his regular life and bringing my story to readable life; Uwe, for knowing where and how to find a home for my book; and Jack, for giving the book a chance to stand on its own two feet. Thanks are also due to Jack's incredible team at ECW: managing editor Crissy Calhoun, sales and marketing director Erin Creasey, art director Rachel Ironstone, copyeditor Peter Norman, and especially project editor Jen Hale, who was positive and patient and understood our vision better than we did sometimes.

And most especially, to my wife, Lena, who has inspired me since the day we first met!

Tony Moss would like to thank his wife, Bridget, daughters Maggie and McCartney, who know all the words to "Summer in the City" (at least they think they do); to John Lewis and *Baltimore Magazine*, for commissioning the article that started us on the journey that culminated in this book; to Dan Di Sciullo, for being a sounding board; and to Rosanne Cash and Mark Oliver Everett, who proved that music memoirs can be things of style and class.

Get the eBook
FREE!

At ECW Press, we want you to enjoy
this book in whatever format you like,
whenever you like. Leave your print
book at home and take the eBook to go!
Purchase the print edition and receive
the eBook free. Just send an email to
ebook@ecwpress.com and include:

- the book title
- the name of the store where you purchased it
- your receipt number
- your preference of file type: PDF or ePub?

A real person will respond to your email with your eBook
attached. Thank you for supporting an independently owned
Canadian publisher with your purchase!